The Reminiscences Of

Vice Admiral Bernard B. Forbes, Jr.
U.S. Navy (Retired)

Interviewed By

Paul Stillwell

U.S. Naval Institute • Annapolis, Maryland

Copyright © 2008

Preface

More than 20 years ago I interviewed Captain Louis Colbus for the Naval Institute's oral history program because he came recommended as an excellent storyteller with a fascinating story to tell. He lived up to the advance building. As a follow-on to that project, he recommended that I interview his Virginia Beach neighbor, Vice Admiral Beetle Forbes, on whose staff he had served in the 1970s. Colbus promised that the admiral also had a great fund of sea stories to share for the benefit of oral history. Alas, when we got to the interviews themselves, Admiral Forbes's health was in decline, and he was already suffering from some memory loss, a situation that continued to worsen. The result is that he often felt frustrated during the course of the interviews in being unable to recall some of the names and situations from his impressive naval experience. Readers of this volume should bear that in mind as they make their way through his account.

That said, many stories were still ingrained in the admiral's memory, and through them we get an interesting portrait of a man who made history himself and observed a good deal more. Throughout his long career, Beetle Forbes was thoroughly dedicated to the Navy, and his narrative demonstrates his great enthusiasm for the service of which he was a part. He spoke of his Naval Academy experience with great relish and then moved on to recount a career that included increasingly responsible billets in his specialties of naval aviation and personnel administration.

He particularly enjoyed his commands: an aviation attack squadron and two ships. He also acquired an unofficial subspecialty in serving as aide and deputy to two noteworthy flag officers, Admiral Felix Stump and Admiral Ike Kidd. Both of them requested that Forbes come back for repeat tours, a testament to the value they placed on his service. The benefit for history is that Admiral Forbes provided vivid word portraits of their personalities and working styles. Admirals Stump and Kidd demanded a great deal of themselves and of those who worked for them.

A facet of Admiral Forbes's own leadership style was the long-held principle that loyalty downward produces loyalty upward. He cites example after example of looking out for the men who worked for him in order to enhance their morale. Probably the most notable was when he ordered thousands and thousands of doughnuts for the crew of his aircraft carrier, the *Independence,* as a reward for their hard work in unloading ammunition. In other instances, he saw to it that Eugene Lovely, a talented enlisted man on board the ammunition ship *Shasta,* got an opportunity to attend the Naval Academy and that Captain Bob Dunn was plugged into the opening when the carrier *Saratoga* needed a new skipper.

I am grateful to Captain Colbus and to Admiral Forbes's widow Betty for reviewing and refining the original raw transcript at a time when the admiral was no longer able to do so himself. I have done some additional editing in the interests of accuracy, clarity, and smoothness. That included rearranging the sequence of the material in a few cases for the sake of continuity. I have also added footnotes to provide amplifying information and corrections.

Finally, the Naval Institute expresses its gratitude to the Tawani Foundation and the Pritzker Military Library of Chicago for their generous financial support of the oral history program that produced this memoir.

Paul Stillwell
U.S. Naval Institute
May 2008

VICE ADMIRAL BERNARD BROWN FORBES, JR.
UNITED STATES NAVY (RETIRED)

Bernard Brown Forbes, Jr., was born in Savannah, Georgia, on 29 October 1920, the son of Bernard B. Forbes and Jennie Ennis Forbes. He attended Sparks (Maryland) High School and Geneva College, Beaver Falls, Pennsylvania, prior to enlisting in the U.S. Navy on 15 August 1938. He had duty in the receiving ship *Seattle* (ex-CA-11) and the aircraft carrier *Yorktown* (CV-5) prior to reporting in August 1940 for instruction at the Naval Academy Preparatory School, Norfolk, Virginia. In 1941 he entered the U.S. Naval Academy, Annapolis, Maryland, on appointment by the Secretary of the Navy. Graduated on 7 June 1944 with the class of 1945 (accelerated course due to World War II), he was commissioned ensign on that date.

Following graduation from the Naval Academy, Ensign Forbes had aviation indoctrination at the Naval Air Station, Jacksonville, Florida, and in August 1944 joined the crew of the destroyer *Barton* (DD-722). During his time on board he held several billets in the gunnery department, including gunnery officer. He served in that destroyer throughout the remaining period of World War II and until February 1947, participating in attacks on Luzon; landings at Ormoc Bay, Mindoro, and Lingayen Gulf; assault and occupation of Iwo Jima and Okinawa Gunto; Fifth and Third Fleet raids against Honshu and Nansei Shoto and the Third Fleet operations against Japan. As a lieutenant (junior grade), Forbes in 1946 took part in Operation Crossroads—the first atomic tests at Bikini Atoll.

In February 1947 he assumed command of the USS *PC-572* and in October of that year was detached for flight training at the Naval Air Station, Pensacola, Florida; the Naval Auxiliary Air Station, Cabaniss Field, Corpus Christi, Texas; and the Naval Air Station, Jacksonville, Florida. Designated a naval aviator in April 1949, Lieutenant (junior grade) Forbes joined Composite Squadron 33 (VC-33). From July 1950 to April 1951 he had duty as flag lieutenant and aide to Commander Air Force Atlantic Fleet, Vice Admiral Felix B. Stump. He had similar staff duty when Admiral Stump commanded the Second Fleet. In that assignment Lieutenant Forbes participated in two major NATO exercises.

In November 1953 he returned to the Naval Auxiliary Air Station, Cabaniss Field, to serve as an instructor until March 1955 and the next month became administrative assistant, flag lieutenant, and aide to the Commander in Chief Pacific/Commander in Chief Pacific Fleet, Admiral Stump. In September 1957 he reported as executive officer of Attack Squadron 15 (VA-15), based on board the carrier *Franklin D. Roosevelt* (CVA-42) and in that capacity participated in a Mediterranean cruise.

From June 1959 to June 1960, Commander Forbes received postgraduate instruction at Stanford University, from which he received the degree of master of arts. Following further instruction, in the senior course at the Naval War College, Newport,

Rhode Island, he joined Attack Squadron 44 (VA-44) in July 1961 and in September of that year assumed command of Attack Squadron 176 (VA-176). That squadron, under his command, participated in a Mediterranean cruise, based on board the carrier *Shangri-La* (CVA-38), and won the Battle Efficiency E. In December 1972 he reported as air officer on board the *Franklin D. Roosevelt,* which won the Flatley Safety Award for fiscal year 1964. In June 1964 he was detached for duty as head of the Manpower Program Branch, Office of the Chief of Naval Operations, Navy Department, Washington, D.C.

In August 1966 Captain Forbes assumed command of the ammunition ship *Shasta* (AE-6), which made a nine-month deployment to the Western Pacific to support combat operations in the Vietnam War. The *Shasta,* under his command, was awarded the Battle Efficiency E for fiscal year 1967. During the period from August 1967 to June 1969 he was Assistant Director for Distribution Control in the Bureau of Naval Personnel, Navy Department, Washington, D.C. From August 1969 to August 1970 he served as commanding officer of the aircraft carrier *Independence* (CVA-62). During his time in command, the ship deployed to the Mediterranean as part of the Sixth Fleet and participated in the North Atlantic Treaty Organization's Exercise Peacekeeper.

In October 1970 he became chief of staff and aide to Commander Sixth Fleet, Vice Admiral Isaac C. Kidd, Jr. In the spring of 1971, during his tour with the Sixth Fleet, Captain Forbes was selected for promotion to rear admiral. In September 1971 he was ordered detached for duty as Assistant Chief of Naval Personnel for Officer Personnel Control, Navy Department. Upon reorganization of the bureau, effective 30 June 1973, his title was changed to Assistant Chief of Naval Personnel for Officer Development and Distribution. In October of that year he assumed command of Carrier Group Six and in July 1974 was assigned additional duty as Commander Striking Force and Commander Carrier Striking Group One. Rear Admiral Forbes served as Commander Carrier Group Two/Commander Task Force 60 in the Sixth Fleet in June-July 1975. He was promoted to vice admiral in August 1975, when he became Deputy Commander in Chief U.S. Atlantic Command and Deputy Commander in Chief Atlantic Fleet. While in that billet he was sidelined by a heart attack in August 1976 and was relieved in September 1976. Vice Admiral Forbes officially retired from active duty in March 1977.

Post-retirement activities included a number of activities, including service as chairman of the committee of retired affairs for the Secretary of the Navy; as first director of the Hampton Roads Naval Museum; and volunteer work for the American Red Cross. Vice Admiral Forbes died 27 June 2002.

Family Personal Data:

Wife:	Betty Joyce Kabler, married 25 November 1950
Children:	Marian Nelson "Nell" Forbes Bater, born 20 July 1952
	Susan Lynn Forbes Snead, born 10 December 1954

Dates of Rank:

7 June 1944	Ensign
1 January 1946	Lieutenant (Junior Grade)
1 January 1951	Lieutenant
1 May 1955	Lieutenant Commander
1 April 1960	Commander
1 July 1965	Captain
1 November 1971	Rear Admiral
1 August 1975	Vice Admiral

Chronological Record of Service:

Aug 1938-Oct 1938	Naval Training Station, Norfolk, Virginia, recruit training
Oct 1938	Receiving ship *Seattle* (ex-CA-11), seaman
Nov 1938-Aug 1940	USS *Yorktown* (CV-5), seaman
Aug 1940-Jul 1941	Naval Academy Preparatory School, Norfolk, Virginia, student
Jul 1941-Jun 1944	Naval Academy, Annapolis, Maryland, midshipman/student
Jun 1944-Aug 1944	Naval Air Station, Jacksonville, Florida, aviation indoctrination
Aug 1944-Feb 1947	USS *Barton* (DD-722), gunnery department billets, XO
Feb 1947-Aug 1947	USS *PC-572*, commanding officer
Oct 1947-April 1949	Flight training, Pensacola, Corpus Christi, and Jacksonville
May 1949-Jul 1950	Composite Squadron 33 (VC-33), personnel/admin officer
Jul 1950-Apr 1951	Staff, Air Force Atlantic Fleet, flag lieutenant and aide
Apr 1951-Nov 1953	Staff, Second Fleet, flag lieutenant and aide
Nov 1953-Mar 1955	Naval Auxiliary Air Station, Cabaniss Field, Corpus Christi, Texas, instructor
Apr 1955-Aug 1957	Staff, CinCPac/CinCPacFlt, flag lieutenant and aide
Sep 1957-May 1959	Attack Squadron 15 (VA-15), executive officer

Jun 1959-Jun 1960	Stanford University, graduate student, master's degree
Jul 1960-Jun 1961	Naval War College, Newport, Rhode Island, student, senior course
Jul 1961-Sep 1961	Attack Squadron 44 (VA-44) (RAG), refresher pilot training
Sep 1961-Nov 1962	Attack Squadron 176 (VA-176), commanding officer
Dec 1962-Jun 1964	USS *Franklin D. Roosevelt* (CVA-42), air officer
Jun 1964-Jul 1966	OpNav (OP-103), head, Manpower Program Branch
Aug 1966-Jul 1967	USS *Shasta* (AE-6), commanding officer
Aug 1967-Jun 1969	Bureau of Naval Personnel, Asst. Director for Distribution Control
Jun 1969-Aug 1969	Prospective Commanding Officer Training
Aug 1969-Aug 1970	USS *Independence* (CVA-62), commanding officer
Aug 1970-Oct 1970	Staff, Chief of Naval Operations
Oct 1970-Jan 1972	Staff, Sixth Fleet, chief of staff
Jan 1972-Oct 1973	Bureau of Naval Personnel, Asst. Chief for Officer Personnel Control
Oct 1973-June 1975	Commander Carrier Group Six
Jun 1975-Jul 1975	Commander Carrier Group Two/Commander Task Force 60
Aug 1975-Sep 1976	Deputy Commander in Chief Atlantic/Deputy Commander in Chief Atlantic Fleet
March 1977	Retired from active duty

Medals and Awards:

Bronze Star Medal
Legion of Merit
Meritorious Service Medal
Navy Commendation Medal
Navy Unit Commendation Ribbon
American Defense Service Medal

American Campaign Medal
Asiatic-Pacific Campaign Medal with four operation stars
World War II Victory Medal
Occupation Service Medal with Asia clasp
National Defense Service Medal with one bronze star in lieu of second award
Vietnam Service Medal
Philippine Liberation Ribbon with one star

Authorization

The U.S. Naval Institute is hereby authorized to make available to individuals, libraries, and other repositories of its choosing the transcripts of two oral history interviews concerning the life and naval career of the undersigned. The interviews were recorded on 27 December 1991 and 7 February 1992 in collaboration with Paul Stillwell for the U.S. Naval Institute.

The undersigned does hereby release and assign to the U.S. Naval Institute the rights and title to these interviews, with the exception that the undersigned retains the right to use the material for his own purposes, as he sees fit. The copyright in both the oral and transcribed versions shall be the sole property of the U.S. Naval Institute. The tape recordings of the interviews are and will remain the property of the U.S. Naval Institute.

Signed and sealed this ___9___ day of ___Feb___ 1997. 2004

_____
Bernard B. Forbes, Jr.
Vice Admiral, U.S. Navy (Retired)

The United States Naval Institute

gratefully acknowledges

Captain Richard C. and Mary Dunn Fay

Captain Richard S. Gardiner, USN (Ret.)

Theodore L. Hoy

Rear Admiral Albert R. Marschall, USN (Ret.)

LCDR John T. Pigott, Jr., USNR (Ret.)

Roger T. Staubach

for their generous support in

underwriting the oral history of

Bernard Brown Forbes, Jr.
Vice Admiral, U.S. Navy (Retired)

Launched in 1969, the Naval Institute's oral history program is among the oldest in the country. Used in combination with documentary sources, oral histories offer a richer understanding of naval history through candid recollections and explanations never entered into contemporary records. In addition, they can help depict the atmosphere of a particular event or era in a manner not available in official documents.

The Naval Institute gratefully accepts tax-deductible gifts to strengthen its oral history initiatives. This support allows the Institute to preserve the life experiences of today's service men and women so they may teach and inspire future generations.

For information about opportunities to underwrite Naval Institute oral history projects, please contact the Naval Institute Foundation at 291 Wood Road, Annapolis, Maryland 21402; by phone at (410) 295-1054; or by e-mail at foundation@usni.org.

Interview Number 1 with Vice Admiral Bernard B. Forbes, Jr., U.S. Navy (Retired)
Place: U.S. Naval Institute, Annapolis, Maryland
Date: Friday, 27 December 1991
Interviewer: Paul Stillwell

Paul Stillwell: Admiral, just to begin at the beginning, could you tell when and where you were born and something of your forebears and your early family life?

Admiral Forbes: Yes. I was born in Savannah, Georgia, October 29th, 1920. My father was then manager of Swift and Company, and we moved around, as I later learned, from city to city.

My forebears on my father's side, the Forbes family originated—this is all written down in the old family Bible in this beautiful Spenserian hand—in Scotland. My great, great, great, great—I guess that's enough greats—granddaddy was a cabin boy on his uncle's ship trading between Aberdeen, Scotland, and Dumfries, Virginia, which was *the* port in the Commonwealth of Virginia in those days.

After his third trip he jumped ship in Dumfries and settled there. He then joined the Continental Army in due course. He was all shot up at the Battle of Guilford Courthouse and, as is written in the book, apparently was shot through the fanny or somewhere near there, because he showed his scars to his children only on Saturday night when he took his bath. He was given 500 acres but no mule in Buckingham County, Virginia. And our family still has 350 of those original 500 acres, and that's where my family on my father's side springs from.

My mother was from a good Irish family, Ennis, and they lived up in Maryland. I lived in Savannah as a youngster. Then my father was transferred to Newport News, Virginia, and I entered school in Newport News. I'll never forget the Stonewall Jackson Elementary School, which is now a parking lot for the Newport News Shipbuilding and Dry Dock Corporation. The school is long since gone. I went there until the sixth grade.

Then my father became quite ill. I'll brag. Back to school. In those days you had one low, one high, two low, two high—I skipped two high and four high, and I'd gotten up to the sixth grade. My father died, and my mother went back with her family, who then lived on a farm up in Maryland, about 21½ miles north of Baltimore. I went back to school up there.

Paul Stillwell: When was this that he died?

Admiral Forbes: That would be about 1930, in that area somewhere. I went to a two-room school there. We had the first, second, and third grades in one room and the fourth, fifth, and sixth grades in the other room, which was a great advantage because you could get the advanced dope on what was going to be taught to you the next year if you kept your ears open. But I went there in the sixth grade, and I finished there in the sixth grade. Then I went to the seventh grade and high school quite a ways away. I had to ride a bus. I was picked up every morning at 7:30 and went to the Sparks High School, where I graduated in 1937. Again I'll brag; I was president of the class, president of the student body. I really enjoyed it down there. Now, do you want to keep going on from there?

Paul Stillwell: Well, please tell me more about your parents and what kind of influence they had on your upbringing.

Admiral Forbes: My mother was a wonderful, wonderful lady: hard working, a very devout Methodist. She made sure that I got the necessities. When my dad died, I was too young to know all the details, but there was very little money left in any estate. And my grandparents on my mother's side were farmers. My grandfather had been a very successful brewery man in his day. By then they were just farming and had a little farm where they raised chickens and sold eggs. I remember that eggs sold for 20 cents a dozen.

My mother wanted to make sure that we received a good education, and she sacrificed to make it so. In those days we had very little cash money, but we got to school. In my senior year in high school, I would take every Thursday off and drive my mother to Towson in the outskirts of Baltimore. She had a little homespun egg route and sold eggs. She knocked on the doors of her regular customers. I never went to school on Thursdays. The principal understood these things in the days of Depression.*

My father was a wonderful, wonderful gentleman. He was just as sharp as a tack. He'd done extremely well. Then he had one of those fluke things: an infection, lost his leg, and died of the consequences. It was a tragedy. He's buried up in the old home church plot up in Buckingham County. My mother lived on for quite some while. I was taken good care of financially by my father's brother, my uncle Arthur, who was the head man in the Federal Reserve Bank in Richmond. He sent money every month to help us through school and just the basic needs.

But it was a very subdued life-style during the Depression, of course. I can't help but laugh when I think back on it. We had no running water, no electricity, no telephones, but we ate well. I mean, it was just very, very basic in those days. Sometimes I get a lump in my throat when I think back. And no car. I rode to school on the bus, and when I got home I was home, period. That was it. When I went to elementary school there, I walked a mile and a half one way to school.

Paul Stillwell: Did you walk when you delivered the eggs?

Admiral Forbes: Oh, no, no. We had a car in my senior year. We got a 1931 Chevrolet, and I learned to drive. I joined the Boy Scouts up there. I had a wonderful scoutmaster, and I've got to tell you my sea story about getting my driver's license.

I had read all the books and done everything. You had to go in and take these tests, and my scoutmaster loaned me his car. I had never driven before. I'd ridden with a lot of people and watched everything. With the inspector in the car, we had to come to a stop on a hill. This was back in the days of old gear shifts. You had to start off on a hill and go on up the hill. I sat there in this Auburn. He had an Auburn sports car; oh, it was something else in those days. I put the Auburn in high gear and let out the clutch, and up

---

* Following the crash of the New York Stock Exchange in late October 1929, the United States was plunged into the Great Depression, from which it did not recover until the nation geared up for World War II at the beginning of the 1940s. The Depression was marked by high unemployment and many business failures.

the hill we went. The inspector looked at me, and he said, "*High gear*? Well, I guess if it'll do it, you can do it. You're supposed to do it in low gear."

That's how I got my driver's license. We just used the Chevrolet for business purposes, not for social. Any high school social activities you had in those days were very, very few. One of my friends lived on the farm two up from us. His parents were quite well to do. I used to go with Howard Bailey and drive with him all the time.

Paul Stillwell: What ambitions did you have as you were growing up?

Admiral Forbes: This may sound strange, but it's true. I always wanted to go to the Naval Academy. I guess the reason was that my mother's youngest brother, Francis Ennis, had been Naval Academy, Class of 1927.[*] He broke his leg playing soccer at the Naval Academy, and it developed into a bad situation. His leg wouldn't heal properly, and they gave him a medical discharge.

Well, all of his midshipman uniforms were still up there on the farm. I used to get them out and look at them and thought they were great. So I always wanted to go to the Naval Academy, but there was no way of getting a political appointment in those days. When a Navy recruiter came to the high school—this was in 1937, during the Depression—he talked about three square meals a day and about running water. I thought, "Running water? We've got a good stream behind the barn. What's so big about that?" [Laughter] I went down to "Bawlmer," as you properly pronounce it, not Bal-ti-more, Bawlmer. I signed up and told the recruiter I'd like to try out for the Naval Academy. Well, I was accepted, and I enlisted on August the 15th, 1938.

Now, in the meantime—I'll brag—I did very well in high school. I had a good principal, Mr. McDonald, Good Lord rest his soul. I took the competitive exams in the state for scholarships, and I won a scholarship to Geneva College in Beaver Falls, Pennsylvania. Now, I'm not a racist, which I'll get to later. But, being raised in the South all my life, I had never been to school with darkies. I went up to that college, and my uncle Arthur took care of the financial end of it, what little money was involved. I completed a year at Geneva College.

---

[*] Midshipman Francis W. Ennis, USN.

Paul Stillwell: This would be '37 and '38?

Admiral Forbes: No, this would be '36. I was lucky—I shouldn't say lucky, I guess, but I graduated from high school when I was 16 years old and went right to Beaver Falls. I graduated high school in June and went there in September 1936 and completed a year. I wanted to try out for the Naval Academy in the worst kind of way. That's when I went down in '38 and enlisted in the Navy in Baltimore.

Paul Stillwell: Well, what did the blacks have to do with this? Did that turn you off on the college?

Admiral Forbes: No, no. It was just interesting for me to go into class and see blacks, because in those days one of the closest friends of my mother and my Aunt Louella, who lived with us, was this old black lady. We had been very close friends of their mother's, Aunt Matilda, and occasionally her sons would bring her up, and they'd sit there and just talk and have the greatest time. But when it came time to eat at lunchtime, my mother and my Aunt Louella and all of us ate in the dining room; Miss Matilda had to eat out in the kitchen by herself. They were still that strict. And you never saw a black in the public schools at all. And suddenly, bang! Just very, very interesting.

Paul Stillwell: How much awareness did you have of the world at large in that time, the developing situation in Europe and so forth?

Admiral Forbes: Practically none. We had no radio. The *Baltimore Sun* was delivered by the mailman, and that was your only contact with the outside world. That was very basic living. The drinking water came from a spring. I used to carry the water from the spring in two buckets, one in each hand. It was about 300 yards from the springhouse to the kitchen. We had wood stoves which you cooked on and which you heated by, and you did your homework while it was still the light of day. Or you had what we used to call a coal oil lamp—kerosene nowadays. And you did all your homework. Everybody went to bed about 8:00 o'clock at night and got up at 5 o'clock in the morning, when you did all the farm chores, including milking the cows. Then you hopped on the school bus at 7:30 and went to school. We took our little sandwiches with us, and that was it.

Paul Stillwell: Probably not a lot of opportunity to go to movies and newsreels then either.

Admiral Forbes: Only once in a while. I had this very close friend, Josh Inser. In fact, we're still very close. I can go into some great details about Josh. Josh lived down near the high school. On certain days—maybe two or three times a year—he and Bill Hurst and I would walk to the Old York Road, which was the main thoroughfare between York, Pennsylvania, and Baltimore. We'd hitchhike into Baltimore and go the movies. When I say, "go to the movies," I mean we'd go and sit there through the show at least twice. Then we'd go again in the afternoon and sit through another one twice. Afterward, we'd get on the streetcar, which was in Baltimore, and go out to Towson. It used to cost a dime, which was a lot of money in those days. Then we'd hitchhike home, and that was it. We used to do that about three times a year. That was our exposure to the modern world. [Laughter] Oh, well. It was a great life.

Paul Stillwell: How did things work out then when you got hooked up with the Navy recruiter?

Admiral Forbes: Well, I told him I wanted to try out for the Naval Academy, and he said, "Well, we've got a waiting list, but are you serious?"

I said, "Yes, sir. I've won a scholarship to college. I've been to college for a year, and I stood number one in my high school class." I did a little—not bragging but I gave him the cold, hard facts of life. And I said, "My uncle went there in the class of 1927 but didn't get all the way through. I just like the Naval Academy, and I've always been interested. I like to sail." When I lived in Newport News I did a lot of sailing on the James River. I didn't go into all that, but I sailed with Captain Hogg, who ran a fishing fleet there. I said, "I'd just like to try out for that Naval Academy."

He said, "All right, Forbes, we'll give you a chance." I was sworn in, and the irony of those days was that I had to go from Baltimore to Norfolk, where the big recruit training station was located. It was one of the big ones in those days. We were sent to Norfolk on the old Chesapeake Bay Line, and we went first class. Here I was, with a little ditty bag and my work clothes, and I was there in the dining room with all of these well-dressed people. It was somewhat embarrassing, but it was a good meal.

Paul Stillwell: You felt a little out of place?

Admiral Forbes: I did feel out of place. However, I had a nice room with two big bunks in it; I lived like a king overnight on my way to Norfolk. The recruiters in Baltimore—this one broke me up—gave me a dime so that I could get on the streetcar in downtown Norfolk, when I got off the ship, and ride out to the base. That's what I did.

That was on August the 15th, 1938, and I met a young man who walked through the gate at the same time. He was Chris Petersen, who lived there in Norfolk and had joined the Navy. He and I went through boot camp together. I'm getting ahead of the story, but we later went through the Naval Academy Preparatory School together, then went to the Naval Academy together. Chris is still in Norfolk, and we are in Virginia Beach now. Chris and I are the closest of friends to this day. Chris is just one great, great guy.

Paul Stillwell: Was he a classmate of yours at the Naval Academy?*

Admiral Forbes: Yes. By the time we were lieutenant commanders, Chris left the Navy. His father operated a big plumbing firm in Norfolk. Mr. Petersen said, "Now, Chris, I know you like the Navy, but I've got to get someone to take over the corporation. I'm getting old. You have to take over this firm." Chris resigned and took over the firm. He's now the President of Coley-Petersen Plumbing, and they do a lot of Navy contract work. He's just one A-number-one individual. I really like Chris. He's a great guy. He'd give you the shirt off his back.

---

* Midshipman Christian Charles Petersen, USN, graduated in the Naval Academy class of 1945.

Paul Stillwell: Well, what do you remember about boot camp? I mean that certainly must have been a contrast to this existence you'd known at home up to then.

Admiral Forbes: Well, in a way. When I was at home, we could volunteer for the CMTC, which as I recall stood for Citizens Military Training Camp, which was one month long. When I was a junior in high school, I put in for it, and I made it. I was sent to Fort Meade, Maryland, where I went to basic boot camp for one month. After CMTC I went home. The next year I volunteered for it again; that was my senior year in high school. This time I was sent to Fort Monroe, right across the way.* There I was in the Coast Artillery training for one month. I received a lot of close-order drill. It was very interesting. Having been raised up to the sixth grade in Newport News, I knew some people here. I used to get back and forth for visits. It was great.

So when I went into boot camp, I was one of the few who'd ever had any military training. Therefore, I became a recruit petty officer first class. We did all the close-order drills, went to all the classes, and it was just a good, very healthy, very busy time there. When I finished boot camp, I was assigned to USS *Yorktown*, CV-5.†

Paul Stillwell: She was just a new ship then.

Admiral Forbes: She was a new ship and had just arrived in Norfolk. I went aboard *Yorktown* in November. My division officer—I'll never forget him—was Ensign Robinson, Naval Academy class of 1938.‡ I said, "Sir, I want to try for the Naval Academy."

He said, "Forbes, you do the best you can with your assigned jobs on this ship, and I'll keep an eye on you." So I did. I had the duty the first Christmas I was on board, naturally. I was mess cook, side cleaner, captain of the head—all the good jobs—but I

---
* Fort Monroe is an Army post in Hampton, Virginia, located at Old Point Comfort, where the James River meets the Chesapeake Bay.
† USS *Yorktown* (CV-5), lead ship of her class of aircraft carriers, was commissioned 30 September 1937. She had a standard displacement of 19,800 tons, was 810 feet long, 83 feet in the beam, and had an extreme width of 114 feet. Her top speed was 32.5 knots. She had eight 5-inch guns and could accommodate approximately 90-100 aircraft.
‡ Ensign Hugh M. Robinson, USN.

worked as best as I could.* Then came time to take the exam for the Naval Academy Preparatory Class. I did that, and Ensign Robinson recommended me. I was very flattered. I was one of the fortunate few that passed the exams.

I went to the Naval Academy Preparatory Class in Norfolk, where you went to school from 8:00 o'clock in the morning on Monday until noon on Saturday, a full day, compulsory study hour every night. You had liberty Saturday afternoon and Saturday night. We had class on Sunday afternoon and study hour Sunday night. That was it— just study, study, study. We were crammed with what could be expected in the Naval Academy exams. I took the entrance exams and was one of the fortunate few who made it. My friend Chris Petersen did, too, I might add.

I went from the fleet in Norfolk to the Naval Academy. We went to Annapolis in an old tugboat; I'll never forget that. We went aboard the *Reina Mercedes* at the Naval Academy.† After arriving in Annapolis on that big day, we were called over, just the Naval Academy Preparatory Class. We then mingled with the civilian youngsters who were coming to the Academy. There was no mass formal swearing in. We were sworn in in small groups at Mem Hall.‡

I'll never forget it! I was standing by this civilian boy whose name was Fay, and mine, of course, was Forbes.§ We were lined up alphabetically. We raised our hands and we were sworn in as midshipmen. The duty officer looked at us, and he said, "You two, Fay, Forbes, your room is 1006. Get over there!"

We went over to our room. Then we drew uniforms and all that. I won't go into all the details of all the gear we were issued. But, as you may recall, in those days your name was stenciled across the front of your uniforms. Well, having come from the fleet, I could do this, and I was stenciling my gear. Dick Fay just looked at me, and I said, "Here, Fay, let me help you." I was stenciling his uniforms, and we were working away. Dick looked at me, and he said, "Forbes, what's your name? Bernard? All right, Bernard, tell me. When do the girls show up around here?" [Laughter]

Now, this was in 1941. I said, "There are no girls at the Naval Academy."

---

* The jobs he enumerated are among the least desirable on board ship.
† USS *Reina Mercedes* (IX-25), a former cruiser captured during the Spanish-American War, served as a station ship at the Naval Academy from 1912 to 1957.
‡ Memorial Hall is a large, ornate space in Bancroft Hall, the Naval Academy dormitory.
§ Richard C. Fay, who graduated with Forbes in the Class of 1945.

"No girls? Where in the hell am I?" This was when I found out he was the only son of a millionaire. He had four sisters, and later I met them all. His father saw the war coming on and had him appointed to the Naval Academy. So Dick said, "No girls? What am I doing? Well, I'll tell you what. If I've got to be in this place, I'm going the best one they've got."

I'm getting ahead of my story now, Paul. But, anyway, as plebes in those days we were allowed to drag twice—to the Masqueraders, and I've forgotten the other function. They were big affairs here at the Academy, later on in the school year, of course. Dick would say, "You guys go ahead. I want to study." At the end of plebe year he stood up near the top of the class.

And I'm getting ahead of my story, because I want to get to Pearl Harbor in a minute. We went home for a short leave. I got back to the room before he did. I was sitting in the room at the desk when he arrived back from leave. I said, "Dickie Boy, how was leave?"

"Beetle, guess what."

I said, "What?"

He says, "I discovered girls."

I said, "Well, good for you."

He said, "You know what else I discovered? I don't have any vices." And he went right down to the midshipmen's store. We only made $2.00 a month cash, with all that formality of the pay line. We had to sign for things in the midshipmen's store. He drew two cartons of cigarettes, and he started to smoke like a wigwam.

And we had John Wilson Brown IV, who lived in the room next to us. He was the son of the president of Forman Distilleries. And his nickname, I might add, was "The Bourbon Bunny." The Bourbon Bunny's father—and this is getting off the record, but the statute of limitations is long since past—kept him supplied with bourbon. Our assigned lockers had this very set format of how everything had to be stored. It included a bottle of Listerine. Well, the Bourbon Bunny's bottle wasn't Listerine. It was bourbon. The Blotter—that was Mo Nuschke—was his roommate, and he had a bottle of bourbon.* Dickie boy started to drink like a fish, and he had one wonderful tour! He dragged every

---

* Midshipman Paul Louis Nuschke, USN.

weekend, and he really enjoyed the Naval Academy.* But if he'd have been there six more months, he'd have bilged out academically. [Laughter] But smart. Oh, he was. But what a great guy.

Paul Stillwell: Well, we just sort of glossed over boot camp. Please describe that and some of the experience of living in the barracks and getting indoctrinated into specific Navy things.

Admiral Forbes: Of course, we lived in the barracks. We were issued uniforms right away, the day we checked in. We went over and stood in line, and the officer looked at each of us and said, "You wear a size umpty-ump." We were issued four white uniforms, blue service, blue uniforms, and we tried on shoes. We were really completely outfitted. Then we were told, "Now, you live over in this wing." We went over to our wing, where we were assigned a bunk. We made up our own bunk. Thank heavens. At first we had hammocks, but they knocked that off after about one day. The buildings are still there in Norfolk where we went through our training.

We were in, I'll never forget, Platoon 37. We got up in the morning at 6:00 o'clock, got dressed, and fell in. Then we marched over to the old mess hall. It has long since been torn down. We went through the mess line with our trays. After breakfast we came back to the wing, brushed our teeth, and did whatever had to be done. Then we fell in again and had just a very full day: march, march, march, drill, close order drill.

We broke for meals, and in the evening we were allowed to go to the movies in the barracks next to ours. For us poor country boys, who rarely saw a movie, this was just the greatest thing in the world. We're going to sit down and watch a Hollywood movie every night? And that was it. We got no liberty. We were restricted to the base, and we went through there. I went there in August, and I guess we were there about three months. It was just a good military indoctrination. We studied seamanship courses, learned how to tie knots, and everything was very basic.

---

* "Drag" was Naval Academy slang for dating girls. A midshipman who dated seldom or not at all was known as a "Red Mike."

Paul Stillwell: Did you get out in rowing cutters?

Admiral Forbes: Yes. We had whaleboats in those days. In fact, the old place there in Norfolk is now since gone. The boat slip we had was filled in over the years. It's now a golf course. [Laughter]

Paul Stillwell: Did you have a position of leadership based on your CTMC training?

Admiral Forbes: Yes, I was the number-two man in my platoon. The number-one man was a sergeant in the Army who got out and wanted to go into the Navy. He had three years of actual military experience and was a great guy. He was from Richmond. I'll never forget that.

Paul Stillwell: I suspect you were probably one of the best educated in the group, too, especially having a year of college.

Admiral Forbes: Yes. That's right.

Paul Stillwell: Was it hard for some of the people to keep up that were in your company, because they weren't as sophisticated or whatever?

Admiral Forbes: No. We had a few who dropped out. They just couldn't take the military training, and they just said, "No way." I don't to this day know how they were ever handled. They were just removed from the company. We also had defectors, if you want to call them that.

Paul Stillwell: Do you think that providing these movies and on-base entertainment was a way to keep you away from the clutches of the sleazy downtown Norfolk, Granby and East Main and that environment?

Admiral Forbes: Yes, because that was in those days, it was sleazy down there. I won't go into—

Paul Stillwell: Well, please do.

Admiral Forbes: There was no drinking. No beer or any alcohol was available to us.

Paul Stillwell: Well, certainly some people were consuming.

Admiral Forbes: Oh, yes. But we made only $21.00 a month as apprentice seamen. When we made seaman second, we went to $36.00, then seaman first to $54.00. And if we advanced to petty officer in our first enlistment, which was four years, we were considered front-runners. Most people ended up their first four years as seamen, making $54.00 a month. So we didn't have that much money.

But the Naval Academy Prep School provided a sea story. When we finished Prep School and had completed the exams, one of my close friends and classmates was Joe Bonds, who was from California. His parents bought a brand-new Buick to be delivered at Flint, Michigan. When we finished Prep School, we had over a month before we had to be back to find out if we were going to the Naval Academy. If we didn't make it, we would be sent back to the fleet.

Joe and I bummed a ride with another classmate there at the Prep School, Bob Bascom, who lived up towards Michigan. His parents came down to pick him up to take him home on leave. We rode with them that far. Then we hitchhiked to Flint and picked up this brand-new Buick, which we drove across country to Joe's parents' home in California. We spent some leave time there and had a great time.

Then we had to get back to Norfolk. We bought a '29 Studebaker for $29.00 on the West Coast. [Laughter] We drove that Studebaker through Yellowstone National Park and had a wonderful trip all the way to Norfolk. We stopped at night and made our own little meals. It was just very, very basic. It was also very, very enjoyable. We arrived back in Norfolk, sat around waiting in the same barracks, and we found out we made it to the Naval Academy.

Then we sold the '29 Studebaker. We had used the Studebaker to go up and visit my mother while we were waiting. We'd take the Studebaker and drive up to Maryland from Norfolk on the weekends. That's when Joe met my sister, whom I'll come back to in a minute, and they formed quite a friendship. When we learned that we made the Naval Academy we sold the Studebaker for—what was it? $15.00 anyway. We went to the Naval Academy from there.

Paul Stillwell: I'm interested also more in your time on board the *Yorktown*. Why did you not get into a regular division? Why did stay a side cleaner and mess cook?

Admiral Forbes: Oh. Well, no. I was in the third division, which was a deck division.

Paul Stillwell: Oh, I see.

Admiral Forbes: Each division in those days had to supply so many mess cooks, so I was assigned mess cook duties for about six weeks. Third division was a deck division with a certain portion of the ship to keep clean, preserve, paint, and shine. That was when I went over the side for cleaning and painting. And we had the heads that had to be cleaned and maintained. When I was assigned those duties, I was called captain of the head. I did all of the various and sundry jobs. Mess cook was a great one. You talk about food. Ooh. It was very interesting and very basic. Nothing fancy.

Paul Stillwell: How strict was the discipline in that ship?

Admiral Forbes: I would say quite strict.

Paul Stillwell: Do you have examples?

Admiral Forbes: Well, I had to go to my division chief to get my liberty card. I had to have a liberty card to go ashore. I then had to go to the quarterdeck, where they looked me over carefully. Then I saluted and said, "Request permission to leave the ship, sir," and then I could go ashore. Well, when you're making only $21.00 a month, there's not much you can do. Of course, things were much cheaper in those days. We mustered for quarters every morning. We were inspected. We had indoctrination talks. It wasn't German-type discipline, but it was very firm, and it was strict. It was a happy ship. I'll say that. It was a happy ship.

Paul Stillwell: What made it a happy ship.

Admiral Forbes: Well, I think the food, the leadership we had, and the mission. We observed flight operations where we saw airplanes land on the ship and take off. This was back in the good old days.

Paul Stillwell: Are there any specific operations you remember? Any trips?

Admiral Forbes: We steamed to the Caribbean and visited Guantánamo.[*] We operated Eventually we steamed around to the West Coast. We transited the Panama Canal.[†] As a boot seaman, it was a real thrill for me to observe the clearance on either side of *Yorktown* while going through that canal.

We had good captains on board; they were all nice men who were concerned about the welfare of their crew. They weren't martinets. The skippers would personally pass the word, "Now we're going to do this, going to do that and watch this, watch that, and look over at that's so-and-so, there's a such-and-such." We went ashore in ports on the Pacific side. We were granted one day's liberty so that we could go ashore and look around and buy souvenirs. Then we went to San Diego and became part of the Pacific Fleet and operated out of there.[‡]

---

[*] Guantánamo Bay, on the south coast of Cuba, near the eastern end of the island, for many years provided a fleet anchorage and training area for U.S. Navy ships.
[†] The *Yorktown* passed through the Panama Canal on 27 April 1939 as part of a large fleet movement to the Pacific.
[‡] For details on the ship's history during that period, see Robert J. Cressman, *That Gallant Ship: U.S.S. Yorktown CV-5* (Missoula, Montana: Pictorial Histories Publishing Company, 1985).

Paul Stillwell: I've seen pictures that show the *Yorktown* moored at North Island after she got out there.*

Admiral Forbes: That was our homeport—North Island. That's where I disembarked to report to the Naval Academy Preparatory School. I had to get back to Norfolk. You've got to remember now, this was back in the good old days. I was assigned to a transport ship there in San Diego, so I went south and east, back through the Panama Canal to Norfolk. Once in Norfolk, we were sent to Baltimore on the Bay Line overnight. (There were two ferries: Chesapeake Line and the Bay Line.) We then boarded a bus and went to the Naval Academy. There we boarded the *Reina Mercedes*, where we stayed until it was time to get sworn as midshipmen.

Paul Stillwell: What were the heads like in the *Yorktown*? That was a new ship compared with the older ones that were in the fleet.

Admiral Forbes: They were stainless steel. There were no toilets as such. There was one stainless steel bulkhead with a trough at the bottom. The seawater came out of a little pipe at the top and went down, so that there was always water flowing; at the bottom was the drain. That was for urination. For other service, there was a nice long trough with water flowing through it constantly and little seats side by side. There were about 20 seats. That was your toilet. No privacy.

Paul Stillwell: What were the seats made of, wood?

Admiral Forbes: Wood, yes. No privacy but very clean. There were big mirrors. There was one bulkhead with attached basins; that was for shaving. I don't think I shaved but about once every few weeks as a youngster, but that was it.

Paul Stillwell: Did you have showers?

---

* North Island Naval Air Station is on the end of the Coronado peninsula, across the harbor from San Diego.

Admiral Forbes: Yes, we did. The next adjoining space, on the other side of the head, was the washroom, which had the showers. Everything was stainless steel. In those days you were only allowed limited water use. The ship was very insistent about this; we got in, we turned on the shower and got wet, then turned the water off. Then we soaped down real good. We then turned the water back on to get the soap off; securing the water was the end of the shower. There was no standing under the shower enjoying the water. These were known as sea showers and aimed at conserving fresh water, which was distilled from salt water.

Fresh water was a critical item in the old Navy. Sometimes, when things would go wrong down in the engineering spaces, and the evaporators wouldn't operate properly, we experienced water hours, or we would have no water at all. Now, I remember once the only water that was available in the ship for the crew to use was in the drinking fountains, which we called scuttlebutts. We couldn't wash our faces or brush our teeth. The ship was having a condenser problem, but it didn't last long. I mean, like two days. It was a different Navy in those days. However, we were always fed well.

Paul Stillwell: What were the messing facilities like?

Admiral Forbes: Great big long lines. We went through the mess line with metal trays. We had wooden tables, and the legs folded up. When we finished our meal, the tables were hung up on the overhead. Then there was the entire empty space in there with just chairs.

Paul Stillwell: That was a carryover from the old Navy when the crew members ate in berthing compartments.

Admiral Forbes: Yes. That's right. When we went through boot camp in those days we were issued a hammock and a mattress. When we were transferred, we rolled our mattress and hammock. We learned to tie it properly. We also had our seabags. We filled our seabags with uniforms, shoes and other baggage, and then wrapped the hammock around that.

Paul Stillwell: That was known as lashing it up in seagoing fashion.

Admiral Forbes: Yes, like a big U, and that's what we carried. That was our luggage.

Paul Stillwell: Well, and on a number of ships in the time you're speaking of men still slept in hammocks.

Admiral Forbes: Yes. That's right. Now, on *Yorktown*, since she was such a new ship, we slept in bunks—three deep and very close together. There was a locker up against the bulkhead—a little square locker. That was yours, and everything a sailor owned had to be stowed in there.

Paul Stillwell: What do you recall about inspections on board the *Yorktown*?

Admiral Forbes: Oh, we had the regular personnel inspections by divisions. Seniors would come by and inspect our haircuts, our shoeshines, and our uniforms to ensure that they were properly cleaned and pressed. It was a good, taut ship, which made for a happy ship. We had a good division officer, Lieutenant Robinson. He was one sharp young officer.

Paul Stillwell: Any of the skippers or other senior officers you specifically remember.

Admiral Forbes: No. We never got to know any of them.

Paul Stillwell: Any liberties you remember from the *Yorktown*?

Admiral Forbes: I remember going ashore in Panama, which was an eye-opener to a farm boy. We got over there and looked all around at all the deals and the sales that were offered. With little money we had very little leeway.

Paul Stillwell: Did you get to see flight deck operations?

Admiral Forbes: Yes.

Paul Stillwell: That must have been very exciting too.

Admiral Forbes: Absolutely fascinating. I can look back in my mind's eye to this day and see those biplanes come aboard in the back and just flop down and grab those wires. We had the old SBDs.* In fact, I got to ride in an SBD after Prep School. Flight operations were just great and mostly in the daytime. There were very few night ops in those days—1938. It was an interesting tour.

Paul Stillwell: Did that develop in you the desire to become an aviator?

Admiral Forbes: No, it didn't. I wanted to be submariner while at the Naval Academy. Aviation came late in the game.

Paul Stillwell: Was the *Yorktown* involved in any fleet operations while you were on board?

Admiral Forbes: Yes.

Paul Stillwell: What do you recall of those?

---

* The Douglas-built SBD Dauntless, which entered fleet squadrons in 1941, was the Navy's most successful dive-bomber in the early part of World War II.

Admiral Forbes: Just the number of ships and the steaming in formation. Ships had to look sharp with nothing hanging over the side. Ships' crews wanted to be shipshape, especially when observed by other ships and crews. We took great pride in our ship. It was clean, sharp, and it was a happy ship.

Paul Stillwell: Did the seagoing way of life appeal to you?

Admiral Forbes: Yes.

Paul Stillwell: What about it?

Admiral Forbes: Well, I liked the routine. I liked being able to stand watches up on the bridge every now and then. Most of the time I was one of the lookouts and observed how that bridge was run. It was sharp and well run. I served as side boy for all the honors rendered to senior and official visitors.[*]

This is where I saw so many of the admirals who later became famous in life: Admiral Bull Halsey, Admiral King.[†] They all came aboard at one time or other to embark in *Yorktown*. I saw them close up when I heard the announcement, "Side boys, man the rail." It was a good life, and we were well fed. Coming off the farm, as I did, and experiencing a poverty-stricken existence made me feel that I was doing quite well in those days, relatively speaking.

Paul Stillwell: Did you have a feeling then that war was coming?

Admiral Forbes: No. None at all.

Paul Stillwell: Were you thinking in terms of a career at that point?

---

[*] Side boys are crew members stationed in two ranks at a ship's gangway on the arrival or departure of officers or officials for whom side honors are rendered. The number of side boys varies from two to eight, depending on the rank of the individual.
[†] Vice Admiral William F. Halsey, Jr., USN; Vice Admiral Ernest J. King, USN. Both were four-star admirals in World War II.

Admiral Forbes: Oh, yes. I wanted very much to go to the Naval Academy. I really worked at that, and when I had the time off I read history books and tried to do a little prepping for what I was going to see on those exams. I had, as I say, a good division officer who helped me. He would suggest, "You ought to read this, you ought to do that." He was very good and helpful.

Paul Stillwell: I guess a point to be made is that now a number of people look at the Naval Academy as just another college or university, but back then you were buying a whole career when you agreed to go.

Admiral Forbes: That's right. It was a new way of life.

Paul Stillwell: What do you remember about that plebe summer indoctrination at the Naval Academy?

Admiral Forbes: Well, I remember when we were sworn in that day. I got Dickie Boy—I call him Dickie Boy, my pride and joy—as a roommate, Richard Chester Fay. They put us in our room down there. Since I had time in the Navy, I had a leg up on these pure civilians who came in right off the college campus or their hometowns. We drilled and learned the ways of military life. I enjoyed it. All the seamanship things I'd done before. I tried very hard not to be a know-it-all; I just worked like everybody else. Plebe summer was a very interesting time, which I enjoyed very much.

Paul Stillwell: Do you remember any hazing that went along with that?

Admiral Forbes: No. My first classman was Abe Carter, who lived in a four-man room. There were Abe Carter, Jig Jig Wallace, Jig Jig Ebnet, and Jig Jig Rowan.* That wouldn't happen again in 20 years in the United States Naval Academy. Three Jig Jigs.†

---

* Midshipman Robert Ross Carter, USN: Midshipman John George Wallace, USN; Midshipman John Joseph Ebnet, USN; Midshipman John Joseph Rowan, USN. All were in the class of 1942.
† At the time "Jig" was the word for the letter J in the phonetic alphabet.

I don't recall any hazing at all. Oh, we had to square corners and do minor things such as going up and down the ladders in a particular manner, as we did for other routine things. In those days we marched to class. There was none of this walking to class. We went by sections, and I'll have to digress. I'll never forget we always had our big navigation P-works on Saturday morning; these were the practical applications. We had the first P-work test like an 8:00 o'clock class, followed by another one at 10:00 o'clock, so on and so forth. We'd pass one class coming back from having completed the test. We were marching to the test class and heard, "Big fix, little fix." So we got the advanced dope on what to look for in that exam, because sometimes these instructors deliberately gave the fix and the readings. When we couldn't get a fix, we'd work even harder trying to get through. "What have I done wrong?" They did it deliberately, so you knew it was going to be a big fix or it was going to be a little fix. It was going to be the kind they wanted you to get. It was hilarious.

Paul Stillwell: Did you get caught up in the spirit of the place, the great pride that so many people feel in the Naval Academy?

Admiral Forbes: Yes, I personally did. I was proud just to think that here was this little country boy who had made the Naval Academy. I was proud as could be, and I enjoyed it thoroughly. I also enjoyed my classmates, especially the people who were assigned to my company.

I've got to tell you my quick sea story, since you've just come back from Pearl Harbor. How I remember Pearl Harbor is almost irreverent.* Sunday. We fell in. We'd finished noon meal. I returned to my room, and I went over to my first classman's room. I said, "Sir, is there anything I can do for you?"

Abe said, "Yeah. We want some ice cream sundaes. Beetle, go down and get us four big chocolate ice cream sundaes." He looked at me, and he said, "And get one for yourself." We made only $2.00 a month

---

* On Sunday, 7 December 1941, Japanese carrier planes attacked and heavily damaged American warships at the naval base at Pearl Harbor, Hawaii. The U.S. Congress declared war on Japan the following day.

I went to the gedunk line, as they called it, down there in the basement and was ordering my ice cream when Pearl Harbor was announced. I finally got my five big ice cream sundaes, and I went back up. Now, these were first classmen; they were going to graduate on the 19th of December. When I went in that door with my tray of five big ice cream sundaes, I heard things like, "I wonder if my ship got hit." "And what do you think of—?" "Do you think they will let us out of here earlier?" They were talking a mile a minute. They were all excited.

I said, "Sir, here's your ice cream."

"Beetle, we haven't got time for that stuff. You eat it." So I went over to my room, and Dickie Boy and I sat down and ate five chocolate ice cream sundaes. That's how I remember Pearl Harbor, unfortunately. It was quite an experience.

Paul Stillwell: Well, you had something of an advantage in terms of maturity over your classmates since you were five years out of high school at that point.

Admiral Forbes: That's right. I really appreciated just being here and knowing what it had to offer downstream. But that plebe year was rough, and a lot of people dropped out.

Paul Stillwell: What made it rough?

Admiral Forbes: Well, the routine. We were up at the crack of dawn in the morning. We mustered in the passageway at reveille, then got cleaned up, got into uniform, and marched down to the mess hall. We had breakfast by the numbers, so to speak.

Paul Stillwell: Well, the daily routine had been a way of life for you for three years, so that probably wasn't a problem for you.

Admiral Forbes: That's right. I adjusted to this very quickly, but people like my roommate Dickie Fay did not. And then we had a four-man room; we had Mike Marschall, known as Mike the Kike, who was, and still is, a wonderful friend.[*] Let me

---

[*] Midshipman Albert R. Marschall, USN.

just digress for a moment and say that roommates were called your wives. Wives at the Naval Academy developed into the closest, most enduring friendships one could ever have. To this day we are still closer than brothers. We talk back and forth long distance on the phone. We correspond. We visit. We are just as close as can be, and this Christmas Dickie Boy put a little handwritten note in his card to me about how much he had appreciated our friendship over the years and how I was the only reason he ever got through the Naval Academy. And I'm being quite frank, I broke down and cried, it was just so touching. And I wrote him back a little note too; we are very close.

Paul Stillwell: It's interesting he would make a point of it this many years later.

Admiral Forbes: This many years later, because we were just close as could be. At the Naval Academy we were roommates, and we were as different as night is from day.

Paul Stillwell: How did you differ?

Admiral Forbes: Well, I was here because I wanted to be at the Naval Academy and be a naval officer. I came out of the fleet and really appreciated everything. This was going first class, so to speak. He was here because his daddy wanted him to be here. Jumping to first-class year, we got the assignments we would have when we graduated. To do that, we went down to Mem Hall, where there was a great big fish bowl filled with little capsules, and they had a number in each capsule. There were 914 graduates in my class; therefore, there were 914 capsules in the bowl. A duty officer was there with the roster, and we were all lined up. We walked up and clicked our heels. I reported, "Midshipman Forbes, First Company, sir." A plebe was there, and he put his hand in the jar and pulled out a capsule—at random, of course. The plebe opened it up and read a number. That was our preference number to determine our chances when we were commissioned.

  I must get back to my buddy and "wife," Dickie Boy, my pride and joy. We were sitting there, and he said, "Now, Beetle, I'm going down there. I want to get one of these big cruisers they're always talking about around this place and get down behind that armor plate they're always talking about, and I want to twist a knob till this war is over.

Then I'm getting out." We went down, Forbes and Fay together. I gave my name, and the plebe pulled out, "Seven hundred and forty-seven, sir. Seven-four-seven." I thought, "Oh. I've had it." Then Dick Fay. The duty plebe pulled his out, "Twenty-five, sir. Two-five."

I thought, "Jeepers, creepers." I wanted to go to submarines so bad I could taste it. Well, 747. I hadn't a prayer of going to submarines. When we graduated, we could either go to submarines directly, or we could to go to the fleet for two years before we could go into aviation or anything else. I was assigned to a destroyer. Now, I'll get back to Dickie Boy. Guess what he put in for and got.

Paul Stillwell: Cruiser.

Admiral Forbes: He got a cruiser, USS *Philadelphia*. Guess where he came from. Philadelphia. As it turned out, he reported aboard in the Med one night. The next morning USS *Philadelphia* got under way and returned to the States for a major overhaul in the Philadelphia Navy Yard. He never saw or heard a shot fired in anger the entire war. However, the Navy realized that they had a sharp officer academically, and they sent him to MIT.[*] He did extremely well at MIT and became an EDO.[†] I've been hurt to this day as to why he never became a flag officer. He was very sharp and did everything for the Navy. He's one great individual.

Paul Stillwell: Well, I talked to one of your classmates, for example, George Steele, who went directly into submarines.[‡]

Admiral Forbes: Well, I've got to tell you my sea story about that. We only had plebe, youngster, and first class years.[§] At the end of our youngster year I applied for submarines. The Navy sent me to New London in the summertime. I was assigned to the

---

[*] MIT—Massachusetts Institute of Technology, Cambridge, Massachusetts.
[†] EDO—an officer designated for engineering duty only.
[‡] Vice Admiral George P. Steele II, USN (Ret.).
[§] During World War II the Naval Academy curriculum was shortened to three years.

O-9, a submarine, where I trained for a month.* I had a ball under way out there in the Atlantic. There was no combat or anything like that but all this training. I had my first alcoholic drink there, too, I might add at the officers' club with the officers that night. And I really enjoyed the food. It was just work, work, work. I enjoyed it. And, boy, did I want to go to submarines!

So when I drew number 747, I knew I was "dead," because everybody wanted submarines. Since only 200 graduates went into submarines that year, I had no chance. But, jumping way ahead, I received orders to USS *Meredith*, DD-726, a brand-new destroyer. I said, "Oh, well. Great, great. I like those destroyers. I saw them steam alongside when I was in *Yorktown*." After graduation, I was still at the academy. One evening, while at dinner, I met two commanders. One of them said, "Forbes, where are you going for duty?"

I said, "USS *Meredith*, sir." And as I look back on it, I remember them exchanging looks. I didn't know it, but they knew it: *Meredith* had been sunk at Normandy!† My orders were changed to USS *Barton*, DD-722, which was the first 2,200-tonner ever built and commissioned. It was, as I subsequently found out, manned by handpicked reserves, all destroyer experienced.

The skipper was Naval Academy, the exec was Naval Academy. There was one officer, no names, out of the class of '44 at the Naval Academy, and then here I came. The officer out of '44 was relieved for cause, I might add, later on. But, anyway, on the humorous side, my sister Marian had gone into the WAVES and gone to Smith College and was commissioned.‡ She and her roommate were young ensigns up there at Smith College, and one weekend they decided to visit the Boston Navy Yard to see the ships. By sheer coincidence, as they walked around they saw USS *Barton* moored there.

My sister Marian didn't know that I was assigned to report to *Barton*. Very properly, these ladies walked up the accommodation ladder to the OOD.§ Marian saluted

---

* The submarine in which Midshipman Forbes trained was apparently another one. The USS *O-9* (SS-70), which had been commissioned in 1918, sank on 20 June 1941 during a submergence test off the Isle of Shoals, near Portsmouth, New Hampshire.
† The destroyer *Meredith* was damaged 6 June 1944 when she struck a mine off Normandy. She was salvaged but later sunk by a German bombing attack on 9 June.
‡ During World War II Smith College in Northampton, Massachusetts, was a training site for female naval officers. WAVES – Women Accepted for Voluntary Emergency Service.
§ OOD – officer of the deck.

very smartly as she'd been taught at Smith College, turned to him, and said, "Sir, Ensign Forbes requests permission to come aboard, sir." My sister told me, "He went white." Then he got it out, "It happened. We've got one!" They were looking for Ensign Forbes, and there she was on USS *Barton*'s quarterdeck. [Laughter]

Paul Stillwell: This was before you reported.

Admiral Forbes: Yes, I hadn't reported yet. She told me all this later. She was invited to the wardroom, where they just howled, and had lunch. Marian told them all about me, so I was no stranger when I finally reported on board.

Paul Stillwell: Did she outrank you?

Admiral Forbes: I think she did. Yes, she did. She graduated Smith before I left the Naval Academy. When we graduated from the Naval Academy in those days, most of us went right to Jacksonville for aviation indoctrination. Half of us went there, and half of us went on leave. We spent a month or so in Jacksonville, then came back and had leave. Then we went to our ships. I left the academy on June 7, and I reported aboard *Barton* on August the 7 of that year. She'd been hit at Normandy, and she was up in the Boston Navy Yard being repaired, and that's when I went aboard.

Paul Stillwell: Well, we haven't really discussed your time as a midshipman thoroughly yet. What do you remember about the academics?

Admiral Forbes: They were thorough, and to this day I smile—I can't help it, that's age—when I went up to see my old room and found these three great big computer sets up there. And I thought, "Jeepers, creepers, all we ever had was a slide rule." Behind your answer you put SRA, which meant "slide rule accuracy." The academics were very demanding. We were in class almost constantly—all day long. We marched to and from class. We'd go down, fall in, have noon meal, and go to class again.

Every day we would go to class, and the instructor would say, "This is what you all had for your studies. Gentlemen, man the boards." We'd go up, and he'd give us slips of paper. Each of us got a different slip with questions. We wrote the answers and were graded, and that determined your class rankings and your grades. There was very little time off.

Saturday morning was the big navigation P-works. At noon we had noon meal formation; we had to go to luncheon. Again, there was no time off. And I'm talking about up through midshipman first class. In the afternoon plebes had to attend athletic events scheduled in this yard. That was a plebe function. So we didn't get to go out in town. There was something all the time. Then on Saturday night we could go to the movies here in the hall and be back for taps. We weren't allowed to go out in town as plebes.

Sunday morning it was reveille, followed by mandatory church service. We either had to go to the chapel, or we marched out in town to the church of our choice. The only person who ever beat the system was my roommate, Mike Marschall. When we had to fill out all the forms, Mike put "Druid" in the blank marked "Religion." Well, this caused all kinds of consternation here. Druid? Well, we don't have any Druid services on the Naval Academy grounds. There are no Druid services in Annapolis. So Mike was allowed to stay in the room. He was the only one that beat the system. Now he's a Deacon of the Presbyterian Church, I might add.

Chapel was mandatory. We returned from chapel and fell in for noon meal. On Sunday afternoon it depended on where we stood. We had a compulsory study hour, or we could dope off around the yard.

We used to do a lot of sailing. That was our one way of getting away from these grounds. When we were first classmen, we were allowed only two weekends off first class year *if* we had a 2.8 grade point average or better. And when we were granted weekends off, that meant we fell out from noon meal formation on Saturday, and we had to be back for evening meal formation on Sunday. But if you sailed—and that was my favorite pastime or sport here—you could leave here Saturday morning when classes were finished. We had access to a yawl, the *Highland Light,* the *Vamarie,* or the

Freedom. These big boats were available for sailing, as long as we were back for evening meal formation on Sunday, and as long as we had an officer on board.

In our company was Mother Becker; he had another nickname, but I won't tell you his real nickname because this is on tape.* Mother Becker's first cousin was a young naval aviator who'd been shot down. He was in our age group, and he was recovering at the hospital in Bethesda; he would come over on the weekends. Well, he was an officer. He was an ensign, and he could go with us, and he filled the requirement. Well, we used to sail down to all these places in the Chesapeake Bay and have a ball. It was all above board. I'll be quite frank about that. But you were just free. You escaped the Naval Academy, and you prepared your own little meals. Or we'd go ashore and eat at a restaurant down there at night. It was all above board and a lot of fun, because you got away from academy and we did that.

Paul Stillwell: Were you involved in any other sports?

Admiral Forbes: I tried out for soccer, because that was the only high school sport we had up in Maryland, and I didn't make the team. Sailing was mine. We did very well. We won quite a few awards and enjoyed it very much. I really enjoyed sailing.

Paul Stillwell: How much competitive pressure did you feel with the other midshipmen in your class?

Admiral Forbes: Competitive in what sense?

Paul Stillwell: Trying to make a better class standing.

Admiral Forbes: Well, nothing was on the derogatory side. People like Mike Marschall had a leg up on us all along. He had two years at Tulane University, where he was expelled for drinking. Mike had been in engineering, so we country boys who had never seen some of these things or even heard of some of these subjects had to work like mad.

---

* Midshipman Merlin D. Becker, USN.

And the Mike Marschalls could relax and didn't have to spend so much time hitting the books, but we were very, very close. There were no hard feelings. We were just great buddies.

Our first-class year we were in room 1423, which was a corner room overlooking the gym. I'll never forget the room next to us. The rooms in those days had a great big main room with little side rooms called bee holes. Well, the room next to us had a great big main room and a bee hole in front of their room on the hall.

We didn't have private showers or heads in those days. You went out in the hall to get to the shower. Well, whoever designed that shower had a window between the shower proper and the bee hole which was adjacent to it. I don't know why. Very little light would come through there. But Dickie Boy, my pride and joy, got an idea. They moved their locker over in front of the entrance to that bee hole, the doorway, and then got all this lacrosse gear and stuff, which was propped up as it was supposed to be on the top and bottom. The regulation required where athletic gear was to be stowed. So the casual observer couldn't tell there was a door behind that locker.

Then they took out the window between the shower and the bee hole and put hinges on it so they could open it. They put a desk, two bunks, and four chairs in this cubicle, which was called the Mark III hideaway. At night, during study hour or after taps, they'd go in there, get up on the chair in the shower, go through that window, and get in that little bee hole. They could keep the lights on and play bridge, and Dickie Boy had a ball.

Then there was Harry Englehart, the good Lord rest his soul.[*] Harry lived next to us, and I've got to tell you that sea story. Harry Englehart was a great guy. Smart. Oh, I mean brilliant would be a better word. He stood high in class standing.[†] Every night, when study hour started, a bell rang. We'd hear from the bee hole adjoining Harry's room, "Bang, bang, bang." He'd hit the bulkhead, which was the signal for my roommate, Dickie Boy, to go over. They played bridge in his little bee hole, where the duty officer couldn't see them.

---

[*] Midshipman Harry A. Englehart, Jr., USN.
[†] Englehart finished number 51 of the 914 graduates in the class of 1945.

As I stated, we had no time off here. First class year, as I said, earned us two weekends off. Harry wanted to go somewhere, so he plotted and planned. He went to the battalion office. Harry wrote the names of three midshipmen in grease pencil up on the bulletin board, as he was supposed to, and put down, "sick bay, sick bay, sick bay." One was an admiral's son, no names; one was Hank Searls; and the third was Harry Englehart.*

This was on Friday afternoon after everyone had gone home. At Friday evening meal formation, muster was taken, and no Englehart, no Searls, and no Blank; however, they were checked. There were these black pads like linoleum which were used with a grease pencil. The pads were used over and over again, and normally they checked "absent, absent, absent." Well, this time the watch standers looked up at the board and said, "Oh, they're in sick bay." So nothing was done.

So on Sunday night, when they came back, no one was around. Harry Englehart went down and very carefully took their names off the board for sick bay. Harry cleaned that up, got the muster pads out for the weekend, and erased out all the absentees. The perfect crime. So the duty officer on Monday didn't know they'd ever been absent. However, the admiral's son, who went "over the wall" with them, was absent. Later his mother attended a function at the academy. (I got this firsthand, because I was a company officer.) The mother was saying how nice it was to have her son home for the weekend. It was just great to see him.

That night the wife of our company officer was talking to her husband and said that Mildred was so glad to have her son home. The company officer thought, "He didn't have any weekend off." So he got the errant midshipman down and quizzed him, and he had to tell the truth. He and his mates were honest. They were all awarded class-A offenses, and they were confined to their rooms, except to go to class and to meals. This was just after Christmas, and the confinement lasted until the day we graduated.

Paul Stillwell: All because of a chance remark by the admiral's wife.

Admiral Forbes: Well, yes. Otherwise it was the perfect crime.

---

* Midshipman Henry H. Searls, Jr., USN.

Paul Stillwell: Well, I'm fascinated by these bee holes. What was the purpose of those spaces and how big were they?

Admiral Forbes: They were little rooms that joined the main room. In our room we had two beds, two lockers, and two desks. There were two middies in the main room. Then the little bee hole was smaller. A bed, a locker, and a little desk could fit into a bee hole. A man could move around but not very much.

Paul Stillwell: I see.

Admiral Forbes: Therefore, we didn't have four people living in this room where movement wasn't possible. There were bee holes in some of the rooms. Our corner room had two bee holes, while the room next to ours only had one bee hole. Some rooms didn't have bee holes at all. We had a four-man room, and one roommate, Warren Taylor, moved out after a while. He got permission to do so because he couldn't stand Dick Fay always bragging about his escapades with all his dates and his adventures. This midshipman stood number two in the class, I think. He just got permission and moved into a room and lived by himself first class year. So the three of us lived there and finished our first class year.

Paul Stillwell: What kind of a fate awaited a midshipman who dropped out or got kicked out, failed scholastically? Did he go into the fleet as an enlisted man?

Admiral Forbes: Dickie and I lived with Mike Marschall and Konrad K. Koch, K. K. K. We were in the Sixth Company during plebe year. K. K. K. was from Oklahoma. After Pearl Harbor he wanted to get into the action. He made no bones about it, so when we took our exams in January, he deliberately bilged out. On his math exam he got a .8, and we said, "K. K., you get a 1.0 for spelling your name right in a math exam." We knew he deliberately bilged out, and he went into the Army Air Corps.* He went through pilot training and bombardier-navigator training. He stood number one in both classes and fought the war in the Army Air Corps.

Paul Stillwell: That, I would think, was an unusual case.

Admiral Forbes: It was. Then we had a few other classmates who came from prep school and out of the fleet with us, and they bilged out honestly. They tried hard, and they went back to the enlisted Navy. Willie H. Kitts was a man I'll never forget. He was killed on a destroyer where he was a fire controlman. I can remember those sailors very well.

Paul Stillwell: What do you remember about class characters?

Admiral Forbes: Oh. [Laughter] Well, let's see. Whom did we have as class characters? Well, we had Hank Searls, who was a millionaire's son. They brought him here to play football. He couldn't even make the junior varsity after he got here, for some reason. I'm trying to think why he was so famous. I don't remember any real class characters, though.

Paul Stillwell: What do you recall of the summer cruises?

Admiral Forbes: We didn't have summer cruises. The first year we finished here at the end of plebe year we had a YP cruise.† We operated out of the Naval Academy. We'd go out for the day and return to port and anchor. One time we transited to St. Christopher and spent the night. We went ashore for a few hours, and that was it. The next year we went on the battleship *Arkansas* and steamed in Chesapeake Bay.‡ We moored in

---

* On 20 June 1941 the U.S. Army Air Corps was officially redesignated the U.S. Army Air Forces and retained that title until the establishment of the U.S. Air Force in 1947.
† The YP was a yard patrol craft used for training of ship handling and seamanship.
‡ USS *Arkansas* (BB-33) was commissioned 17 September 1912. Following modernization in 1925-26 she had a standard displacement of 26,100 tons, was 562 feet long and 106 feet in the beam. Her top speed was 21 knots. She was armed with 12 12-inch guns and 16 5-inch guns.

Norfolk once over a weekend. That training lasted a month. And, as I said, I was sent to a submarine instead of going on leave. We didn't have the good old historical-type midshipman summer cruises.

Paul Stillwell: Was it that experience in that O-boat that got you interested in being a submariner?

Admiral Forbes: I guess it was. We left New London and went to sea in the Atlantic for four or five days at a time. The training was interesting and challenging. Those officers were superb, and I just thought this was where I wanted to serve.

Paul Stillwell: Did you get any opportunity for social life as a midshipman?

Admiral Forbes: We could date, yes. We could invite a young lady to the academy. Now, remember, I made $11.00 a month as a first class midshipman. That was cash. Of course, we had an account at the midshipmen's store. However, as far as cash in hand we received $11.00 a month.

Paul Stillwell: That's less than an apprentice seaman made.

Admiral Forbes: That's right. When I would invite my high school girlfriend down, Mary Jane Cleveland, Good Lord rest her soul, she and a few others would come together. Various houses in Annapolis would rent their rooms. The girls had to pay for their own rooms, and they had to pay for their own meals. We would have them here for dances, teas, and special events. That was the social life, and it happened on Saturday.

A quick sea story about Mike Marschall, who was from New Orleans. His parents wrote him and said that his cousin wanted to come to the Naval Academy and bring her roommate with her. They asked when the girls could visit. He looked at me and said, "Beetle, if she visits here, would you date that roommate of hers?"

I said, "Okay, Mike. For you, I'll take a blind date. So what?" Mike wrote his mother, and, sure enough, she got the schedule. Mike and I went to the Greyhound bus to meet them that Saturday afternoon, and they were the last two people to get off the bus. You talk about big! Mike said, "Eunice, is that you?"

"Mike!!" And she gave him a big hug. And she introduced me to her roommate. They were professional wrestlers. Mike said, "Boy, talk about being bricked, Beetle." That was the old expression around here if you got a real bad date.

They didn't bring suitcases. They brought a footlocker between them, so Mike and I went down Maryland Avenue carrying this footlocker to where they were going to stay. We took them out for a cross-country walk and did things like that so no one would see us with them. [Laughter] It was grim, and Mike and I to this day still howl about those cousins of his that his mother was so insistent we date.

Your girlfriend paid for everything, and you brought her to the dance. Then we were allowed so many minutes, almost an hour, from the time they ended the dance—the hop as they called it in those days—till you had to be back in Bancroft Hall and get checked in. Then we had to go to church on Sunday. And that was it. That was your social life.

Paul Stillwell: Well, there must have been something appealing about dating midshipmen if the girls were willing to pay all the expenses.

Admiral Forbes: Well, I guess the glamour of the place attracted them. I mean the war, the uniforms, the orchestras we had here. Jeepers, creepers. Some of the big-name bands would come in and play, and we'd just have a ball.

Paul Stillwell: Do you remember any of the big names from these bands?

Admiral Forbes: No. I wanted to say Glenn Miller.

Paul Stillwell: Well, he was killed during the war.

Admiral Forbes: Yes. We had a few who just brought down the house. They played the midshipman type of music, which provided us casual weekends. But, as I said, one couldn't do anything with so little money. In those days you could not have a car; you couldn't drive a car; you couldn't ride in a car. When Dickie Boy's parents would come down in that huge monster of a car they had, we couldn't even sit in the car, much less ride into town with them. We had to walk out there and meet them. We were not allowed to have anything to do with cars at all.

Paul Stillwell: Do you have any idea what the rationale was for that?

Admiral Forbes: I don't to this day.

Paul Stillwell: Well, I think midshipmen had a higher relative social status then than now. Would that be fair to say?

Admiral Forbes: Yes, very much so. If you were a midshipman, I can recall that you'd be introduced and people would say, "Oh, United States Naval Academy!" Quite frankly, we were a grade above everybody else.

    Now I've got to tell you about this nickname "Beetle."

Paul Stillwell: Please do.

Admiral Forbes: In the good old days as plebes you had to go down and stand in line in front of this nice great big old fat black lady to get your laundry. You had to walk up at attention and give your three initials, and I was christened Bernard Brown Forbes, Jr. I'd say, "B. B. F." Well, the first couple of weeks I got C. D., E. D. and everything else, always somebody else's laundry. I then had to go through all that formality of taking it back and trying to get my own laundry. I remember one day I was standing and waiting to get my laundry. My turn came to go before her, and I said, "B. B. F., Lady. B. B. like in Beetle Butt." Now, I don't know why I ever said that, but Dickie Boy was standing there and he said, "Beetle Butt. That's a lot better than calling you Bernard." So at that moment I became Beetle Butt. When I became an admiral, they dropped the Butt. I'm serious. That's how I got the nickname. Oh, my.

Paul Stillwell: I think that's another custom from back then was the assigning of nicknames. I don't think that's done as freely now.

Admiral Forbes: Probably not. In my company we had the Bourbon Bunny, the Blotter, Head Tremaine.* He wore an eight and three-eighths hat, and the Navy didn't have any that fit. When he came here as a plebe, he didn't have to wear a hat. They had to special order hats for him till they finally got them, and he became known as Head Tremaine. There was also Mother Becker and some that I can't use since this is being taped, but it went on and on.† Everybody in the company, if you were anyone, you had a nickname. Norman Bagnall Bessac, our other roommate, was Buzz Bessac. Albert Rhoades Marschall was Mike the Kike. It went on and on and on. My future brother-in-law was known as Jo Jo, the Dog-Face Boy. Joe Bonds.‡ We all had nicknames.

Paul Stillwell: What do you remember about the disciplinary structure in Bancroft Hall? You had your company officers and battalion and so forth on up to the commandant. What do you recall about that organization?

Admiral Forbes: I remember our company officers. I'll never forget first class year in our little four-man room. We got a new company officer, Lieutenant Commander Pugh.§ He'd only been aboard about two days. One Sunday afternoon, we were studying in our room, and here he came. It was customary in those days to use their academy class ring to bang, bang on your door, and that meant they were going to come in. This was the custom. That was the routine, and we jumped to attention. The door opened, and in walked this brand-new company officer, Lieutenant Commander Pugh, with his sword and all the trimmings.

He never said a word. He walked over to the desk and took the chair and pulled it up against the bulkhead and got up on the chair and put his hand down behind the wainscoting. We just noticed the thing around the wall. We never thought anything

---

* Midshipman Mark G. Tremaine, USN.
† Midshipman Merlin D. Becker, USN.
‡ Midshipman Joseph E. Bonds, USN.
§ Lieutenant Commander Donald E. Pugh, USN.

about it. We didn't know there was a space behind it. Lieutenant Commander Pugh pulled out an empty liquor bottle. He never said a word. He got down off the chair and put it on the desk. Then he said, "Now, who's got a knife?" I gave him my knife; we'd all been issued knives. He went into the shower and got down and unscrewed the drain and picked it up and, lo and behold, there was a piece of wire hanging on there; that's all. He said, "Must have rusted off."

He put it back down, came over, and took the knife. We weren't allowed to have radios till we were first classmen. We had the little wooden AM. That's all we had in those days. The radio on the desk had a nice piece of white cloth over the back so you couldn't see inside, where the tubes and wiring were located. He took out the thumbtacks that were holding the cloth, then used his white gloves to go over all those tubes. The gloves came out gray. He looked at me and said, "Room in gross disorder. That will be ten and three." We were all standing there at attention. He turned and started away, got to the door, and walked out. Then he came back and pointed to that liquor bottle and said, "I put that there when I lived in this room." He was a character. His nickname, of course, right off the bat, was Stinky. Stinky Pugh.

I was fortunate. I was the company officer with three stripes. When Thanksgiving came along, Stinky called me down to the office, and he said, "Now, Forbes, my wife and I would like to have you come over and have Thanksgiving dinner with us."

I said, "Sir, thank you, but, Commander, with due respect, the midshipmen in this company could tell you a lot better things to do with that turkey than eat it." I thought he'd die. Oh, he was a character. Three of us wound up going over and had a nice dinner. And he served wine. Well, in those days anything alcoholic here was an absolute no-no. We all looked at each other, and he said, "Drink it. That's grape juice, and you can drink grape juice." And he was serious. He was great. We got along with him wonderfully well. He was just a character. And we had Marriner Bertholf—I'll never forget him—another wonderful character.[*] We think back on them very fondly. They're all dead now.

---

[*] Lieutenant Commander Charles Marriner Bertholf, USN.

Paul Stillwell: Why was the whiskey bottle still there?

Admiral Forbes: Well, I don't know. I didn't know about the space down behind that. Only he knew, and it had been hanging there on that piece of wire all these years, I guess.

Paul Stillwell: Was there anything in it?

Admiral Forbes: No, it was empty. Somebody may have found it. I don't know. We didn't know it was there.

    Dickie Boy was the character in the class, in our company, and in our room. Buzz Bessac was a star man. We had no free time to call our own. We had to stay in our room and study. We fell out when the bell rang. We could go to the head, and that was about it. But, Dickie Boy left to see Harry Englehart and play bridge. He would open that window and get out. Now, we were up on the top deck. The great big bronze or copper gutter ran along the edge of the roof. I bet you if he ever fell he'd be dead, but that's how he went back and forth. We had a good company, I'll tell you.

Paul Stillwell: One of the great challenges for midshipmen has been beating the system. Do you remember some of your attempts along those lines?

Admiral Forbes: Well, we were beating the system on playing bridge at night and having the Mark II concealing that room all blocked off, because we had a 0400 reveille and standing to be mustered. Dickie Boy and the lad next door would run in the shower, which was okay. We had an old chair that they'd use to jump and go through that window and go back to bed. We had two bunks in there. Well, that's where they used to play bridge or just dope off. That was the way they beat the system.

Paul Stillwell: What about Frenching out?*

---

* "French out" is midshipman slang for leaving the Naval Academy without authorization.

Admiral Forbes: No. With no money what were you going to do? I never did that. Some midshipmen used to try to go over the wall once in a while. I'll come back to that. Now, who was it that fell? We had one that fell and was really injured. I can remember that, going over the wall. But that wasn't very common.

Paul Stillwell: One of the assignment policies for officers apparently, for instructors and company officers, was to bring in men whose ships had been sunk in combat. Did you have any encounters with these combat veterans during the course of your studies?

Admiral Forbes: No. I don't recall a soul ever coming back.

Paul Stillwell: I would think that would be a real advantage in giving you some personal touch with the war.

Admiral Forbes: I don't recall a one.

Paul Stillwell: How much were you able to keep in touch with the progress of the war and to learn about it?

Admiral Forbes: Primarily from the newspaper. We all had the newspapers delivered to our door every morning, and that was the only way. There was so little time off. You were virtually confined to the Naval Academy grounds by virtue of the study pattern and the monetary situation.

Paul Stillwell: Looking back in retrospect, how well did the Naval Academy education and training prepare you for your assignments in the fleet?

Admiral Forbes: Very well indeed. But the thing that I think back on is academically we didn't use a thing that we learned here except in navigation. Well, I shouldn't say that. If you were a snipe, yes.* You knew basically what was going on. It helped. Overall, you

---

* "Snipe" is a slang term for someone in a ship's engineering department.

had a wonderful background to acclimate to anything you experienced out there, but you put down your slide rule and your pen and pencil when you went aboard ship and you went to work.

Paul Stillwell: The other thing it did was teach you to look in books for the answers.

Admiral Forbes: Yes.

Paul Stillwell: Because there is a host of technical manuals and instructions manuals and that sort of thing. What about in terms of leadership and dealing with men?

Admiral Forbes: You know, I personally think that's an individual personality trait—how one meets and gets along with other people and how they relate to you.

Paul Stillwell: But those skills can be developed. It's not necessarily something you're born with.

Admiral Forbes: That's true. That's true. I can't think of anything in particular. We were well trained at the academy. The regimen and the standards were all excellent. When we left the trade school, as we called it in those days—I don't know if they still call it that or not—we ran into other officers who hadn't had that background. We wondered how they could do things differently and saw that their standards were so much lower than yours. It was sometimes embarrassing, and it was always interesting and puzzling.

Paul Stillwell: What can you say specifically about those standards? In what areas did they exist?

Admiral Forbes: Oh, the importance of being the officer of the deck, for example; your uniform and how well you were attired; how you wore your .45. While these were perhaps minor things, they determined the image you created as the officer of the deck.

Some would hang their holstered .45 and its belt on the stanchion by the brow. They would be out of uniform because the old man wasn't on board to see them. They were lax, had no personal pride, and only responded to close supervision. They were there because they had to be there. Period. They didn't feel an obligation to do well.

Paul Stillwell: Is there anything else you want to put on the record about your time as a midshipman?

Admiral Forbes: Well, I enjoyed it. I profited from it. I was flattered by the fact that I was a three-striper for two sets.

Paul Stillwell: What was involved in that?

Admiral Forbes: Well, your leadership qualities and class standing had something to do with it, I'm sure. A midshipman couldn't be a bucket; he was selected. It was a selection process that was all done at the officer level, and I was fortunate. I had the first set in the first company as a three-striper, and then Bill Barnes had the second set. There was a third set, the final set. I was a three-striper and Bill Barnes went on to the regimental staff as I recall. He's a great guy. He was one of the most academically brilliant gents here at the academy and also one of the nicest persons we had in our class.*

Paul Stillwell: Anything you remember from going to the athletic events, such as the varsity football games?

Admiral Forbes: Oh, yes. Again, I was fortunate. I was on the press detail, as they called it in those days. I worked up in the press box with the announcers and went to all the football games. I enjoyed it very much, especially explaining about the goat being our mascot. I'll never forget; I can still hear those reporters sitting there just hilarious. They said, "Bill, the goat. What kind of goat is he?"

---

* Midshipman Willis C. Barnes, USN, stood fifth among the graduates in the class of 1945. He later went to MIT and into the Navy's nuclear power program.

I replied, "That's a he goat." I don't know why I ever said that. I thought they would die laughing. I worked very closely with them. I provided the names of the players and their numbers. I would help them in their reporting and the announcing of the football game.

Paul Stillwell: Well, both the Military Academy and the Naval Academy had a couple of the top teams in the country back then.

Admiral Forbes: Yes, and while I was here we never lost to Army. In fact, every morning when I still—and I hate to say this, but I will—put on my Army bathrobe, I think back. We had no money, so we used to bet articles of uniform. I have an Army sweater which was far superior to the Naval Academy sweater in those days and that long gray, in those days almost down your ankles, Army bathrobe. We bet trousers and things like that.

Paul Stillwell: Anything more on the football games?

Admiral Forbes: Well, we enjoyed them and everyone attended. We had no option in those days. Everyone had to go to the football games. We all wanted to go anyway. And we won; Navy had a good team. We could never beat Notre Dame, but we beat Army, and that made or broke your season—same as this year, I'm sure.

Paul Stillwell: What do you recall about the experience of graduating finally in 1944?

Admiral Forbes: We had the graduation ceremony, and I'll never forget throwing our hats in the air. That was a great thing; then I went straight home. In those days we went to Jacksonville for naval aviation indoctrination. This was the big thing then. We flew in PBYs and SNJs for a month, and then we had a month's leave.* They were very proper

---

* The PBY Catalina was a twin-engine flying boat that performed extensive service before and during World War II. The SNJ Texan was a training aircraft manufactured by North American Aviation.

about that. We were split up into sections. Then we went to our first assignments. Graduation was a great, great ceremony.

Paul Stillwell: Probably a relief from all this incarceration you'd been through for three years.

Admiral Forbes: Oh, yes, because it's hard to realize in this modern day and age the restrictions we had. They were very politely done, but you just were not allowed out in town. As I say, even as a first classman, you were not allowed to even ride in a car. Your little $11.00 a month pocket money didn't give you any latitude. It was very restricted, and we studied. We went to class. We had to hit those books to get through. But it was a great. I look back, and I get a lump in my throat. Those were three great years. I have no regrets whatsoever. I enjoyed it thoroughly. And the friendships I make, as I mentioned earlier, are memorable.

Paul Stillwell: Do you have a facility for memorization? That certainly helps in a curriculum like the Naval Academy's.

Admiral Forbes: I don't follow you.

Paul Stillwell: Well, I mean the ability to memorize and retain it so you can feed it back on a test or in a daily recitation.

Admiral Forbes: No. Not that I know of.

Paul Stillwell: So that requires more study than it might.

Admiral Forbes: Yes.

Paul Stillwell: Well, you've described the process of getting your assignment to the USS *Barton* and how your sister paved the way for you.* Please describe the experience itself on board that ship.

Admiral Forbes: Well, I went aboard, and I was the boot ensign—unexpected, unprogrammed. This was the interesting thing. I'll tell you who was on board at the time who really impressed me. It was Robert Montgomery, the popular Hollywood movie actor.† The ship had just returned from D-Day over in Normandy. It had been hit over there by one of those big German shore batteries.

Quick sea story about that and my good friend whom I met on board, Howard Fashbaugh, who was one of the snipes. When the shell hit, it came down into the engine room unexploded. The sailors ran and said, "What do we do in a case like this? Let's get to damage control. Unexploded shell." And old Fash got the enlisted snipes around him and said, "Come on fellows. I'll show you what we're going to do with it." And they picked this great big 16-inch shell up and dropped it out the hole it came through into the water. That was the end of that.

Small repairs were completed, and we left the shipyard. We steamed to Norfolk, spent a couple of days, and then on down and through the Panama Canal. We went out to Pearl, where we loaded ammunition. We received a full deck load. I was the fire control officer and a junior officer of the deck. The officers on there were all handpicked reserves. Now, I'm not being derogatory, but it amused me. With Robert Montgomery, I just sat there in awe of him.

I wasn't allowed to eat with the other officers, because there were too many of them. I always ate by myself. I was the junior ensign. There were two tables, with two sittings at each table. I was normally at the third sitting, which was the one officer and maybe the duty officer who was coming off watch. I'll never forget Lieutenant Robert Montgomery, when he said to the fellows, "Okay, we've been through Normandy. Now

---

* USS *Barton* (DD-722) was an *Allen M. Sumner*-class destroyer commissioned 30 December 1943. She had a standard displacement of 2,200 tons, was 376 feet long, 41 feet in the beam, and a draft of 19 feet. Her design speed was 34 knots. She was armed with six 5-inch guns and ten 21-inch torpedo tubes.
† Lieutenant Commander Robert Montgomery, USNR. He had earlier served with the U.S. naval headquarters in London and in the White House map room. In 1945 he starred in the film *They Were Expendable* about U.S. PT boat operations around the Philippines early in the war.

we're going out to the Pacific, and I've had enough of this blank-blank. I'm getting off here." He received orders, and he departed the ship.

But all those experienced reserves had destroyer duty. And I remember we had three union organizers in the combat information center, CIC. These were the enlisted sailors who operated the radars and electronic gear. All of them were just crackerjack people. Good to know. I was the fire control officer. Well, *Barton*, being the first 2,200-tonner put in commission, had three twin 5-inch/38 mounts. Do you want to go into all the details about destroyer duty?

Paul Stillwell: Well, in a minute, but I'm interested in more on Montgomery. Was he part of ship's company?

Admiral Forbes: Yes, he was in the wardroom.

Paul Stillwell: Did you have any contact with him at all?

Admiral Forbes: Just to see him, you know, the short time he was on board. When we went to the Pacific, as I say, he left USS *Barton*.

Paul Stillwell: Well, please tell me all about destroyer duty.

Admiral Forbes: Let me just jump ahead about USS *Barton*. That ship has had a reunion, which included the wardroom and the crew, every year since 1950. Their 42nd reunion is coming up in May of this year. We come back in droves. I'll never forget back in the good old days when the captain said, "Now, gentlemen, remember, as the years go by, those Jap shells will get larger in caliber and those misses will get closer." It was and is a very closely knit crew—officers and enlisted—just a great bunch.

Paul Stillwell: Did you have any special training in the fire control equipment before you reported?

Admiral Forbes: Never saw it. It was very modern, and I was assigned there. My chief fire controlman, who was better known as Jake the Fake, was absolutely superb. I'll get back to him later, because he's the kind of man who makes this Navy what it is today. I worked on that computer down there, and we would plot and plan and boom-boom-boom-boom-boom and my ship, *Barton*—which I call my ship because I was on there longer than anyone—still holds the Navy record for the greatest number of rounds of 5-inch/38 ammunition ever fired by a ship in the United States Navy. You'll note my hearing aid.

In Okinawa alone, and it's all documented, we fired 28,848 rounds of 5-inch/38. By then I was the gun boss. Now, I'll never forget when we went off the firing charts that the Bureau of Ordnance figured and provided. The ordnance experts were assigned to what was called the Bureau of Ordnance in those days. BuOrd calculated the number of rounds permitted for a barrel. I wrote to BuOrd and said, "We fired more rounds per barrel now [and I gave them the number] than shows on your charts. What do we do?"

And they came back in due course: "Keep shooting. Tell us what happens." Well, after that large number of rounds at Okinawa, I got the barrels star-gauged, and they were 5¼ inches in diameter instead of the normal 5. We could hear the rounds rattle in the worn barrels. We went alongside a tender and had six new gun barrels installed. The repair personnel had just finished dropping those things in over a couple of days when our radioman ran out on the deck and said, "It's over. It's over. The sons-a-bitches have given up." The Japs had surrendered. So we never fired those new gun barrels. I enjoyed my destroyer duty. I could go into sea stories by the hour on what we did out there.

Paul Stillwell: Well, please tell some of them.

Admiral Forbes: Well, we arrived in WestPac, and, being the first of a new class of destroyer, we participated in all of the Philippine actions.[*]

Paul Stillwell: When did you get out there?

---

[*] WestPac – Western Pacific.

Admiral Forbes: We sailed in September, and we got out there in early October. We visited Pearl Harbor, loaded ammunition, and went out. We had the squadron flag embarked, and we were engaged in all of the Philippine campaigns. You name it: Leyte, Mindoro, Tacloban—all of those.

Paul Stillwell: Well, let's take them one by one. What do you remember about the Leyte campaign?*

Admiral Forbes: Just shooting. We conducted shore bombardment, shore bombardment, and more shore bombardment. We fired at kamikazes.† With our gun gang we never missed a round. They never missed a round. The crew performed perfect maintenance on those weapon systems and we fired, fired, fired, as I said. I've forgotten the exact number, but we were credited with 20-some kamikaze shoot-downs. They were good. We had a great gang out there.

Paul Stillwell: What can you say for the Mark 37 director?

Admiral Forbes: It worked well. Our gunnery officer was John T. Pigott, who could buy and sell us all ten times over today. He's a millionaire settled on the West Coast. As I said, these were all reserve officers.

As for those VT fuzes, we had very poor luck with them.‡ We went back to the time fuzes, particularly against the kamikazes. The only time we ever were hit, quote and unquote, was when we shot down a Japanese aircraft that was almost on his back. The cockpit scraped off our side as the plane and pilot went into the water. In about 20 minutes one of my gunner's mates came running up. "Here, Boss. These are for you.

---

* On 22 October 1944 the U.S. Sixth Army under Lieutenant General Walter Krueger made an amphibious invasion of the island of Leyte in the Philippines.
† Kamikazes were Japanese suicide aircraft that began showing up in the Philippines campaign in the autumn of 1944. The pilots attempted to crash their bomb-armed aircraft directly into American warships. Hundreds of them successfully hit their targets and inflicted great damage.
‡ The proximity fuze for 5-inch antiaircraft projectiles was also known as the VT, or variable time, fuze. It contained a small radio transponder that detonated the projectile when it got near a target, thus eliminating the need for a direct hit.

This is your souvenir of the shoot-down." He handed me two of that Japanese pilot's teeth. [Laughter] Oh, my. Yes, we had a good crew and they never missed a round. As I say, I was very proud of them.

Paul Stillwell: Where was the ship during the Battle of Leyte Gulf?*

Admiral Forbes: We were in the screen there and provided shore fire support. We were always supporting either the Marines or Army on the beach. In fact, that's where we took aboard some of General MacArthur's staff and put them ashore to join the general.†

I was the mess treasurer because I was the junior officer; that was one of my beautiful jobs. The skipper said, "Take care of those people. I want that colonel and those people to know they've been in the United States Navy." When we anchored and they were going to leave the ship, the captain came down and said, "Now, Colonel, I trust everything was to your satisfaction."

The colonel turned to him and said, "Captain, I would never ride one of these buckets again if my life depended on it."

The old man said, "Sir, what did we do?"

He said, "There's no way to dig a foxhole in these steel decks." [Laughter] We did take good care of our Army passengers.

Paul Stillwell: Who was your skipper?

Admiral Forbes: Well, at first we had Commander—they were all Commanders—Joe Callahan.‡ He was relieved by Commander Edwin Boardman Dexter, who was at the Naval Academy when I was a midshipman. When he left to be a destroyer division commander, we got Commander Harrison Perry McIntire, class of '35. He was known as Meanie McIntire. He, too, was quite a skipper.

---

* The Battle of Leyte Gulf was a complex engagement that lasted from 23 to 26 October 1944. The Japanese lost the carriers *Zuikaku*, *Chiyoda*, *Zuiho*, and *Chitose*, along with the battleships *Musashi*, *Fuso*, and *Yamashiro*; ten cruisers; 13 destroyers, and 5 submarines. U.S. losses were the light carrier *Princeton* (CVL-23), two escort carriers, two destroyers, and a destroyer escort.
† General Douglas MacArthur, USA, Commander Southwest Pacific Force, was in command of the amphibious forces that invaded of Leyte in October 1944.
‡ Commander Joseph W. Callahan, USN, was the commanding officer when the ship was commissioned.

Paul Stillwell: I just saw Dexter a couple of months ago. He was out of '28.

Admiral Forbes: Yes, and very active. To this day I hear from him. We visit. He is one great gentleman. In fact, as the boot ensign on board I took part in a little show for him when he came aboard. We were anchored, and we reenacted some the things we had done at the Naval Academy, and I thought he would die laughing. We had a little makeshift orchestra on board; the crew members were the ones who played. We'd had Glenn Miller at the academy. We played a couple of his tunes, and I made some of the comments that he'd made. Again, I thought the new captain would die laughing. To this day he is the leader of this annual reunion we have. Eddie Dexter and his girlfriend Betty are always there.*

Paul Stillwell: He's also big on the USS *Meredith*, which was down at Guadalcanal and was sunk.

Admiral Forbes: The new *Meredith* was named after that, and that was sunk too.

Paul Stillwell: Right.

Admiral Forbes: Yes, he was a good skipper. He let you run your part of the ship, and as long as you did it right, he never bothered you.

Paul Stillwell: Best kind of skipper to have.

Admiral Forbes: To this day I really admire Eddie Dexter.

Paul Stillwell: You've talked about the quality of the reserve officers. What can you say about the quality of the enlisted men in the *Barton*?

---

* Dexter died 19 October 1994, subsequent to this interview.

Admiral Forbes: A-number-one ichi ban is all I can say. They were crackerjacks. They knew and did their jobs. Now, I've got to tell you my quick sea story about the chief fire controlman, George Miller, better known as Jake the Fake. That was his nickname on the ship. He could fix anything. When we lost power once, he ran emergency lines with a couple of youngsters running that Mark 37 director so that the lines wouldn't get tangled up during the kamikaze attacks. As I said, we never missed a round. He could do anything.

One day after a heavy kamikaze attack, when we shot down the one that grazed the ship, he turned to me and said, "Boss, we came through another one." He then said, "If we get out of this alive, I'm going to do what I've always wanted to do."

I said, "What's that, Jake?"

He said, "I want to be a doctor."

And I thought to myself, "A doctor? You must be 40 years old, you old fud. What do you mean be a doctor?" Well, I never gave it any further thought. But years later, when I was in the Bureau of Naval Personnel as the deputy director, my secretary came in and said, "Sir, there's a gentlemen here who would like to see you."

I didn't know who it was, but I said, "Send him in." And in walked Jake, immaculately attired.

I jumped up and gave him a—and I said, "Jake, what are you doing?"

"What did I tell you I was going to do, Boss?"

I said, "Oh, come off it."

He said, "Yes, I am. I went back and went to medical school. I'm a cardiologist in New York City." He smiled and said, "If I do say so myself, I'm doing quite well."

And I said, "You always did well. That's why we're both here today alive." That's because he could fix anything, and he was one great individual. Unfortunately, he died very suddenly and very unexpectedly. His last request, and they came to me about it, was to be buried in Arlington National Cemetery, so I arranged for his funeral. He was a bachelor. No family but what a great guy.

One more story about my chiefs. As gunnery officer I had the torpedoes and all the ship's ordnance. The chiefs invited me down to eat with them one day, which was a great mark of honor. This was during the war. We were having noon meal there, and in those days you had what we called "bug juice." It's known as Kool-aid now. We had all the different colors. It all tastes the same to me. I was eating my lunch, and I picked up my glass of bug juice, and I said, "Boy, this certainly beats anything we've ever had in the wardroom. What did you put in this bug juice? What kind of stuff is this?"

My chief torpedoman looked at me and he said, "Boss, you know that report you sign every month about the evaporation of torpedo alcohol in this heat out here?"

And I said, "Yes. Sometimes it's several hundred gallons."

He said, "You're drinking it." [Laughter] Well, the torpedo alcohol was 100% pure grain alcohol. I never put him on report, because they did such a wonderful job. We had to bend the rules a little bit, as they were a great bunch.

Paul Stillwell: Well, tell me some more stories like that. What other ways were the rules bent?

Admiral Forbes: I'm trying to think. We had no contact with the outside world. We just went boom-boom-boom all the time.

Paul Stillwell: Did you get caught in that big typhoon in December '44?*

Admiral Forbes: Yes. Did we ever. We were one of the ships in that typhoon. I remember we cracked our upper superstructure one place from heavy rolling. We were with the destroyer that sank. Those poor souls, as I recall, had pumped out their salt-water ballast, and they were so light. We rolled 40 degrees. I remember that. Well, that was grim. I was the junior officer of the deck.

And speaking of destroyers, I hate to admit—and I laugh when we say this—but I lead my Naval Academy class in the number of collisions at sea as officer of the deck. [Laughter] I'll never forget that. One of the first carrier strikes on Japan, we were steaming at 25 knots in this great big carrier formation. It was pitch black, the middle of

---

* While operating off the Philippines, ships of the Third Fleet ran into a ferocious typhoon on 18 December 1944. In all, three destroyers—*Hull* (DD-350), *Spence* (DD-512), and *Monaghan* (DD-354)—sank, and a number of other ships were damaged. For details, see C. Raymond Calhoun, *Typhoon: The Other Enemy; The Third Fleet and the Pacific Storm of December 1944* (Annapolis: Naval Institute Press, 1981).

the night, and pouring rain. It was miserable! We were zigzagging; they called it swinging on the code. They wanted to change the base course, which required going through quite a routine. USS *Ingraham* of our squadron was in the screen, and we later found out that they missed the signal. I noticed her getting off station, and in those days you had a sea return about as big as a silver dollar in those old radar sets.[*]

Paul Stillwell: PPI scope?[†]

Admiral Forbes: Yes. And I told the radarmen, "Keep an eye on that guy," because she disappeared into the sea return. We executed the change to the new base course. Coming out of this black pouring rain upwind of us I saw this destroyer at the last second. And I mean when I say last second I mean last second. We collided at an angle that split our bow.[‡] The part above her main deck went into the number one mount. Below her main deck our bow split and went up her side, so that we had a V-shaped split. No one was hurt, thank heavens.

We got that all unscrambled. We had the squadron commander on board. He had to be transferred as were going to get this bow fixed. As I said, we were steaming at 25 knots when we collided with the *Ingraham*. I had the conn when we collided, and my famous statement was, "[Blank], we've hit." [Laughter] And the first word rhymed with hit. Classmates heard about this later on. They had a little bronze plaque made with this statement engraved on it, the date, and who said it. That plaque was mounted in Mem Hall with a little piece of velvet over it. [Laughter] Along with John Paul Jones and "I have not yet begun to fight." "And we have met—" and all those famous statements. Oh, that broke me up.

Paul Stillwell: Did you get any repercussions out of this. Was there an inquiry?

---

[*] In this context sea return means electronic clutter on the radar scope that makes it difficult to distinguish targets close to the ship.
[†] PPI—plan position indicator, a type of radar that presents essentially a geographical picture with one's own ship in the center of the scope and surrounding ships, planes, and land areas shown in their respective positions in terms of range and bearing.
[‡] The collision with the *Ingraham* (DD-694) was on the night of 16 February 1945, when the ships were operating as part of the fast carrier task force off the island of Honshu, Japan.

Admiral Forbes: Oh, yes. Well, I'll finish my sea story. We transferred the commodore and his staff. We were creeping into this anchorage all by ourselves just off Japan when we intercepted a Japanese convoy at 2:00 o'clock in the morning. It was pitch black. Our second salvo hit the tanker, and it blew up. And then we got both escort ships and sank them. We didn't shoot the guys in the lifeboats. We were above board.

We steamed to where the inquiry was conducted. We were exonerated. We found out later that the officer of the deck in *Ingraham* had missed a signal and gotten off station, but he didn't call his commanding officer. The captain was in his sea cabin, but the officer of the deck was going to try to get back on station himself. And he missed everything in that heavy weather. He was really barreling, trying to get back on station when he saw us. As he admitted—he was quite honest—instead of giving left full rudder, he gave right full rudder. He came right into us. So we were exonerated and, of course, sinking that Japanese convoy didn't hurt things either.

Paul Stillwell: Right.

Admiral Forbes: They were given the full blame. That was my first collision.

Paul Stillwell: Well, when the tape recorder wasn't running you mentioned something about March 19, 1945. What happened then?

Admiral Forbes: That was when we were up at Iwo Jima supporting the Marines.[*] We really worked with the Marines during that war. They came back and said, "Your shells aren't exploding." Well, with all that volcanic ash, these base fuzes, which were supposed to activate on impact to blow the shell, there wasn't enough impact to activate the fuzes. We were getting all these duds.

The Navy came out with a very quick fix. They provided modified nose fuzes. We had to take the white phosphorus shells, bring them up, screw off the regular fuze,

---

[*] On 19 February 1945, U.S. Marines invaded the island of Iwo Jima, approximately 660 miles south of Tokyo, and captured it in a fierce campaign. The objective was to provide a forward airfield—an emergency landing site—to support the U.S. bomber offensive against Japan.

and then screw in this new one. It had something like a ten-penny nail sticking out the nose. When it hit—"boom," it blew up.

Well, I had it all organized, and the chief gunner's mate devised a handmade wrench to work those fuzes. The sailors would bring the projectiles up and set them down. The chief would use his wrench to loosen the old fuze, and another guy would screw it off. I put on the new fuze, and then they'd tighten it up. We'd been doing that for about a half hour when all of a sudden there was this little wisp of smoke when they took the fuze off of one of the white phosphorus shells. I had the presence of mind enough to spin on my heel. Thank heaven, since we had this low-order detonation and the shell blew up.

The explosive powder in the shell was sealed from the fuze by a plastic sheet. The board of investigation concluded that it had been cracked; that let the air in and the white phosphorus in there just ignited. Anyway, I came to in the lifelines, and I still had my belt on and my boondockers. Everything else was blown off. I mean, my shirt and the trousers, the whole nine yards. They got me over to a hospital ship. There were about 16 of us, and the chief who had been holding the shell and I were the two who were really banged up.

At the hospital ship—this I'll never forget—I was lying there on a table and they come with little pincers. They'd see where the white phosphorus would smoke and then go in there and take that piece out and throw it away. I had white phosphorus in my arm, the back of my legs, and my back. Every time I take a shower I think of that. They wrapped me up like a mummy with all this grease and stuff on these burns. I was in the hospital ship, and so was the chief. The poor chief later died of poisoning. He just reacted to the anesthesia they gave him, and that was a tragedy.

I was released from the hospital ship and sent back to Saipan. Now, this was during Iwo Jima, and all the Marine wounded were back there in droves. They couldn't figure out why I was there; they thought I was a Marine. In fact, when I left there they issued me an entire Marine outfit—trousers and all. I kept saying, "No, no, no." And I'll never forget lying there in that bed, and when the doctors came in, they said, "See that thing? That's a Naval Academy graduate. He's not a Marine." They laughed because Naval Academy graduates were rare indeed.

Then I was sent back to Aiea, the big naval hospital on Oahu there in the Hawaiian Islands. I'll never forget, when we arrived by plane, the hospital corpsmen said, "Now, this ensign—" And the chief said, "We don't have an empty bed for the ensigns or the junior officers. Put him upstairs with the senior guys." And he said, "Someone will die tonight, and we'll put him down there tomorrow morning." So I was carried off on this stretcher and delivered to the top deck in the hospital there.

Down the hall was a room with two nice, big beds. One of them was occupied by this old senior-looking—I thought granddaddy—lying there. He said, "What in hell's going on?" They explained the situation to him, and he said, "Okay, put him over there."

They put me in the other bed, and this man asked me some questions. He was a commander, Carl Lewis Estes from Texas.[*] He was a multimillionaire, and later I found out he had bought his way into the service. He could arrange anything. He had been in the back of a TBM and was shot down.[†] That's why he was there in that hospital recuperating. He asked me all about myself when I came in.

The next morning someone came up and said, "We've got a space for you."

Commander Estes said, "You leave him right there." Well, I found out he practically ran the hospital. Our room was the last room on the morning sick call. All the doctors and nurses would come in there to chat and tell sea stories. He'd ask, "Now, how many Marines checked in here last night from Texas?" And they were prepared to give him the answer, and he'd say, "Send them up." The Marines who were ambulatory would come up, and he'd ask them where they were from, what they did and all that. Then he'd say, "Go buy yourself a beer," and give them a $20.00 bill. He kept money up there.

He had his own private phone. When things were happening, he'd call his wife because he ran some newspapers back in Texas. I'd sit there and listen to him, and the censor would get on. He'd say, "Get off the line. This is ComSackPac speaking." [Laughter] That's what he called himself. But he was one great gentleman, and I got to know him very well and we got along very well.

---

[*] Carl Lewis Estes (1896-1967) was a newspaper publisher and industrial leader. He served in the cavalry during World War I.
[†] The Grumman-built TBF Avenger was the U.S. Navy's standard carrier-based torpedo plane from mid-1942 through the remainder of World War II. The General Motors-built version of the Avenger was designated TBM.

When I got so I could walk and get around a little bit, I went down to the first deck of the hospital. I wanted to go to the store. I got on the elevator up on the top deck, and there wasn't a soul on there. Before the door closed, in stepped Admiral Halsey.* I remembered Admiral Halsey from when I was the side boy on *Yorktown*, way back in the good old days and he was a carrier division commander. Now I was an ensign. I stood at attention. He had a great big black eye. We went all the way down to the bottom floor, the door opened up, and I was still at attention. He got off, and then he turned around, came back, looked at me, pointed to his eye, tapped it with his finger, and said, "Beer bottle." Then he turned around and walked away. [Laughter] I almost died.

My roommate, Commander Estes, had a Jeep assigned to him. Now, don't ask me how he did these things. He couldn't drive, so I drove him around. He said, "Forbes, you certainly like these Jeeps, don't you?"

I said, "Yes, sir. This is quite a deal."

He said, "I'll tell you. When the war's over, you get in touch with me, and I'm going to buy you a Jeep for every day in the week."

And I said, "Well, thank you, sir."

Anyway, I recovered so I could go back to the ship. I was the only one who returned from the original group that were wounded or blown up. The chief died, poor soul, but all the rest of them they sent back to the States. I returned to *Barton* because I was the gunnery officer.

Paul Stillwell: Well, how much were you incapacitated by this?

Admiral Forbes: Well, I was just delicate. I couldn't touch anything. I mean, ooh, if anybody touched on my elbow, back, or leg, that was all. I had to be very careful. I had all these scars—very, very, very sensitive.

Paul Stillwell: How long did it take to heal?

---

* By this time Halsey was a four-star admiral in command of the Third Fleet. He and his staff were ashore in between operations at sea.

Admiral Forbes: Oh, months. It was a mess. Anyway, I went on back to the ship.

Paul Stillwell: How long were you off the ship?

Admiral Forbes: Two months. From March the 19th to May the 19th. I remember exactly, because I returned when the big Okinawa campaign was in progress. That's where we shot those 28,848 rounds.

Paul Stillwell: Well, please tell me about how the replenishment went. How did you keep that much ammunition coming aboard?

Admiral Forbes: You went alongside the ammunition ship, though we didn't do it then very often. Every third morning we went into Kerama Retto, which is one of the little atolls there in the Okinawa complex.[*] That's where there was a great big ammunition dump. That's where the ammunition ships were. We'd load ammunition, which was an all-hands job—I mean, everyone except the skipper and the exec, even the officers. Everyone was carrying 5-inch projectiles and powder to load up. Then we'd go right back out on the line.

Well towards the end of the campaign, we went in one day, and I went to the exec and said, "Sir, these kids have been working their butts off. We've shot this place up. You know, we've been carrying that beer around in that locker room down there in the stern since we left the States. What do you say we let the guys get over on the beach for a little while and give them some beer? They certainly deserve it."

"I'll check with the captain."

And the captain said, "Hey. Not a bad idea at all." And he looked at me and said, "You take them." So we got all the boats when we were done loading ammunition that day, and we went over there on the beach. I was not a beer drinker, but I remember we had what was called Acme beer. We took it over there by the case. Each of them got two cans, and the young kids who didn't drink beer would sell their cans of beer to those who

---

[*] Kerama Retto is a group of small islands off the southwest coast of Okinawa. It was used as an anchorage and logistics base during the Okinawa campaign.

did for $6.00 a can. Boy, when you were making $21.00 a month, $6.00 was a lot. Anyway, they all enjoyed their beer and had a ball and they went back to the ship, and away we went. Bang-bang-bang-bang-bang. That's how you kept morale up, little things like that.

Paul Stillwell: I'm surprised that the guns weren't replaced before that. That's an awful lot of rounds to pump out.

Admiral Forbes: It is that, and I think we were the first destroyer to have the guns replaced like that for just actually wearing out the barrels. But thanks to the people like Jake the Fake, we never missed a round. Those gunner's mates were all just A-number-one gents, I tell you.

Paul Stillwell: Did you have to trim the rifling off the end of the barrel? Was it extruded out the end?

Admiral Forbes: No.

Paul Stillwell: Well, that metal was going somewhere if you got up to five and a quarter inch diameter.

Admiral Forbes: Well, it was wearing out on the shells. We had a little extrusion, but it was so small you could barely see it at the end of the barrel itself. But, no, we set the record. When the war ended, we were the only ship of our destroyer squadron that steamed back under our own power. They'd all been hit by kamikazes. We were fortunate except for that one little skinny, where we got the cockpit. That's all we ever got hit.

Paul Stillwell: I'm surprised that you say that the VT fuze didn't work all that well, because others had great success with it.

Admiral Forbes: No, it was brand new when it first came out. They just wouldn't explode at all. I mean, it would get close enough. We could almost see the thing. We just had very, very poor luck with them. As the boot ensign, I had to log every serial number of every VT fuze we received. I had to keep track and report back. The fuzes couldn't be tracked the way they were fired. Of course, if you fired when a kamikaze attacked, we could tell which VT fuzes worked and which ones didn't. We'd send back the message, giving them the success of the VT fuzes. These results were very closely held and classified. We weren't allowed to say much about them in those days.

Paul Stillwell: What kind of a reaction did you have when the war ended?

Admiral Forbes: Well, the sailors just cheered when the young radioman ran out screaming, "It's over. It's over." The crew just screamed and turned on all the lights and blew the whistle. We were at anchor, installing those new gun barrels. Typical of *Barton* luck, we received a message the next morning to get under way and steam to Iwo Jima to pick up the New Zealand delegation for the surrender ceremonies.

We buttoned up everything, and I got my gunner's mates together and my chiefs. We talked about how we were going to have to take the roller path data and all the readings for the new gun barrels. Oh, we had everything worked out. We steamed into Iwo, which was the forward-most operational airfield still going strong. We boarded the New Zealand delegation and then steamed on to Tokyo Bay.

We went alongside *Missouri*, put the lines over, and put this delegation aboard.[*] Then we were sent in to anchor right off the Yokosuka Naval Shipyard.[†] We were the closest ship in to the Japanese beach. And they had the surrender ceremony. The captain called me up, and he called me "Rabbit" because I was so junior. By the way, I had many nicknames. When I was christened Bernard Brown Forbes, Junior, that was at my mother's request. My father wanted to name me Peter Alexander Forbes after his father. My mother won, but he and all of his side of the family always called me Pete. I was never called Bernard. He never called me Bernard in his life. I was always called Pete.

---

[*] The battleship *Missouri* (BB-63) was the site of the Japanese signing of surrender documents in Tokyo Bay on 2 September 1945.
[†] Yokosuka was the site of a major Japanese naval base and ship-repair facility.

And my sister, who visited *Barton* in Boston, had talked about her brother Pete. When I later went on board, I was so junior they called me Peter Rabbit, then later just Rabbit. Getting back to Yokosuka, the skipper called me up and said, "Rabbit, I've got orders to send an officer over to Yokosuka to see what's going on over there, what we can expect." He added, "You're the one."

And I thought, "Yeah, I'm the boot ensign. So I strapped on my .45, got the whaleboat, and went over. I was the first naval officer to set foot in Japan after the war ended. I went up in that big shipyard, and I was just amazed. They'd just left work and gone home. Everything was right there. In the rooms where they did the drafting, the utensils were still out. The charts were out. As we later heard, they left and went to the hills. They heard the ugly Americans were coming ashore. And walking around, I finally came across a policeman. He saluted very smartly, and I saluted back, and then I walked around some more. I finally found a firehouse that was manned. That was it.

Barton went back to Okinawa to support the Marines. There was a Marine colonel as the head man. One day during the break we let him take a hot shower, fed him a good meal, and gave him two cases of oranges. And, of course, he had to say to the Captain, "Sir, what can we do for you?"

We'd already briefed the old man, and he said, "All those Jeeps you've got over there. Can we get a Jeep?"

Well, I had been to the skipper. I said, "You know, get these kids something to do. Boom-boom-boom all the time. But, no liberty, no ending."

The colonel said, "Yes." So he had the last laugh. They gave us a Jeep out of a shell hole over there. Well, they brought it out and put it up on the main deck and that's what we needed for those youngsters on the ship. That was their car, and they worked on that thing. I mean, they virtually overhauled it in their spare time.

When the war ended, we put that thing ashore in Japan, and we could go all around. I'll never forget. Being the boot ensign, I got to sit in the back once in a while. We saw Yokohama and all those places as we drove around. The destruction over there was unbelievable. You had to see it to believe it. There were blocks of nothing but concrete slabs where houses had been. And every so often there would be a big iron safe where a store had stood or a building had been. Streetcars were still on the track, completely gutted, with the trolley up on what used to be the wire. Everything was gutted by fire for miles and miles. They really suffered from that shore bombardment. But that was it.

Paul Stillwell: Did you see any of the other people as you made these travels? Any civilians?

Admiral Forbes: No, I didn't see any civilians until I went back there after the war. When that was all over and when they let us go back to the States, we went back by ourselves and we went into Everett, Washington, I'll never forget, October 27, 1945.

Paul Stillwell: Navy Day.

Admiral Forbes: Navy Day.* We moored. With the exception of one, two, three—there were three of us, and then the skipper and exec, I'd forgotten them, for a total of five of us—that entire wardroom fell in on the pier, waved at the old man and said, "Bye-bye, sir." They were all reserves. They had the points to get out.† I mean, this had all been cleared ahead of time. They just didn't abandon ship. The captain realized he was going to lose them all. They fell out on the pier, and they all marched off waving. The only time we've ever seen them since is at the reunions; they come back.

Most of that crew were, as I say, handpicked reserves. They had time to burn, too, as far as getting out of the service. And they left. So we had a skeleton crew. Then a contingent of 21 officers reported aboard. We had Naval Academy class of '46—oh, you name it. Not one of them had ever been to sea before. We didn't have a single—I mean, no experience. Howard Fashbaugh, who's a very close friend of mine to this day,

---

* Theodore Roosevelt was President of the United States from September 1901 to March 1909. He was such a strong advocate of naval power that for many years his birthday, 27 October, was observed in the United States as Navy Day.
† For the demobilization of the U.S. armed forces after World War II, the services had a point system to determine individual priorities for leaving the service. Points were awarded for length of service, overseas service, battle stars, decorations, and dependent children. Those with the highest number of points were the earliest discharged.

was the engineer left on board, and he was a young jaygee.* I was still an ensign, and that was it. We manned the ship right then and there.

I'll never forget the first thing he and I did when we got time to get off the ship. The old man let us go, and the first thing we did was to go into a restaurant and get a glass of milk. We hadn't had a glass of milk in so long that the first thing that came to our mind was to drink some fresh milk. And that was the last time I got ashore, because then the old man's family arrived. Since I was the only qualified OOD he had, I had all the duties every day.

Of course, Howard being a snipe, couldn't stand deck watches. We trained the youngsters we received. From the class of '46 was Bill Polhemus; I can rattle off all their names.† We'd be having luncheon in the wardroom, and the captain would look up and say, "Bill, you don't look very happy. What's wrong?"

"I've got the duty tonight, sir."

He said, "And you just got married before you came aboard, too, didn't you?"

"Yes, sir."

"Well, you poor soul." He looked at me and said, "Rabbit, you take his duty tonight."

Paul Stillwell: Oh, gee.

Admiral Forbes: And finally I got the duty all the time. I was his only qualified OOD. We were laughing about it the other night. From December 24, 1945, until January 3, 1946, I had the duty, solid, on that destroyer. Oh, well. It was great. I really enjoyed my destroyer duty.

Paul Stillwell: What sort of a mission did the ship have after the war ended?

Admiral Forbes: Okay. We got a quick overhaul and had everything fixed up. Then we were chosen—all the classification has been taken away now, I'm sure—to be the ship to

---

* Jaygee – lieutenant (junior grade).
† Ensign William B. Polhemus, USN.

take the atomic weapons out to Bikini for those tests.* The skipper knew it. He got me up, and I was briefed by the people. We had these senior people on board, and then an Army group came on board in uniform. This was later on. Then we received the bomb itself—not just the fuselage of the bomb, but the brains, the innards, the nuclear component part, which they stowed in one of the staterooms, and we had this special Army team of guards.

It was Bill Polhemus's room; he had to move out. I said, "Bill, we're just boot ensigns. These people are senior to us, and that's why they're taking your room."

"Okay, okay. I guess that's the way it goes."

I knew why they were there. The weapons were there, secured under the bunk; they weren't very big. They had two of those people on guard 24 hours a day, on a Navy ship at sea. Once Bill forgot about the guards. He explained to me, "Hey, Rabbit, I went to get the shirt I forgot, and some guy stuck a .45 right in my face."

I said, "Well, you know how those Army types are. They don't know what's going on." And we both laughed. He laughed with me, and we dismissed it that way. When we got to Bikini, we very carefully unloaded it. Of course, the crew knew that that big thing up on the boat deck was the body of the bomb; we didn't make any bones about that. And, I'll never forget, we had to have the exact depth of water in the sound, in case anything dropped over the side. Then we were the closest ship to the actual explosions.

Well, now, I'll have to digress for a moment. We arrived there days before they had the actual bomb drop, because they had to reassemble the components. So while the preparations were being completed, we found out that this was the breeding ground of the yellow fin tuna out there in that atoll. They wondered if the bomb blast would have any effect on the fish.

There was an old World War I minesweeper on station. It was one of these old, old buckets. A classmate of mine was skipper of this ship, and he had—I learned the word for the first time—an ichthyologist on board from San Diego. They cruised around the atoll fishing, and they'd log the kind of fish they caught and the sex and all that. Everything was very proper. I got permission to visit the ship one day while *Barton* was

---

* In July 1946 a joint Army-Navy task force conducted tests at Bikini Atoll in the Marshall Islands to determine the effects of atomic bombs on moored warships. Along with an array of U.S. ships were captured German and Japanese warships.

anchored. I'd never caught so many fish in my life. We saw gear carried away. These were great big yellow fin tuna. I'll jump ahead and say fortunately it had no effect on them.

As I said, we were the closest ship to the drop point. I'll never forget when that big bomber came over and dropped that thing.* We had the people on board; we had the special camera on our fire-control radar. I'd helped them with that. I said, "Why don't you just mount it on my fire control radar?" We just tracked that bomb right down. Oh, it was great. We just tracked it in till it exploded. We got all the pictures for them.

After that we steamed downwind and chased that cloud for I've forgotten how many—oh, it seemed like forever. We then came back and took water samples every so often. That's when we caught so many sharks. We came back and were there for the underwater explosion, which really didn't hurt the fishing either, as they later found out. Then we returned to the States. The services were being cut back. I'd been promoted to executive officer then.

Paul Stillwell: Was there any monitoring to see if you'd been exposed to radiation?

Admiral Forbes: Yes. For years after that, I had to go every so often for a complete physical and I'd get these letters from on high about what they'd found and all this, that and the other.

Paul Stillwell: Was there any effect?

Admiral Forbes: No. And I was the one who was with those tests all of the time.

Paul Stillwell: What do you remember about your duties as exec?

---

* Operation Crossroads involved the testing by U.S. forces of two atomic weapons, detonated at Bikini Atoll in the Marshall Islands on 1 July and 25 July 1946.

Admiral Forbes: We were getting ready to decommission *Barton*, and the ship's company was being transferred. We did the best we could with what we had. Authorities came on board one day and said, "Now, sir, we want to get all the clocks off this ship."

I said, "Fine," and they took them all off. On the pier was a man with a great big sledgehammer—boom. I said, "What in the world?"

The man in charge said, "We don't want these things on the black market."

And I thought to myself, "Well, you're not going to get the one in my room." So I just took mine off and I kept it, and to this day I still have it and it's going strong in our den. Cameras and other things of value were removed and destroyed right there on the pier. Workers stripped the ship, and we were kind of the point of contact for all this business. Then the ship was put out of commission.* Bang, just like that.

Paul Stillwell: How sophisticated was the mothballing process?

Admiral Forbes: I didn't think it was very sophisticated at all. We cleaned the ship up and got rid of all the ammunition. We also accounted for all of this, that, and the other. We inventoried everything, created a lot of records, and closed up the ship. That was it.

Paul Stillwell: Was there any dehumidification gear put on board?

Admiral Forbes: Not that I know of. I didn't see any. And that was in San Diego. I left there on February 1, 1947. I'd gone aboard on 7 August 1944. I had the longest tour on the ship of anybody.

Paul Stillwell: What then?

Admiral Forbes: Well, out there during all those carrier strikes and working with the carriers, I saw naval aviation, and I thought, "If you can't go to submarines—" Boy, I was really impressed. So I wanted to go to flight training, and I applied for it. In fact,

---

* On 22 January 1947 the *Barton* went out of commission in reserve at San Diego. She was recommissioned in 1949 and then served in active duty until 1968.

while we were still out there during the war, one time we came in to load ammunition, and the old man let me go over to the tender which was there and take the flight physical.

I filled out all of the papers, and I passed. Now, Eddie Dexter, the old man whom I still think the world of, didn't like naval aviators. I'd put in my request, and his only endorsement was "Forwarded," which in Navy terminology is the kiss of death. Not "Forwarded recommending approval." Just "Forwarded," which is the nearest to saying nothing you can. So I was not accepted then, but I kept applying.

All of a sudden, out of a clear blue sky, when we were decommissioning *Barton*, I got orders as commanding officer of *PC-572* in San Juan, Puerto Rico.[*] I thought, "Jeepers, creepers."

Well, anyway, when I left *Barton*, I bought a car, and I'll never forget that. It was about a '29 Essex, which didn't cost very much money. Bill Polhemus and I drove to his home way up in the Middle West somewhere; I've forgotten where it was now. I dropped him off and, then I drove on back to Maryland. I left the old car there, and I got a flight down to Puerto Rico.

I went down there as a sharp young jaygee, because I made lieutenant (j.g.) on 1 January 1946. I went to *PC-572*, which was moored. The gangway watch was a young seaman, and he had what I later found out was called a director's chair on the quarterdeck. His .45 was hanging up over the stanchion on the brow. I stepped on board and saluted very properly, you know, a destroyer sailor. He looked at me and said, "Who are you?"

I told him, "I'd like to see the commanding officer."

"Well, let me see if I can find him."

Finally the commanding officer came out; he was a lieutenant. I introduced myself, and he said, "Well, we're getting ready to have lunch. Come on in, Forbes." I went in this little wardroom, and there were he and two young ensigns. He gave me a seat, and they brought out the tea. I was going to put sugar in my tea; I drank tea with sugar in those days. As I took the lid off the sugar bowl, a cockroach ran out. That was my first hint about what I was getting into.

We had lunch, which very simple. Then he excused himself and he left, and I said, "Where's he going?"

---

[*] PC – patrol craft.

The answer was, "Oh, sir, he's engaged to the admiral's daughter, and he just comes and goes as he sees fit. He's the commanding officer."

Well, the admiral was Com 10, as I later found out.* When I had the chance, I told him I was there to relieve him. He said, "I know that. What do you need?"

I said, "Well, can I see the records?" This, that and the other. I had all the technical names in those days.

"Aw, I don't fool with that stuff." I couldn't get anything out of him, and I was there about two weeks trying to get all of this squared away. I got a message from the Bureau of Naval Personnel saying, "You've been there two weeks and you haven't relieved. What's wrong?"

I said, "They can't find this, they can't find that."

I got this message back: "Relieve under protest. We've got to get him off." Well, this is off the record. I later found out the admiral was waiting for him to be relieved by me, so he could marry his daughter. They had set a wedding date and all that. So we had a short change-of-command ceremony. And so help me, I hadn't had command of that ship two hours, and I was summoned over to the admiral's office.

I walked in there, he stood me at attention, and chewed me out for having a ship in such horrible shape. It hadn't been under way, I later found out, in over 45 days. And about having the ship in such horrible condition, etc., etc., etc., etc. He said, "Get that thing squared away and get over to Cuba."

Well, later I found out that he had orders to the fleet training group at Guantanamo Bay, Cuba, but he'd always put it off and had certain backing there to do this, so I had to get under way. Well, the gyrocompass was out of commission. And my petty officer first class was in jail. Anyway, I got real hot, and I got the guy out of jail. It was some trumped-up charge. And we got everything. I got a couple of chiefs up, and I said, "Now, we got to do this, this and this,"

They said, "Well, sir, we'll do the best we can."

I said, "Okay, you've got my support," and so forth. And we got under way. Well, fortunately I had been in the Caribbean before, so I could almost dead-reckon

---

* Com 10 – Commandant of the Tenth Naval District.

navigate from Puerto Rico around to Guantánamo Bay, Cuba, and we went into the Guantánamo.* We got in there on time and anchored.

The inspecting party came aboard before we started the course. They left, and about two hours later I got a call, "Report to the admiral." I went up there, and this other admiral just chewed me out. He said, "Forbes, my people tell me this is the lousiest ship they have ever seen. Everything about it. Dut, dut, dut, dut, dut—" He went on and on and on. When he got all done, he said, "You got anything to say?"

And I said, "Yes, sir. One thing, Admiral, if I may, sir. I relieved under protest four days ago."

He looked at me. He said, "You did?"

I said, "Yes, sir."

"All right, Forbes. It's up to you." So we worked. That was a good crew. We worked and I changed the menu, we did everything. We got everything pretty well organized. We went through that training, and we came out with flying colors. We passed this, that, and the other. Then I got orders to go south to Trinidad, which was a long way. We got under way and cruised to Trinidad, where there was a relief.

I received a call from the Bureau of Naval Personnel, and the detailer said, "We certainly gave you a bucket of worms when we gave you that set of orders. Anything we can do for you?"

I said, "You know, I put in for flight training for years and I've never got it."

Oh. And they came back and said, "Would you like to go to a battleship as division officer?" and this, that and the other.

I said, "No, but I put in for flight training. I'd like to go to flight training."

They came back in another message and said, "Consider it done." When I arrived in Trinidad, my relief, who was a full lieutenant, arrived there also and took over the ship. I got orders to flight training. I went by transport back up into Norfolk, and that's how I went to aviation.

---

* Dead reckoning (short for deduced reckoning) is a method of navigation whereby one plots a direction and amount of progress from the last well-determined position. The result, known as the DR position, amounts to the best estimate of one's actual position at a given time.

Paul Stillwell: Your not going into submarines right out of the academy was the luck of the draw, but was there not an opportunity to apply later?

Admiral Forbes: Yes, but in the meantime I had become so enthralled by naval aviation, watching out there in the Pacific, all those strikes and working with those people that I'd said, "That naval aviation is great." So I wanted to try out for that.

Paul Stillwell: What was the routine that you got into at flight training?

Admiral Forbes: Well, I checked into the great big brick BOQ down there at Pensacola and lived up on the top deck. I was out of the class of '45. There were Henry Jonathan Hosmer Cooke out of the class of '43 and William Alexander out of the class of '44.[*] I'm trying to think of my roommates right around that little area there.

We started the basic flight training and flew the SNJs at first there at Pensacola and went through that.[†] Then things changed. We went to Cabiniss Field and went through training in TBMs.[‡] Then we went to Jacksonville. We were kept moving around in this flight training. I finished up flight training in TBMs in '49. Then I received orders to VC-33, which was a brand-new squadron that was just commissioning at Naval Air Station, Norfolk and flying TBMs.[§]

Paul Stillwell: What do you remember about the training process itself? How well did you take to airmanship?

Admiral Forbes: Pretty well. I wasn't a natural-born aviator, but I tried very hard. I studied everything, and I got through.

Paul Stillwell: How capable were the instructors?

---

[*] Lieutenant William H. Alexander II, USN.
[†] The SNJ Texan was a training aircraft manufactured by North American Aviation.
[‡] Cabaniss Field at Corpus Christi, Texas.
[§] VC-33 – Fleet Composite Squadron 33.

Admiral Forbes: A-number-one. In those days they were all wartime pilots who were very good and very thorough. I sat up in that SNJ, and the instructor was in the back seat and what he did, he said, "Now, Forbes. Now, don't do it this way, do it that way." And then they gave you your solo hop. The instructor stood down on the ground and watched you bring that SNJ around and land. And, of course, in those days we used grass landing fields so much. And I'll never forget that one instructor I had. We'd land in these grass fields. "Okay, Forbes. You know what to do now, don't you?"

"Yes, sir." I'd get out and go over to a watermelon patch and cut out a couple of big watermelons. I would bring them back and put them in the plane under my feet. "Okay. Here we go." Phsew. We used to get watermelons all the time. He was a great guy. They were thorough. They were good.

Paul Stillwell: What about tactical training and formation operations?

Admiral Forbes: Yes, we got that. That was also good. Everything was demonstrated first. You sat in that SNJ with them and went through all these maneuvers and the loops and the rolls and the formation flying and how to keep this and that like the throttle—very detailed. They were all experienced. And then you did it and they sat in the back seat and watched you for a couple of times, and then you did it solo by yourself. I thought it was thorough training.

Paul Stillwell: How sophisticated was instrument work then?

Admiral Forbes: Not very. You had an altimeter and a compass and a horizontal indicator, which showed the angle of the wings. We made a lot of radio approaches. The radio was tuned in, and we would go out and come back in a regular pattern and so forth and so on. It was, for its day and age, thorough enough.

Paul Stillwell: How did you get into the attack community? Did you request that?

Admiral Forbes: Yes. I didn't want to be a fighter puke.

Paul Stillwell: Why not?

Admiral Forbes: I don't know. [Laughter] I put in for attack. You didn't have much choice. Regardless of what you requested, you were assigned where you were needed. I went to this new squadron that was just forming, and I fortunately had some old buddies from Pensacola. We flew the TBM and the XBT2D-1 in Norfolk.* We were an antisubmarine warfare squadron. We did a lot of night work and a lot of instrument work. I tell you, we really got the time in.

Paul Stillwell: What sorts of weapons did the plane carry?

Admiral Forbes: We carried torpedoes and bombs.

Paul Stillwell: Was this primarily an antisubmarine torpedo?

Admiral Forbes: Yes. And then we had torpedoes for ships. We wore two hats.

Paul Stillwell: Well, that was kind of an obsolete role at that point, wasn't it? Was there much expectation that you would torpedo surface ships?

Admiral Forbes: Well, I don't know. That's what we did because we're talking about 1949. We were four years away from the end of the war.

Paul Stillwell: So that was still considered a viable mission, I guess.

Admiral Forbes: Yes.

---

* The Douglas BT2D Dauntless II was an attack plane, later to be known as the AD Skyraider. The X indicated it was still an experimental model.

Paul Stillwell: What was involved in dropping an aerial torpedo? The old Devastator had the low and slow approach that was fatal at Midway.* Had that situation been improved any?

Admiral Forbes: Nope. We came in and went down a certain height over the water and maintained a certain speed. We used seaman's eye to establish a lead angle on the ship and determine how fast the ship was going, then dropped by seaman's eye. There were no instruments that measured the factors. Most of our operations involved looking for submarines, practicing ASW, and dropped the little sonobuoys for listening.

Paul Stillwell: So the TBM was equipped with sonobuoys?

Admiral Forbes: Yes.

Paul Stillwell: What about radar?

Admiral Forbes: I don't recall radar, to be quite frank about it. We went from Norfolk to Atlantic City, New Jersey, where we got the ADs.† They were AD-4Ns, which were instrument-configured or weapon-configured ADs. They weren't just bombers. We did a lot of antisubmarine warfare work with those.

Paul Stillwell: Did the N indicate night work?

Admiral Forbes: No, but they were equipped for that. They were all-weather aircraft, and when we went from the TBM to an AD-4N, it was just like going from night to day.

Paul Stillwell: In what ways?

---

* The TBD Devastator, built by the Douglas Aircraft Company, was a monoplane torpedo bomber. After TBDs were essentially annihilated in the Battle of Midway in June 1942 they were withdrawn from operational service.
† Douglas AD Skyraider propeller-driven attack planes first entered fleet squadrons in late 1946. The AD-2 version was 38 feet long, wingspan of 50 feet, gross weight of 18,263 pounds, and top speed of 321 miles per hour. In September 1962 Skyraiders still in service were redesignated A-1s.

Admiral Forbes: Speed. Oh, Jeepers. Maneuverability. And the power! Great day. The power of that AD was in the 3,250-horsepower engine.

Paul Stillwell: That was an Ed Heinemann plane; I noticed his obituary just a few weeks ago in the newspaper.*

Admiral Forbes: Yes. I saw that he died, but I didn't see the obituary.

So that was in Norfolk, and while we were in Norfolk I have to tell you my sea story. I lived in the BOQ there, SP-17 at NAS, Norfolk.† In those days you had your own little bedroom with an adjoining bath. The guy on the other side of you also had a little bedroom. Each had two bunks, but they tried to keep it so you had your own room.

The fellow who shared the bath with me was Lieutenant Paul Kissling.‡ I'll never forget him. Great guy. He was aide and flag lieutenant to Commander Air Force Atlantic Fleet, one Vice Admiral Felix Budwell Stump.§ I'd come up to the BOQ some nights from the squadron, and Paul would be sitting on the side of his bed, his head in his hands, just kind of shaking. "Paul, what's wrong?"

"That man. That man, Beetle."

I said, "Oh, my goodness." I didn't know what an aide was.

The same guys we'd gone through flight training with, Hodge McCook and Bill Alexander, were in the same squadron. Even though they were senior to me, we all ended in VC-33. We ate in the wardroom and flew at night. We had a busy life, and we enjoyed it. One day in early 1950 I was at the squadron. The phone rang. When I picked it up, I heard, "Beetle, Paul."

I said, "What can I do for you, Paul?"

"Beetle," he said, "you're an old destroyer sailor. What's this about some kind of a flag on the ship that tells you the commanding officer's not on board?"

---

* Edward H. Heinemann was a long-time aircraft designer for Northrop and later for Douglas Aircraft. He was particularly noted for planes such as the SBD Dauntless and the A4D/A-4 Skyhawk. His memoir, written in conjunction with Rosario Rausa, *Ed Heinemann: Combat Aircraft Designer* (Annapolis: Naval Institute Press, 1980). Heinemann, who was born 14 March 1908, died 26 November 1991.
† NAS – naval air station.
‡ Lieutenant Paul T. Kissling, USN.
§ Vice Admiral Felix B. Stump, USN, served as Commander Air Force, Atlantic Fleet, from December 1948 to 11 May 1951.

I said, "Oh, you mean the third repeater, the absentee pennant?"

"Thank you, Beetle. Thank you." And he hung up.

So that night up in the room I said, "Paul, what was all that about today on the phone?"

"Beetle, Admiral Stump and I were going down. You know, *Coral Sea* and *Midway* are both down at Pier Seven. One's on one side and one's on the other. We were going down about 10:00 o'clock this morning, and the admiral turned to me and said, 'Paul, is the commanding officer of *Midway* on board?' Well, I thought to myself, well, it's 10:00 o'clock Wednesday morning: 'Yes, sir, he's on board.'" Paul continued, "We started up on the quarterdeck, and the admiral said, 'I want to see the commanding officer.' The OOD saluted him very smartly, and he said, 'Sir, the commanding officer's not on board.' 'Thank you.'"

They went down the brow, and this time the admiral turned to Paul, and he said, "Now, Kissling, is the commanding officer of *Coral Sea* on board?" Paul said, "Beetle, I couldn't be wrong twice in the same morning. I said, 'Yes, sir.' So this time we walked up, and the OOD looked up, and he said, 'Sir, the commanding officer's not on board.'"

As they were walking down the brow, the admiral looked at him and said, "Kissling, don't you know anything about how to tell whether the commanding officer's on board?" That's when he found out that his aide and flag lieutenant had been a P4M driver, a big old shore-based plane, all through the war based in Alaska and had never been aboard ship in his life. Never. Admiral Stump then started giving Paul a plebe year, so to speak. And I was getting all these calls about, "Beetle, what's this, what's that?" I'd answer him about the speed pennants. It went on, and the admiral was just running him with all these questions.

We went to the wardroom, and the three of us trade school types, Hollis McCook and Bill Alexander, and we were having dinner. Paul was all upset, so we asked, "What's wrong, Paul?"

"Well," he said, "you know *Missouri* went aground. I've got to go out tomorrow and ride the carrier in, and the admiral wants me to check the pilot's navigation." He said, "What does all that mean?"

We gave him a cram course in Naval Academy piloting, and I said, "Now, Paul, when that admiral of yours is there at your charts, you say, 'Admiral, get that coffee cup off of my chart. There are enough corrections entered already.'" which is an old destroyer thing.

I came back from the squadron after a hop late the next afternoon. I was the administrative officer, and there was a note on my board, "Beetle, call me immediately. s/C.O." Below that, "Beetle, as soon as you call the C.O. call me. s/X.O." And below that, "Beetle, you poor S.O.B." signed, the Big A, who was Bill Alexander. I thought, "What in the world?"

I called the skipper, who said, "Beetle, glad you called. While you were gone, Admiral Stump had me over, and he wants you to be his aide."

I said, "I don't want to be an aide, Captain."

He said, "I know that, and I want to keep you in this squadron. I did everything I could. I even lied, but for some reason it's you and you alone." So then I called the other ones.

Anyway, I got up to the room that night after dinner, and I had never put two and two together. Paul was in there, and I said, "Paul, how did it go today out on the carrier?"

"Beetle, you guys saved my ass," he said. "And Beetle, guess what? I told Admiral Stump about that coffee cup, and he looked at me he said, 'Hold it, Kissling. Someone has been giving you a lot of answers for me over the last month, but who told you to tell me that?'"

Paul gave him my name, and I thought, "Jeepers, creepers."

I was going to be the smart young jaygee, so I reported on the third of July, because I thought, "Well, I'll have the next day off." I went into Paul Kissling's office there in Norfolk, and we went in to see Admiral Stump. He looked at me, and he said, "Who in the hell are you?"

I told him. I said, "Sir, I've been ordered to be your aide. Frankly, sir, I don't want to be your aide because I plan to get married this fall." This was when aides were never married. They were all bachelors.

"Local girl?"

I said, "No, sir. She lives in Lynchburg, Virginia."

"At least you won't be tomcatting around every night like Kissling is then, will you?"

I said, "No, sir."

"Out." We went out.

I became his aide, and the next thing I knew, he had me in and said, "Stand there!" And he gave me ten questions such as, "Who's commanding officer of *Coral Sea*?" "Who's the executive officer of *Midway*?" "What's the state flower of Idaho?" I knew about four Navy questions, and the other six I didn't know. Like a plebe I said, "I don't know, sir, but I'll find out."

I studied like mad, and every day it was the same thing. I went in there and stood at attention while the admiral asked ten questions. He said, "I'll give you a point four on every correct answer." So I got to thinking one day, and I thought, "He really doesn't know all this stuff." I had all the Navy answers down, and he wanted to know, "What's the state flower of Texas?"

I said, "The cactus, sir."

He looked at me. "What's the state bird of Louisiana?"

I said, "The penguin, sir." I didn't know what they were.

Then he looked at me with a kind of a grin, and he said, "You're learning, aren't you?"

I said, "I'm trying, sir." That was the end of that. He never called me in again. He didn't know the answers either to all those other questions. They were off the top of his head. I became aide and flag lieutenant to Admiral Felix Budwell Stump from Stumptown, West Virginia, the son of a Baptist minister. I say that very carefully.

Paul Stillwell: Is there anything else from the TBM squadron to relate? How did squadron life compare to wardroom life in a destroyer, for example?

Admiral Forbes: Well, it's not so close, because you're not confined to that hull, and once flight ops end for the day, you're free. You can go anywhere you want. And you live in the BOQ. It wasn't so confined. When you were on board the carrier, yes. That ready room was a very close-knit group. We argued about the movie we were going to have that night and all of that. We were right together. We couldn't disperse as we could on the beach. That was the only difference.

Paul Stillwell: Did your squadron spend some time on board a carrier?

Admiral Forbes: Oh, yes.

Paul Stillwell: Which one?

Admiral Forbes: We were in the old *Franklin D Roosevelt*. We were in *Shangri-La*. I can go on.

Paul Stillwell: Well, please. Did you make some deployments in that squadron?

Admiral Forbes: No. It wasn't a deploying squadron then.

Paul Stillwell: You just went out for local ops?

Admiral Forbes: Yes, local ops and carquals to keep proficient.*

Paul Stillwell: Well, you haven't talked about your first carrier landing. How did that come about?

Admiral Forbes: Well, we went through all that training in Jacksonville and went to sea that day in that SNJ. I did everything I was told to do. I came around, watched the LSO's flags and just checked to make sure of my speed and that I was lined up.† And when he said "Okay, three," I pulled that throttle and caught that wire, thank heavens.

---

* Carquals—qualification landings and takeoffs on an aircraft carrier.
† LSO – landing signal officer, a naval aviator, who stands on a platform on the port side of the carrier at the aft end of the flight deck. He signals to incoming aircraft in order to coach them onto the deck for recovery. The plane then catches an arresting wire with its tailhook in order to come to a stop.

Paul Stillwell: What ship was that?

Admiral Forbes: Oh, I've forgotten which one it was now. It wasn't the old *Lexington*. I know that.

Paul Stillwell: Well, they had the *Monterey* down there for a while, I think, one of those CVLs.

Admiral Forbes: I've forgotten what we were aboard in those days.

Paul Stillwell: I take it you just took the thing in stride.

Admiral Forbes: Yes. That's very demanding. Carrier pilots have to be on the stick, so to speak.

Paul Stillwell: What was the TBM like to fly? I get the impression it was sort of a sluggish airplane.

Admiral Forbes: It was. It was heavy. It didn't have that much power. But very stable, and the pilot sat up there in that cockpit. I almost had to take off my harness to get down and shift anything because the cockpit was so big, and it was a single place, of course. We had places for crew, but we didn't carry crewmen. It was all solo stuff. But it was a good bird. Very stable, very dependable. We didn't lose any of them.

Paul Stillwell: Well, I think the shift in mission was illustrated when you got the AD, which did not have a torpedo capability.

Admiral Forbes: That's right. It didn't. We had all kinds of equipment on there. The electronics were out of this world. When we first got those ADs, we didn't get any of the books that come normally with an aircraft. We tried to fly them like we flew the TBM.

I'm glad I can still sit here today and talk about it. Jeepers, creepers—no comparison whatsoever.

Paul Stillwell: Just in terms of power and maneuverability?

Admiral Forbes: Power and maneuverability.

Paul Stillwell: Well, I've even heard about some ADs being used like fighters in Vietnam, so that tells you something.

Admiral Forbes: Well, later, when I commanded my own squadron, it was a special weapons squadron, and it had all the verification. We had to sign all kinds of papers, and everybody in the squadron had his own target in Russia. We were a special weapons squadron, and we had the loft low-altitude bomb system. That was the procedure where you went in and lofted the plane at a certain G, and at a certain point you pressed the button. That shape went off, and we used to bomb there in Florida day in and day out. It was quite a squadron.

Paul Stillwell: Did it make any difference in your squadron operations when the Korean War started?[*] That was just shortly before you got pulled over by Admiral Stump.

Admiral Forbes: No. We kept on training on and flying.

Paul Stillwell: Anything you remember about the skipper, exec, or other senior officers in that squadron?

---

[*] The Korean War began on 25 June 1950, when six North Korean infantry division and three border constabulary brigades invaded South Korea. The troops were supported by approximately 100 Russian-made T-34 tanks. In New York that same day the United Nations Security Council adopted a resolution condemning the invasion.

Admiral Forbes: Yes. The skipper was Commander R. M. Lindsey, who was a highly regarded naval aviator.* He treated me very nicely. He did very little flying in the squadron.

Paul Stillwell: He was a spectacular LSO in the *Enterprise* during the war.

Admiral Forbes: Yes. He was quite the gentleman and he gave me all the paperwork, and he did it very politely. He would say, "Please do this this way and that," and I'd report to him and did all the paperwork. I've got his fitness reports in here. They're very interesting. And then our exec, poor soul. We were out operating on the carrier, I'll never forget, because I had just gotten out of the plane and was walking in. He came around, made a beautiful approach, and lined up, and we'll never know to this day what happened, because he had thousands of hours. That nose went down and he—you know how the ramp comes over like that—he hit that ramp just like that. The engine and the prop came cartwheeling down the deck, and the rest of the aircraft went down below and he was decapitated. Oh, it was awful. They put me in charge of the funeral arrangements and all that. He was a bachelor. Thousands of hours and highly regarded. That really hurt. First carquals.

Paul Stillwell: You knew you were getting into a dangerous business.

Admiral Forbes: Yes, sir.

Paul Stillwell: What was Lindsey like as an airman and as a leader?

Admiral Forbes: Well, he was very personable. He had a charming wife, who was great socially. I don't ever remember his flying. He didn't do much. I'm not being derogatory. I just don't recall.

Paul Stillwell: Was that because the squadron had limited flight hours or what?

---
* Commander Robin M. Lindsey, USN.

Admiral Forbes: No. We flew as a group. I don't ever remember flying with him. I did a lot of flying with the exec. He also was very nice, very personable, and very senior. He was a very senior commander, which was normal for that job. Somewhere I've got all that in here.

Paul Stillwell: Well, Admiral, please tell me about that wonderful character who hired you, Admiral Stump.

Admiral Forbes: Admiral Stump was an unusual individual, and I say that in all due respect and admiration. He was over six feet tall. A good operator. Very demanding but very fair. I worked for him, and he took me everywhere he went. In those days, it was Commander Air Force Atlantic Fleet. Now it's Commander Naval Air Force Atlantic Fleet. The name was changed.

We got our flight time in together. In those days, even a three-star admiral had to get in four hours a month. I'd call over and get the SNB, that little twin-engined plane they had over there at the air station in Norfolk, and away we'd go.* I've never seen or known an aviator who could consistently land that plane so smoothly, and it had a history or reputation for being such a bumpy lander.

But he did not believe in anything electronic. In 1917 he'd gone through flight training, and therefore he knew every buoy, every farm, every point of land in the Tidewater area.† He always went by that. None of this radio stuff. And we would go in and land. He'd grease that thing on the deck, and I've got to tell you one quick sea story.

We came back one day, and I was wearing the radio earphones coming back into Norfolk when I called for landing instructions and was told, "You're not cleared, umpty-ump."

I told Admiral Stump. I said, "Admiral, we're not cleared to land." He just looked at me and brought the thing on around and made a beautiful landing. We taxied up to where his official car was waiting for him near the tower. The command duty

---

* The SNB Kansan was a training aircraft manufactured by Beech Aircraft Company. The Navy first ordered a version of the airplane in 1941; the Army designation of the equivalent plane was AT-11.
† Stump graduated from the Naval Academy in 1917 and went through flight training in 1919-20.

officer, who was a commander, was out there with his group. As soon as we were out of the air and stopped the engine, the command duty officer, of course, jumped on me, because they thought the aide was flying. He said, "What did you land that plane for? I told you not to land it."

Admiral Stump had gone over toward his car. He came back and he said, "Forbes, do you have a problem?"

I said, "Yes, sir. The command duty officer wants to know why I landed when I was told not to land."

He looked the commander in the eye, and he said, "I had to pee. Any further questions?" [Laughter] The commander walked off. Admiral Stump was like that. He was quite a fellow.

When he became Commander Second Fleet, he took me as his aide.* We made all of the NATO exercises.† We embarked in *Iowa* most of the time and worked with the Brits and the French and the Norwegians. It was just a fascinating seagoing experience. I'll never forget being on that battleship. On his staff at that time he had Captain Ulysses Simpson Grant Sharp, who later became Admiral Oley Sharp.‡ And he had Captain John Sylvester, who later became Vice Admiral John Sylvester. He had a talented group on that staff. He placed me on watch up on the bridge of the flagship, because I was the only qualified watch officer on the staff. I had done all that duty in destroyers, so he assigned the officers on the staff who had never been to sea as my assistants. We had a good time. It was a very educational tour of duty.

Paul Stillwell: Specifically what sorts of things was he involved in when he was ComAirLant.

Admiral Forbes: Well, as ComAirLant he was involved with the training and safety of all the squadrons and the ships, particularly the ships, who was operating what and how they were doing. He was *the* boss, and he had a lot of good people working for him and he

---

* Vice Admiral Stump commanded the Second Fleet from March 1951 to June 1953.
† NATO—North Atlantic Treaty Organization, which was established in 1949 as a means of coordinating defense against a potential attack from the Soviet Union.
‡ The oral history of Admiral Sharp is in the Naval Institute collection.

worked through them. And, as I said, he was getting his flight time every month. He'd steam out on the carrier, fly off the carrier with someone, and come back around and land. He was good.

The admiral was married. It was his second marriage. His first son was John Morgan Stump, who's Naval Academy class of '51, as I remember. In his second family he had little Felix Budwell, Jr., who was four years old and his sister, who was six years old, so he was a very, very interesting gentleman.

When he left Second Fleet he called me in and said, "I want to take you to CinCPacFlt with me, but it's time you got back to doing something worthwhile."

I replied, "Yes, sir. I've got to get back to flying."

He said, "I know that. Where do you want to go?"

I said, "Well, the best place to go, I guess, is the training command. Get more flight time in."

"Okay." So I got orders down to Cabiniss Field, Texas, as a flight instructor.

Paul Stillwell: Well, before that I'm interested in hearing more about these two tours that you served with him. Did he come to confide in you after you'd gotten to know him pretty well?

Admiral Forbes: Yes.

Paul Stillwell: What sorts of things would he talk about?

Admiral Forbes: He'd talk about personalities, people, what he had in mind, what he would like to do, what he would like to try, things of that nature. I was always just a bit—bedazzled would be the best word to use—at his trust and confidence and the things he told me in discussions. Of course, he knew I'd keep my mouth shut, but he had to talk to someone about these thoughts.

Paul Stillwell: He needed a sounding board to bounce his ideas off.

Admiral Forbes: I won't jump ahead at this point, but I was his aide when he was CinCPac-CinCPacFlt. I'll go into great detail then on what he did then. Admiral Stump was just a good boss, and I represented him and took care of everything when I was the aide and flag lieutenant.

Paul Stillwell: During this time as ComAirLant was he involved in getting carriers ready to go around to operate in Korea?

Admiral Forbes: Yes, and the workup of the aviation squadrons. He was responsible for everything, and he took his responsibilities to heart. He was very conscientious about it. The admiral was a hard worker. I think he took Christmas Eve off. That was about it.

Paul Stillwell: How did this work for you? Did you wind up not getting a lot of time off either?

Admiral Forbes: None. [Laughter] Ask my sweet wife.

Paul Stillwell: You've mentioned that you were planning to get married. When did you get married?

Admiral Forbes: Well, he was very nice about that. He let me have Thanksgiving weekend off, because we weren't going to work on Thursday and he said, "We don't work on Saturday."

I thought to myself, "When did that start?"

So Admiral Stump gave me Thanksgiving weekend, and then he laughed. He gave us a whole week, so we got married on that Thanksgiving weekend and went to New York on our honeymoon. I told him where we were going to live. When we got back—I'm not exaggerating—there was a note on the front door, the first I was ever in this house, to call the duty officer immediately. I called the duty officer, who said, "Admiral Stump wanted me to tell you that you and he are going to Washington tomorrow morning bright and early. Be out here." [Laughter]

I was out there bright and early, and off to Washington we went and stayed two days. He said, "I thought I'd give you a little break." That's all he said. We stayed at the old Army-Navy Club. He had business there in the Pentagon. They had him over. But he was like that. He treated us very nicely. There was never any fraternizing or anything like that.

Paul Stillwell: How had you met your future wife?

Admiral Forbes: Very simple. When I was in VC-33 here, one of my favorite uncles, Uncle Pat, and his wife lived in Lynchburg, Virginia. One weekend I left here on Saturday and went up to see them. I was going to spend the night, and the rest of this I get from the other side of the fence. They knew Betty, my sweet wife-to-be, and her family. They were old friends. She'd just graduated from James Madison. It wasn't called James Madison.

Paul Stillwell: It was Madison College.

Admiral Forbes: Madison College.* They told her, "Our nephew's coming up this weekend, Betty, and we'd like you to come over and have dinner with us on Sunday."

And she says now she that said, "Oh, I don't want to do it." But she thought it over and said, "All right. If you want me to, I'll come." So that's how we met; it was on that Sunday, and that was it. It was just bang. You know how those things are. Then Admiral Stump gave us the time off to get married. He was very solicitous. Admiral Stump was very nice that way.

Paul Stillwell: Okay, that was in Thanksgiving 1950.

Admiral Forbes: Yes.

---

* The institution, now known as James Madison University, is in Harrisonburg, Virginia.

Paul Stillwell: What more do you remember about this process of getting squadrons and ships ready to go to Korea? What was involved in all that?

Admiral Forbes: Well, the commanding officers were involved in the work-up, determining how much experience the personnel had. Do the best you can with what we've got here. That was about it. The admiral would get the various skippers in and the bigger bosses and his subordinates down the line, and he'd talk to him. He told them what they could do, what was expected of them out there, and so forth and so on. He was very thorough in that respect.

Paul Stillwell: What was the role of an aide in that kind of a situation?

Admiral Forbes: Well, he used me—I'm trying to be polite about this—as his living tape recorder. In later years every meeting he went to he insisted politely that I accompany him, and I'd be the only other person there. The only other time, and we'll come to that later, was with President Eisenhower. That broke me up and broke up the President too. But, in any event, when we came out of a meeting, he'd discuss with me what was discussed, and I would say, "Yes, sir, and they said this and that." And that's how he used me.

Paul Stillwell: So did you then write a written report on this afterward, after the meeting?

Admiral Forbes: Oh, not to him personally. We'd discuss it. If any report had to be made, I'd draft it, and he'd go over it and put his touch in there, naturally.

Paul Stillwell: So he just wanted you to confirm his memory? Was that it?

Admiral Forbes: Yes. Confirm it and add anything that I picked up from the subordinates when we mixed in the coffee breaks and things like that. If he had trust in you, he had trust in you, period. He was a very responsible gent.

Paul Stillwell: Was he the sort that would have you run errands for him?

Admiral Forbes: No. I never—oh, a couple of little things I used to do on trips, such as pick up something. We used to get our flight time in together. That was an experience in itself. He flew me to Stumptown, West Virginia, that round spot in the road down there with the filling station. Things like that. No, he wasn't very demanding in that respect. He was good.

I was responsible to keep him in cigarettes. He smoked unfiltered Kools, which we used to say were the cheapest cigarettes you could buy in those days. I used to buy a carton of cigarettes for him every other day. He smoked incessantly, from the time he got up in the morning till the time he went to bed at night. He didn't die of any cancer of the lungs or anything, but he was an inveterate smoker.

Paul Stillwell: How was he toward, say, captains and commanders, people senior to you? Was he brusque to them?

Admiral Forbes: It depended on the individual. I can put it that way. It depended on the individual. He was somewhat unapproachable. He stayed in that office. When he got out, he went out and looked things over. He'd just walk into a mess somewhere and see what was being fed, things like that. Unannounced, unexpected. He was never rude but very sharp, if I may say so, in a country-boy sort of way. He did not socialize. They gave the Christmas party for the staff in his quarters each year, but as far as back and forth, give and take or anything like that, you know, no. That was it.

Paul Stillwell: It sounds like he started off his relationship with you as sort of a hazing thing, and I wondered whether he went through that with other people too.

Admiral Forbes: I don't know, to be perfectly honest with you. He didn't mingle much. He worked right through his little inner staff. Now, he had a secretary, a WAVE first class, Mary Barry. I'll never forget her as long as I live. She could take dictation, type, and do just everything. But whenever she went to take that test for chief petty officer she'd get checkitis or whatever you want to call it, and she couldn't pass it. After two of these he got on the phone with the Chief of Naval Personnel, who was Admiral Holloway.* He told him all about her, and he said, "Now, Jimmy, she's one sharp young lady. She gets checkitis, and she'd make a good chief petty officer. I need her. She's earned it." She was promoted to chief petty officer and continued to work for him. She even went out to Pearl Harbor with Admiral Stump. She was on his staff till he retired. She was right with him. One sharp, sharp lady.

Paul Stillwell: Well, if he was not one to socialize, did he use you as a buffer to keep people away sometimes?

Admiral Forbes: Well, when I say socialize I'm talking about parties, cocktail parties, and things like that, and he didn't—

Paul Stillwell: I see. But he didn't fend people off that were coming to see him officially.

Admiral Forbes: Oh, no. No, no. He was always delighted to see people when he could see them officially. Admiral Stump was quite a gentlemen.

Paul Stillwell: His second wife must have been a fair amount younger than he was.

Admiral Forbes: Oh, was she ever. And that was one of the first jobs I had to do. He called me in one day. I'd been his aide about a week. "Forbes, I want you to go up to Washington."

I said, "Aye, aye, sir. What may I do for you, Admiral?"

"Take these dresses back." I've forgotten the name. Some big store. And this is when I found that a dress could cost $200.00. I almost dropped my eyeteeth. I flew up to Anacostia and went over in the town, where I returned these dresses and got the refund

---

* Vice Admiral James L. Holloway, Jr., USN, served as Chief of the Bureau of Naval Personnel from 2 February 1953 to 31 January 1958. His oral history is in the Columbia University collection.

check. I flew back, and that was that. He used to use you for little things like this as an aide.

But, no, she was much younger, and I'm speaking in all due respect, a different type of person. They didn't entertain in Norfolk, because she stayed home with those children. She had a driver who took her where she wanted to go. Now, this wasn't exactly legal-legal, but it was their car, and Warner was his driver. She just stayed very much to herself. She didn't socialize with the other wives. She was very, very withdrawn, and, as I say, she was quite a bit younger than he was.

Paul Stillwell: Well, he must have been in his mid-50s, and what was she? Maybe 30?

Admiral Forbes: Twenty-something. And they had John Morgan Stump by his first marriage. And John Morgan Stump, Naval Academy class of '51, went into naval aviation. And I remember I got a TBM out of the old FASRon Three there at Norfolk.* John Morgan Stump was up at Quonset Point, so I logged my flight time to pick him up.† I brought him back to Norfolk, so he could see his parents for the weekend. He was one fine young man, and I really liked John Morgan Stump.

Paul Stillwell: Well, please tell me more about the time in Second Fleet. Sounds like a crackerjack staff.

Admiral Forbes: It was. It was a crackerjack staff.

Paul Stillwell: What do you remember about Sharp and Sylvester specifically?

Admiral Forbes: Sharp is sharp and very polite. Admiral Sylvester is a most gracious gentleman. In fact, we were laughing the other night at home. Talking about protocol—we were living in a little rented house here in Norfolk and, lo and behold, one Sunday afternoon came a knock on the door at 4:30 on the dot, and here were Captain and Mrs.

---

*FASRON—Fleet Aircraft Service Squadron.
†Quonset Point, Rhode Island, was the site of a naval air station until the mid-1970s.

Sylvester paying a call on us. Well, we almost dropped our eyeteeth. You know the old Navy formality. But he was like that. Just as nice as he could be. And Admiral Oley Sharp, as they called him, was a good man to work for. I enjoyed being with both of them.

Paul Stillwell: Any specifics about either one that you remember? Was Sharp the chief of staff?

Admiral Forbes: Yes. And Captain Sylvester was the operations officer. They were both very efficient and very productive.

Paul Stillwell: How large a staff was it?

Admiral Forbes: Not very large. I don't know the exact number, but we were in one little teeny wing of the building in Norfolk. ComAirLant was on one side; the naval station and Commander Second Fleet were over in one corner. We were embarked in *Iowa* most of the time. Did several major NATO exercises working with the Brits and the Norwegians. I stood watch flag plot. I was one of the few qualified OODs on the staff. In one case I had two captains working for me when I had the watch. It was a lot of fun.

Paul Stillwell: Well, it wouldn't have been Sharp and Sylvester. They sure didn't need any help.

Admiral Forbes: No, but we had others on board that had never had command or were operationally experienced with surface ships.

Paul Stillwell: Did Commander Second Fleet take tactical command in these kinds of situations?

Admiral Forbes: Once in a while we did. The admiral ran the whole show. As Commander Second Fleet we had the carriers and the destroyers. We worked in these joint exercises. Peacekeeper was a NATO exercise I remember. Then we'd meet and critique them afterward.

Paul Stillwell: How was a Stump at sea? That's a different environment than at AirLant.

Admiral Forbes: He was a seagoing sailor. He knew what he was doing. He liked it and he ran a good show. He was sharp. And he got things done.

Paul Stillwell: What do you remember specifically about the *Iowa*? That's an impressive ship.

Admiral Forbes: That it was very large, that we had good quarters on there. I even had my own bunk all by myself in a little teeny room, which for the aide was unusual. But it was well manned. It made a good flagship.

Paul Stillwell: How were the communications?

Admiral Forbes: Good. I can't remember any problem we ever had with communications.

Paul Stillwell: Did you run the flag mess?

Admiral Forbes: Yes.

Paul Stillwell: What was the atmosphere in there?

Admiral Forbes: It was good. Admiral Stump was never gregarious; I guess that is the correct word to use. But he was very polite.

Paul Stillwell: Did people feel they could talk freely?

Admiral Forbes: Oh, yes.

Paul Stillwell: What do you remember about working with the foreign navies in some of those exercises?

Admiral Forbes: Well, Admiral Stump knew exactly what he wanted to do and he did it. Then we had the conferences afterwards with the Brits. He'd discuss what we accomplished and what we wanted to try to do. It went off very well. We worked with the British and the Norwegians mostly.

We'd have the "hot washup" sometimes on the British battleship. I'll never forget—quick sea story—going aboard the battleship with Admiral Stump. The British admiral invited us down to his mess. Prince Philip was there, doing his active duty.* It was a nice long table. I sat in the middle somewhere, and there was a flag officer at each end. We had this nice meal, and when the meal ended they passed this little canister with a little spoon. I noticed all the Brits took and made—I can't do it—they made a thing in their hand like, between their thumb and their forefinger. This was snuff. They all had to put a little thing of snuff all the way around the table. And then when the mess treasurer said, "And now, Gentlemen," they all had a sniff. The first one that sneezed had to buy a round of drinks for the table. [Laughter] Only the Brits could do that. It broke me up. Oh, yes. They had a little open bar on there—quite the gentlemen.

Paul Stillwell: What was the focus of these exercises? Was it ASW or strike warfare or just what?

Admiral Forbes: Both. The exercises covered the entire field of naval operations. We refueled. We went alongside that British battleship once to refuel and to watch Rum Day, or whatever it was called in the British Navy. There was a huge wooden keg that was about 8 feet in diameter and about 8 feet high. The keg contained the rum for all

---

* Prince Philip is the husband of Britain's Queen Elizabeth II. He was an officer in the Royal Navy.

those youngsters. All the sailors lined up with their little cups getting their ration. And our sailors, who couldn't even have a beer, were looking over and watching them drink rum. You ought to have heard the comments. Ah, it broke me up.

Paul Stillwell: Did you visit any foreign ports during the course of that?

Admiral Forbes: Oh, yes. In England, Southampton was the one we always visited. From Southampton we would travel by car to London and places like that to talk to people, professionally and personally, but we always anchored or moored in Southampton.

We went to Copenhagen once and on to Oslo, which I'll never forget; it was June 21.[*] The admiral was invited to a reception on the beach. We went over there with him, and at 11:00 o'clock at night they teed off. That was the first mistake our hosts made. They thought that this great big club would be a treat for us visitors. But Admiral Stump hated golf with an absolute passion. They teed of at 11:00 o'clock at night, and at midnight the sun just barely touched the horizon, and they had a big drink and toasted Happy New Year and all that. Not Happy New year but—

Paul Stillwell: Mid Summer's Night.

Admiral Forbes: Yes. Then the sun rose, and we stayed there till about 2:00 o'clock in the morning just playing and partying with the Brits. Admiral Stump wasn't a drinking man. Perhaps he drank a little on the side, socially and personally, but he was a very proper person, and he knew he had to do it to please the senior Norwegians who were there. It was a very nice and memorable evening. That's how they celebrated the longest day of the year. They had a big feast at midnight.

Paul Stillwell: Did you get involved any in amphibious warfare in that job?

---

[*] The longest day of the year is on 21 June, and the effect of long daylight is pronounced in far northern latitudes.

Admiral Forbes: Not intimately, no. Observed, yes, but never participated.

Paul Stillwell: What did you learn being that closely associated with seniors?

Admiral Forbes: You learned, one, how the Navy really works, I guess, is the biggest thing, and you learned personalities. You got a feel for what's right and wrong—I mean, acceptable. It was educational. And you got to meet so many, many people. Admiral Stump took me everywhere he went—from the President of the United States, and I'll get into that later on—to Pope Pius, with whom he had a long chat. Everywhere he went, he made sure that his aide spoke to the dignitaries. He always introduced me, including to Madame Chiang Kai-shek, and we'll get around to that. That was interesting. And, of course, the Generalissimo and so forth and so on. It was an education.

Paul Stillwell: You said you learned how the Navy really worked. What were some of the insights you got?

Admiral Forbes: The personalities. Secretary of the Navy, CinCLant, CinCLantFlt. How they thought. And what was right. All of us have idiosyncrasies and likes and dislikes; I was very much impressed. I never found anything really wrong. Everything was done right by the book. A little personality's put in there, a little play here and there. But the main objectives were accomplished and done well.

Paul Stillwell: Was it in any sense a surprise how much influence one individual can have in that kind of a situation?

Admiral Forbes: Well, I guess I could say "Yes." His influence, his personal thoughts and what he thinks and what he demands, regardless of what it says on a piece of paper.

Paul Stillwell: Well, just as an example, I talked to Admiral Hyland, who had Seventh Fleet back during the Vietnam War.[*]

Admiral Forbes: Oh, what a great gentleman. He was on the Pacific Fleet staff at one time, John J. Hyland.

Paul Stillwell: Well, he had a thing about beards, and this is long before it became against Navy policy, Navy wide. So no beards in Seventh Fleet, and that came from one man.

Admiral Forbes: Yes, I remember Admiral Hyland well. He and his sweet wife.

Paul Stillwell: Well, anything more about your time on the Second Fleet staff?

Admiral Forbes: No, it was just a busy time. A lot of sea duty. I learned early on that Admiral Stump was going to become CinCPac-CinCPacFlt.[†] Aides were not allowed to smile or to say anything till it was released to the press. No one else on the staff knew it. But it became evident early on from little bits of things I'd take in to him that he'd been selected to be CinCPac-CinCPacFlt.

Paul Stillwell: How did your bride adjust to this regimen when you were so busy?

Admiral Forbes: Oh, she said, "Ye gads, you work all the time. Look, everybody else has the afternoon free. It's Wednesday afternoon, they're off, and you're out there."

And I'd say, "That's right." And we'd go to work on Saturdays. Towards the end of his tour, though, he stopped working Saturdays, when he went from ComAirLant to Com2nd Flt. At that time, you had to give up your quarters, as there were no quarters for

---

[*] Vice Admiral John J. Hyland, USN, served as Commander Seventh Fleet from 13 December 1965 to 6 November 1967. The oral history of Hyland, who retired as a four-star admiral, is in the Naval Institute collection.

[†] Admiral Felix B. Stump, USN, served as Commander in Chief Pacific and Commander in Chief U.S. Pacific Fleet, 10 July 1953-14 January 1958. After he was relieved as CinCPacFlt on 14 January, he remained in the joint billet as CinCPac until 31 July of that year.

seagoing commands. Admiral Stump bought a house on Bradon Avenue in Norfolk, and so he generally took his Saturdays. He came in early in the morning and then went right home and took the weekend off. We didn't have to work Saturday and Sunday. But later on, at CinCPacFlt, though, he worked 365 days a year.

Paul Stillwell: Well, you said you went to the training command. I'm a little surprised that you wouldn't want to get into a fleet squadron at that point.

Admiral Forbes: Well, I wasn't eligible to go to a fleet squadron. I had to complete this training command. In those days there were check-off lists one had to complete.

Paul Stillwell: I see.

Admiral Forbes: And Training Command was one of them, so I went down to Cabiniss Field in Texas, which is at the end of the—well, it's not so bad as Beeville. That was in the good old days when in the city of Corpus Christi there were no television stations, because they would advertise beer.

We lived in this little civilian community. In Texas in each and every yard and, I'm not exaggerating, there was a big telephone pole and on the top of that telephone pole there was one of these TV antenna arrays so they could pick up San Antonio or any other place when on those freak days when their signals would be right, they'd run and scream, "It's on, it's on!" Then they all ran in and turned on their televisions sets to see television. When we arrived there, we didn't know about it, so we had ours stored away in the closet in the hall. And I said one day, "I wonder if ours will work." So I rolled our TV out, put the rabbit ears up, and got the same picture.

The training command was an interesting tour. When my wife would get upset about Texas, I'd drive her down to Beeville. Then she'd come back to Cabiniss Field and think we were back in hog heaven again.

Paul Stillwell: What was so bad about Beeville?

Admiral Forbes: It's right near the Mexican border. There was nothing. Oh, there are little teeny houses. We bought a brand-new house there in Corpus, which was quite nice, not a bad environment at all.

Paul Stillwell: How did you feel about getting back to flying again?

Admiral Forbes: I enjoyed it. First they made me a ground school instructor. I had to teach ASW, having come from VC-33. I enjoyed teaching, but I wanted to get back into flying. I finally got the captain down there to let me get back into action. I said, "I came down here to fly, sir."

"Yes, but you've got more ASW experience than anybody around here, and I need you to teach these students."

"Aye, aye, sir."

So I did it, and then finally they let me go. That's when the Marines were building their air arm. Now, this was in ADs, and I'd get six young Marine second lieutenants in a flight. I'll never forget. This is all true. The first day they arrived in their dress blues. Now, don't ask me why. I'd have them sit down in the briefing room, and I'd say, "Now, Gentlemen, before we begin this course, who here can give me the translation of the Marine Corps motto 'Semper Fidelis'?"

They'd all sit there at attention. They'd been told, I guess, never to volunteer.

And I'd say, "And none of you gentlemen know? Well, let me tell you. Literally. Semper Fi—dumb but faithful." And to watch the expression on their faces, you got a feel for whom you had in that flight. I enjoyed working with them.

One of the meetings was the debrief with the skipper after about a couple of weeks, and I couldn't resist. He asked, "Any of you have any questions or comments?"

I said, "Yes, sir. You know I've got all these Marine students. Sir, may we change the number of blades to 10 instead of 12?" In those days on the AD you had to count 12 blades before you could turn on your switch.

Paul Stillwell: What do you mean 12 blades?

Admiral Forbes: On your propeller. You see, you had a four-bladed propeller and it had to turn three complete revolutions. You had to count 12 blades. Then you could turn on your switch to start the engine. This was just to get the oil flowing and all that.

Paul Stillwell: How was it turning around, by hand?

Admiral Forbes: No, electrically. It's just like the starter on a car.

Paul Stillwell: Okay.

Admiral Forbes: But you couldn't turn the gas with the switch. The skipper asked, "Why do you want to do that?"

I said, "Well, sir, these Marine pilots are having a devil of a time getting that boot back on after we count to 12. They've only got ten fingers. They've got to count two toes." [Laughter] I thought he would die.

So he said, "Well, just make it ten." I enjoyed working with the Marines.

Paul Stillwell: Well, antisubmarine warfare seems an odd mission for Marines.

Admiral Forbes: No, no. This was an AD. This was straight flight training now.

Paul Stillwell: Oh, I see. This was after you got out of ASW.

Admiral Forbes: Yes. I taught ASW. It was all part of the training for the other people. But for the Marines, it was strictly the ADs, which were the strike aircraft. We took them through that, making it a good tour.

Paul Stillwell: Well, how did the Marine pilots compare with the Navy pilots once you got down to business?

Admiral Forbes: They were about the same. Now I want to tell you my sea story. We were working away down there. We'd bought this house, and we had our second child there. Little Susan was born in the hospital, and everyone was very proud.

One day a squadron mate came to me and said, "Sir, you have a long-distance phone call from Washington." This was before we had autovon and all these modern communications.*

And I said, "I do?"

"Yes, sir, for you."

I went over to the office from the line and said, "Lieutenant Forbes here."

I heard this voice that I recognized right away. It was Admiral Holloway, who was the Chief of Naval Personnel. He said, "Beetle, do you own a home in Corpus Christi?"

"Yes, sir.'

"You poor son-of-a-bitch."

I said, "Sir?"

"Felix called me last night. He just fired his executive assistant, his aide and flag lieutenant, and his administrative assistant. He wants you to come out there and fill those billets." [Laughter]

I said, "But, sir, I've been his aide. I don't want to be his aide again."

"Beetle, I know that, but you apparently are the only white man in the Navy who can keep him happy."

I said, "I don't have any choice to say 'No,' do I?"

He said, "Won't do you a damn bit of good. Now, get ready."

I said, "I want housing.'

He said, "I'll do the best I can by you." So we got hot. We put that house on the market, and we sold it. It was probably the greatest real estate transaction that ever transpired. We made a total of $60.00 on the house—60 bucks. We went back to see Betty's folks and my folks and my mother with a brand-new baby. Then we took off and

---

* Autovon, short for Automatic Voice Network, was U.S military phone system built in 1963 to survive nuclear attacks.

drove across country and took the old Mars, that flying seaplane, out to Hawaii.* Got there on April the 10th. I'll never forget.

Paul Stillwell: What year?

Admiral Forbes: That was 1955. Admiral Stump had a car waiting for us. We went right up and into the set of quarters that was one door from his quarters—the big official guesthouse. It was a nice bungalow right next door. We settled in there on April 10. We left August 17, 1957, at 4:30 in the afternoon. I can give you the exact time.

That gentleman worked every day of the year except one day while I was with him. And when I say worked, I'm talking 7:30 in the morning until 6:00 o'clock at night, and we were on the road constantly.

In all of those quarters the public works people had placed these nice signs: "Captain So-and-so," "Rear Admiral So-and-so." They looked at me and said, "You're just a lieutenant. We can't put a sign up for you." So we had this nice set of quarters with no sign. I made lieutenant commander while I was out there, and they put up a little teeny "Lieutenant" and a great big "Commander." We were the only junior family in the area. Everybody else in those quarters was either a flag officer or senior captain. We had that nice set of quarters on Makalapa Drive. Very nice.

Paul Stillwell: Why did he take one day off from work in two years?

Admiral Forbes: Well, on Christmas Eve, the second year, I said, "Admiral, what time will you come to work tomorrow, sir?" He knew what I meant. He had a habit—deliberate habit, I might add—of coming in anytime he chose, from 5:30 in the morning until sometimes 11:00 o'clock, and he expected his staff to be there. Well, those poor souls didn't know whether he was going to come in at 5:30 tomorrow morning or not, and it was getting kind of demoralizing. He said, "What do you want to know for?"

---

* The Martin-built PB2M Mars was a four-engine Navy flying boat.

I replied, "Sir, if you're not going to come in till 11:00 o'clock tomorrow morning, I want to let the two yeomen stay home and celebrate Christmas morning with their families."

"Tomorrow's a holiday, isn't it?"

I said, "Yes, sir, but it doesn't mean much around here."

"Don't you come near this place."

I said, "But, sir—" And he looked at me, and I said, "Let me send the messages up to you."

"Don't you come near this place." And that's the first day he never came to work. I shamed him, I guess, into that. [Laughter]

But every other time he was right there on Sunday morning. Then he'd take a break and he'd say, "Let's go," and we'd go to the chapel. He'd sit there through the service and then go back to the office. He'd call the yeoman in and dictate a memo to the chaplain, taking either exception to what he said or agreeing. Admiral Stump's father had been a minister. It was always hilarious that he'd send a memo to the chaplain about the sermon, what he thought about it, etc., etc.

He took me everywhere he went. The only meeting I never sat in on with him was when President Eisenhower called him back. President Eisenhower was in Augusta playing golf, and Admiral Stump hated golf with a passion. We went out to the golf course, and the President came off the course. They went in one of those little golf shacks; it looked like a little privy. And for 49 minutes just the two of them were in there together discussing things. He came out, and we got in the admiral's plane, an R6D, number Zulu 128427—I will never forget.[*] He had two of them. Back to Hawaii we went, and then off to Taiwan. We were on the road all the time in that job.

Paul Stillwell: Did he tell you what he had discussed with President Eisenhower?

---

[*] The R6D Liftmaster was a four-engine propeller-driven transport built by Douglas as the military counterpart to the DC-6 civilian passenger plane.

Admiral Forbes: They were discussing working with Generalissimo Chiang Kai-shek in Taiwan and getting the people out of Vietnam, the Catholics and so forth and so on.* We went to Taiwan, where the Generalissimo put us up in their guesthouse, which was right there. That evening he had us to dinner. There was a nice little table, and Madame sat on my left on one end of the table. The Generalissimo in his little black velvet skullcap sat at the right side of the table. The interpreter and I sat on this side, and Admiral Stump sat across the table. There was just a total of five of us at dinner. Early on they dismissed the interpreter. Admiral Stump said, "I don't need him." They dismissed him, so that just left the four of us. Well, of course, Madame Chiang Kai-shek speaks fluent English, and he didn't speak a word of it. She did all the talking to Admiral Stump.

We were having this beautiful Oriental dinner, and there were the chopsticks. I'd just come out of the training command in Corpus. Chopsticks! How in the world? I was having the devil's own time trying to get those things to work, and I heard this voice. Madame said, "Lieutenant."

I said, "Yes, ma'am."

She smiled and said, "If you look beside your plate you'll find a knife, fork and spoon." She'd had them bring in a knife, fork and spoon so I could eat. They talked shop the entire meal, and she would translate for the Generalissimo. I can see him sitting there now. She was really the brains. I mean, she was one impressive lady. Then I noticed that when the servants would come in and bend over to serve, I could see their .45s they had tucked in the back of their trousers. They all were armed.

The next morning, when the Generalissimo went to his office, there were three great big limousines lined up. They were identical in color and everything else. I later found out that he would choose the one in which he was going to ride, but all three of them went to the office so if any terrorists were out, they wouldn't know which car he was using. So he chose whichever car he was going to ride in every morning. And for Admiral Stump, I put all the information into a back channel. Oh, that coding. Oooh. These reports were sent back right to the President. We had CNO cut in too.

---

* Generalissimo Chiang Kai-shek served as President of Nationalist China on the mainland from 1943 to 1949 and as President of the Republic of China on Taiwan from 1950 until his death in 1975.

Paul Stillwell: What was the substance of it?

Admiral Forbes: They were talking about getting the people out of Vietnam and the threats of Communist China against any moves we may make. Oh, we went to Southeast Asia. With Admiral Stump I went to Cambodia, Laos—all those places—where we visited and talked to the ambassadors. It was absolutely fascinating to see the relationships over there.

Paul Stillwell: Well, there'd been that evacuation of the Tachen Islands.[*] That was right around that time. Wasn't it a matter that Chiang kept demanding this protection or support from the United States when he really didn't have a lot to offer?

Admiral Forbes: That's right.

Paul Stillwell: But I guess Admiral Stump was being solicitous—trying to give him what he wanted, it sounds like.

Admiral Forbes: Yes, they sent all this back to the Joint Chiefs of Staff and the CNO and to President Eisenhower, who wanted this information firsthand what was going on. I think back on all those forms we used and all those back-channel messages. It was something else.

Admiral Stump went on around and talked to additional people. Then he got a message that the Pope would like him to stop by.[†] So we stopped in Rome, which I'll never forget. We had an audience with the Pope. Mrs. Stump was along with the admiral. While we were waiting, the admiral asked me, "Who do you think ought to come?"

I replied, "Well, sir, both your yeoman are devout Catholics. This would be the highlight in their lives if they could meet the Pope."

---

[*] The small Tachen Islands, north of Formosa (as Taiwan was then called) were subject to attack from mainland China in the early 1950s. On 7 February 1955, on the advice of the U.S. Government and with the assistance of the U.S. Seventh Fleet, the Nationalist Chinese evacuated the Tachens.
[†] Pius XII was Pope from 1939 to 1958.

"Okay. Get 'em in here." I asked them to come with us, and entered the receiving area. There were two yeomen, Mrs. Stump, Admiral Stump, and myself. I was on the right, and I noticed out of the corner of my eye that as the Pope came walking in, he stopped just outside the door and turned to his aide. I guess he was asking, "What am I seeing this U.S. Navy officer for?" They briefed him, and he entered this nice room. He could not have been more gracious. The Pope shook hands all around and, of course, those yeomen were just overwhelmed. They dropped to their knees and kissed his ring. It was really a touching, touching scene. It didn't last long. It was just a formality, but it was a nice formality. The Pope thanked Admiral Stump for his participation in saving this, that, and the other.

Then we flew to Washington. Admiral Stump took his wife to the White House. Right outside the White House proper was this little putting green. President Eisenhower was apparently quite a golfer. And we were talking about that. His little grandson was staying there with him, and he ran out and got on this green. His granddaddy said, "Get off of that green. I don't want those footprints on the green to ruin my stroke." The President was just being human.

Paul Stillwell: I can imagine that Admiral Stump's wife would have had some awkwardness relating to the wives of other senior officers because of the age difference.

Admiral Forbes: Well, not only that but every time they entertained up there in CinCPac-CinCPacFlt, which was frequently, I would have to be there. I was the aide, but it used to amaze me. Dinner was at 7:00. He had a fixed routine, which used to break me up. He was a nut on time. He kept two watches, and he had a time tick built into his telephone so he could pick it up and check and make sure it was right on the spot. He said, "If you cannot be on time, never be early, but don't be late either."

He was an absolute fanatic on time; that's the correct word to use. I would have to contact, privately, each family that was invited and say, "Now, sir, when he says 7:00 o'clock, he means 7:00 o'clock, not five minutes of or not five minutes after."

So I'll never forget the night, Oley Sharp was a guest. He, too, was very punctual. Admiral Sharp arrived with a stopwatch. He and all the other guests gathered at this nice big hedge just outside Admiral Stump's quarters there on Makalapa, in front of his front door. As you went in the entranceway, there was a break through this nice big heavy hedge. I was over there because I had to introduce everyone. The guests gathered outside with Admiral Sharp, who had his stopwatch out, and at five seconds of 7:00 the whole group walked in—right on the dot. [Laughter]

The situation of introductions was embarrassing to several people. I had to introduce each guest, including next-door neighbors. I mean immediate staff, like Mrs. Sharp and Mrs. Sylvester. I had to introduce them to Mrs. Stump. She could not remember them from one time to the next, because she never mingled with anyone. She used Admiral Stump's driver at times, but she also had her own driver and her own car. She did everything on her own, and she stayed mostly in seclusion. She was just a different type of lady.

Paul Stillwell: Did you have to work with the stewards to set up these parties?

Admiral Forbes: Oh, yes.

Paul Stillwell: What went into that?

Admiral Forbes: Well, what we're going to feed tonight and what time it's going to be. They were sharp, and we got along very well. They knew what the situation was. They'd been there, and they were right on the dot. Admiral Stump would invite Betty and me quite often to these dinner parties. He did his share of entertaining of everyone you could think of.

Vice President Nixon came to visit. I got a call at 3:00 o'clock in the morning from the duty officer. "Hey, Beetle. Vice President Nixon's on his way out here."

I said, "Well, I know that. He gets here in the morning."

He said, "Yeah, but you don't know this and why I'm calling you." He said, "I just got a call from his plane. He wants his suit cleaned and pressed as soon as he arrives here."

I said, "We've got all these 24-hour-a-day cleaning and pressing places in Honolulu. Give one of them a call, and we'll pick his stuff up and send it down and that's it."

He said, "Beetle, I've been on the phone. I've been trying. None of them are open."

I said, "We've got our own, don't we? I hate to bother 'em."

He said, "Okay." So we got hold of our ship's service officer and got everything set up. I went down the next morning with him to meet the Nixons when they came in. They were coming in from Miami. They landed, taxied up, and they got out of the plane just as gracious—oh, I have to jump in. I'm a great admirer of the Nixons. They were so gracious, and they had their one aide with them. Only he wasn't an aide. He was on the plane. It was an official aircraft. He got off with two suitcases. I asked, "Where's the rest of the gear?"

He said, "That's all there is." And he said, "You know, we've got to get that suit cleaned. When we came out of Miami, we hit a bad air pocket. The Vice President was drinking a beer. It went all down the front of him. That's the only suit he's got."

In those days it was a brand-new material; we'll call it wash and wear. I got his suit and took it over there and had it cleaned and pressed. Then I took the suit to the guesthouse, which was right next to where Betty and I lived, in the next set of quarters. Mrs. Nixon was most gracious.

Then Admiral Stump said, "Mr. Vice President, what can I do for you?"

Mr. Nixon replied, "You know we've got the meeting on."

The admiral replied, "Yes, sir. In the meantime, what can I do for you?"

Vice President Nixon said, "I want to try some of this Honolulu sun and beach." So I put the Nixons in the car and took them down to the beach, where they went in the water and had a ball. They could not have been more gracious.

I asked the aide, "Where's the rest of the luggage?" And I'm getting back again on that.

"This is all they've got. They only carry two bags."

I said, "How about Mrs. Nixon?"

"That's all. Everything is here in two bags." They were going around the world.

I said, "Ye gads. When we go anywhere, we've got eight suitcases and four big hanging bags. It's a truck load."

He just smiled and said, "That's the way they travel." Anyway, they were delightful. I shouldn't say they *were*; they *are* delightful.* They are just as gracious and friendly and nice, we enjoyed their visit very much. They talked about why he was going and where he was going.

Paul Stillwell: Was the Secret Service part of this? Did they go with you to the beach?

Admiral Forbes: No. No. With me tagging along, it was just the three of us who went to the beach.

Paul Stillwell: Wouldn't happen today.

Admiral Forbes: No, it wouldn't happen today. In later years, when I came back to a tour of duty in Washington, the Nixons had Betty and me over to the White House.† I was really touched, as well as flabbergasted. They were just as gracious as could be.

How we entertained! All the dignitaries who came through our area were hosted by Admiral Stump. He'd give them the guesthouse or arrange other accommodations if they wanted to stay downtown.

Paul Stillwell: I interviewed Vice Admiral Tom Weschler, who was Admiral Burke's aide when he came around on his orientation tour before becoming CNO.‡ He said that he was very touched by the warm reception he had from Admiral Stump. Some of the other seniors were condescending, but Stump was not at all.

Admiral Forbes: I was there, and I think the world of Tom Weschler. He and I got along wonderfully well. I'll never forget Admiral Stump taking Admiral Burke aside and

---

* The Nixons died subsequent to this interview: Thelma "Pat" Nixon on 22 June 1993 and former President Richard M. Nixon on 22 April 1994.
† Nixon was President of the United States from 20 January 1969 until his resignation from office on 9 August 1974.
‡ See the Naval Institute oral history of Vice Admiral Thomas R. Weschler, USN (Ret.).

saying, "Arleigh, you are the world's worst public speaker. Now, you can't be CNO and not be able to say ah, yes or no. Now do something about it." And Admiral Burke went to a special course in public speaking. Because I had heard Admiral Burke, and I agreed with Admiral Stump. He'd stumble; he'd read his notes; he'd go back and repeat himself. Admiral Burke took a special course in public speaking. We went back to Hawaii, and we stayed with the Stumps at the guesthouse a few times. We often saw Tom Weschler and Tina. What a wonderful couple.

Paul Stillwell: Well, Weschler's view was that the fact that Stump was so gracious and receptive was probably why he managed to stay in his job so long because he was CinCPac for about five years, I think.

Admiral Forbes: I'll never forget when he was extended. I was there, and I remember that and I thought, "Jeepers, creepers." When he was extended he finally released me. I had said, "Admiral, I can't be your aide forever. I'm a naval aviator. I've got to get into flying."

"Okay."

Admiral Stump finally detached me at 4:30 on Saturday afternoon, the 17th of August. Betty and our two little girls, Nell and Susan, were already in the ship. We returned to the mainland in the *Lurline*. I was watching the clock, because I was concerned about boarding the ship.

Finally, Admiral Stump said, "Well, it's 1630 Saturday afternoon, Forbes. Let's call it a day."

I said, "Aye, aye, sir." Then I said, "Admiral, I won't be here tomorrow morning."

"Where in the hell are you going to be?"

I said, "Sir, I've been detached. I'm leaving aboard *Lurline*. It sails in 30 minutes."

"Well, okay. Bye." [Laughter]

As I went out the door, I thought, "You mean to tell me after two aide tours and all the time, that's all I get?" Lo and behold, the admiral came right after me, gave me a big hug, and said, "Beetle, when you get on the ship read this." Admiral Stump gave me this sealed envelope. Then his driver took me screaming down to the ship.

When I boarded *Lurline*—I'm serious—Betty was in tears, standing on the brow. The word was passed, "All ashore that's going ashore," and all that. I came running aboard and just barely made the sailing. And that letter, which I have in my files, is just one of those touching things, thanking me for all the help that I'd been to him over the years and much praise and platitudes. Just prior to Admiral Stump's death—when he was so ill—Admiral George Anderson, the former CNO, called me and said, "Beetle, I'll take care of the funeral arrangements in Arlington."[*] Admiral Anderson added, "You know him better than anyone else. Would you take care of informing all of his close friends of his imminent death?"

I replied, "Yes, sir, I will." When he died, which was shortly thereafter, within the hour, as I recall, I got on the phone. I was on duty in the Bureau of Naval Personnel, and I called all the various and sundry people to whom he was so close. Then there was the funeral; he was buried in Arlington. Admiral Stump's last request was that he not be buried with the flag officers but that he be buried next to his son, John. This was accomplished. Betty and I attended the funeral and saw him off. It was just a touching, touching ceremony.

Paul Stillwell: Do you ever hear from his widow?

Admiral Forbes: No. Unfortunately, we've lost complete track. Admiral Stump's charming daughter Frances became an airline stewardess and was with the airlines a long time. What a good-looking gal she was. The admiral's nephew, John Stump, recently visited me here in Virginia Beach. John was here planning a ship's reunion. He served in the destroyer escort Navy and is now a retired lawyer living in Northern Virginia. I don't know whatever happened to Mrs. Stump.

Paul Stillwell: Well, she was in her 20s. I guess she'd be in her 60s now.

---

[*] Stump died 13 June 1972, when Admiral Elmo R. Zumwalt, Jr., USN, was CNO. Admiral George W. Anderson, Jr., USN, was Chief of Naval Operations from 1961 to 1963.

Admiral Forbes: Yes, easily. She was a good-looking lady. She stayed to herself. She didn't mix. She didn't get to know any of the wives.

Paul Stillwell: It sounds as if the admiral doted on her, though.

Admiral Forbes: Well, he did.

Paul Stillwell: What more do you remember about the substance of all this work that occupied him day after day after day?

Admiral Forbes: Well, it was educational, in that you met all these interesting people. You heard what went on. You learned to keep your mouth shut. You never talked about your job. I had a lot of close friends and classmates in Pearl. What little socializing time we had, we'd mix with them, and they were smart. They'd never quiz me except to pull my leg about working long hours. They'd say such things as, "Well, Beetle, it's 10:00 o'clock Saturday night. You'd better get hot. You've got to be at work tomorrow morning." However, it was a very educational assignment in that I knew that I had the admiral's trust. He counted on me, and I kept my mouth shut. I observed, and I answered his questions and tried to help as much as I could. That is what it really boiled down to. And he employed his staff all the time. I used to argue with him on things.

Well, one more quick sea story. I looked up from the desk one Sunday morning, and here in Pearl Harbor stood this small gentleman. He was wearing a dark blue suit with a vest and had a hat in his hand. I recognized him as Admiral Rickover.* We didn't know he was anywhere on the island. Admiral Stump insisted that the door between his inner office and my little aide's office, where the yeomen and I sat, was always kept open so I could "learn what was going on in the Navy," as he used to say. It was one of these

---

* Hyman G. Rickover was considered the father of the nuclear Navy. He ran the U.S. Navy's nuclear-power program for many years, from 1948 until he eventually left active duty in 1982 with the rank of four-star admiral on the retired list. Rickover Hall at the Naval Academy is named in his honor, as is the nuclear-powered attack submarine *Hyman G. Rickover* (SSN-709), which was commissioned 21 July 1984.

swinging doors with louvers in it. I jumped up and said, "Good morning, Admiral Rickover. May I help you, sir?"

"I'd like to see Admiral Stump."

I said, "One moment, please." I went into the admiral's office. Admiral Stump was reading the paper, and I said, "Sir, Admiral Rickover's here. He'd like to see you." It was total shock, because we didn't know he was anywhere near. In a stage voice that could be heard all over Makalapa, Admiral Stump said, "What does that little Jewish son-of-a-bitch want with me?"

I said, "He can hear you." Then I said, "You're not doing anything. Sir, you can see him."

"All right. Send him in."

So I went out and said to Admiral Rickover, "Admiral, he'd be delighted to see you, sir. Would you come this way?" I know he heard him. I escorted Admiral Rickover in, and that was it. Discussions.

Admiral Stump gave dedicated service to the Navy. He listened to people, but his personal traits were different.

He didn't like speeding in Makalapa, which included exceeding ten miles per hour on those little roads. He directed his public works people to place great big railroad ties across the road to create bumps, which became known as "Stump's Bumps." Well, he had one put up in front of his quarters. The doctor who lived on the right-hand side of Admiral Stump was Doctor Dement.[*] Doctor Dement came in the next morning, and you could hear him talk. He said, "Admiral, that boom-boom in front of my house—I don't want it. I want it out of there."

The admiral looked at me and kind of gave a little shrug of his shoulders. So I had public works take out the tie; however, they didn't fill in the hole. That became known as the "Dement's Dent." [Laughter] So it was between "Stump's Bumps" and "Dement's Dent." To this day you can still see just a little ridge where that railroad tie was located. It broke me up when I was out there the last time. Oh, well.

---

[*] Captain Donald E. Dement, Medical Corps, USN.

Paul Stillwell: Well, you were talking also about his fetish about people bringing alcohol back from trips.

Admiral Forbes: Well, Bill Lederer brought back a liter of scotch.* Admiral Stump saw it and made him send it right back to where he got it. He wouldn't let him bring it in the country. Did it right there at Pearl. He said, "You send that back. It's not coming in." The only alcohol that was ever brought in was a case of White Australian Hock that was given to him as a farewell. He couldn't turn that down, so that had to come in with us, but that was it.

Paul Stillwell: Why did he have this thing about alcohol? Do you know?

Admiral Forbes: I don't know. He wasn't a drinking man. I don't think he'd ever had a drinking problem but just one of those things. He had a number of fetishes like that—time being probably the most obvious and known.

Paul Stillwell: What do you remember about Lederer's role on the staff?

Admiral Forbes: It was very unusual in that he had direct access to Admiral Stump. They got along wonderfully well. Bill Lederer was always writing and traveling. He was the public affairs officer. Jeepers, all he did was work on books and things like that. He was very complimentary. He could be the most gracious gent in the world. He traveled a lot with us.

Paul Stillwell: *The Ugly American.*†

Admiral Forbes: *The Ugly American.* He wrote that when he was on the plane half the time. He gave me those pages in longhand. The story was based on people there on the

---

* Captain William J. Lederer, USN, Pacific Fleet public information officer.
† William J. Lederer and Eugene Burdick, *The Ugly American* (New York: Norton, 1958). This was a popular novel of the period, later made into a movie. It depicted the role of Americans working overseas in the 1950s.

island and on the staff. He was very productive. He did a lot of traveling on his own, and for some reason Admiral Stump and Bill Lederer hit it off and got along well.

Paul Stillwell: When the tape recorder wasn't running, you told me also about your trip to Australia. That bears repeating.

Admiral Forbes: Well, we went to Australia to represent our President during their big celebration, which in those days was Coral Sea Week. I don't know whether they still do that or not. We were celebrating the Battle of the Coral Sea.* In that role, representing the President, Admiral Stump had to go to various and sundry cities all around Australia. At one of the cities, on a Sunday afternoon, there was going to be a big reception hosted by a prominent local gentleman. Admiral Stump, the Australian admiral, and the host were in the quarters talking. I was outside with the Australian aide. There was a fire blazing in preparation for the lamb chops that would be cooked over an outdoor flame. I said, "Boy, all we ever do is hot dogs."

My fellow aide said, "Hot dogs. I wish we could do hot dogs. But we can't afford hot dogs. They cost umpty-umpty-ump. That's why we're having lamb chops. They cost—" It's the other way around in the States. Oh, well. Admiral Stump mingled, talked, and ate. Everywhere he went he was a most gracious U.S. representative. He related well with the Aussies. Then we went to New Zealand. We went just about everywhere. We went around the world twice paying calls for the President and working in WestPac. We went to Japan, but we never went to China. Other than that, you name it, and we were there.

Paul Stillwell: Well, a lot of these things seem like political and diplomatic ventures.

Admiral Forbes: They were.

Paul Stillwell: What did he do on the fleet side of his job?

---

* The Battle of the Coral Sea took place in early May 1942. It was a standoff tactically but a strategic victory for the United States, because it prevented the Japanese from landing in Port Moresby, New Guinea, which would have been a good jumping-off place for invading Australia.

Admiral Forbes: He had Ulysses Simpson Grant Sharp and George Anderson.* They did most of that.

Paul Stillwell: So he brought them out from the Second Fleet staff too?

Admiral Forbes: Yes. Oley Sharp was out there. Admiral Anderson was the Deputy CinCPac and did a superb job.

Paul Stillwell: What do you remember about him specifically?

Admiral Forbes: Well, Admiral Anderson was very gracious, very nice, very outgoing, and athletic. He was the epitome of a gentleman. He was always friendly, as was that gracious lady of his too. She was very nice and outgoing. So was Mrs. Sharp.

Paul Stillwell: Was it really necessary to work all those hours that Stump did, or was that just a reflection of his personality?

Admiral Forbes: A little bit of both. With that time zone difference out there and Washington calling, there were a lot of direct calls in those days. There were back-channel messages that only Admiral Stump had the code to break. I used to break them for him. But a lot of it was just his individual personality. He didn't play golf. He played tennis. I'll give him credit for that. He just stayed at that desk or on the road.

Paul Stillwell: And then after you left, the job got divided up so there was a separate CinCPac and CinCPacFlt.

Admiral Forbes: Just before I left he moved from the old CinCPac-CinCPacFlt. He became solely CinCPac and moved to the old Aiea Naval Hospital. It was converted up

---

* Rear Admiral U.S. Grant Sharp, USN, later a four-star admiral; Vice Admiral George W. Anderson, Jr., USN, later a four-star admiral.

on the mountain there. The hill became CinCPac headquarters, and he went up there. But I understand he still spent a lot of time in the other place because it was so close to his quarters and he liked it there. Kind of force of habit. He moved into another set of quarters, too, I remember. The old naval station.

Paul Stillwell: What else do you remember about that job?

Admiral Forbes: Well, the hours. The responsibility staggered me as a boot lieutenant and then as a lieutenant commander. He delegated authority, which I could have misused. Oh, jeepers, I could have done all kinds of things using his name, and people knew I worked closely with him, so if I said "this," it was done.

Paul Stillwell: Maybe the reason he picked you is that he knew you wouldn't.

Admiral Forbes: Well, that could very well be. Just the traveling and observing what went on in the world was overwhelming. The politics involved among the various countries and what they wanted, really, and what they asked for in public were amazing. And how things worked. It was just absolutely fascinating.

Paul Stillwell: Did you develop a little cynicism between public appearances and what was really going on?

Admiral Forbes: No, no, I guess not. My sweet wife seldom saw me. Betty said, "You're always on the road." We had a nice set of quarters there, and Nell and Sue were in school—well, one in school. Little Sue was only three months old when we went out there.

We had quite a few classmates there. As I say, we got together with them—at least Betty did—quite often. We were invited to functions. It was a fascinating job, because the admiral put so much trust in his people, and he expected his staff to produce. He made no bones about it. In a nice way he was a very demanding boss. If you could produce, fine; he gave individuals credit. His fitness reports were generally one or two lines. He was quite a gentleman.

Paul Stillwell: Well, you said that Admiral Holloway told you that you were the only white man that could keep him happy. What did he mean by that?

Admiral Forbes: Well, he fired his other aide.

Paul Stillwell: Why did he say white man?

Admiral Forbes: Oh, it was just an old Southern saying. [Laughter] That's all it is. You hear that in the South. You know, "Only a white man can make him happy," or something like that. Then when Admiral Stump retired, he went to the Freedoms Foundation up in—was it?

Paul Stillwell: Valley Forge?

Admiral Forbes: Valley Forge. I went there to see him once. His secretary said, "Am I glad to meet you."
I said, "What do you mean, Ma'am?"
She said, "Every now and then he yells out your name, 'Forbes!' at the top of his lungs, and I wonder who he's calling for. Now I know." [Laughter] But it was just a habit. He never used anything electronic. He used to always bellow. You could hear him all over Makalapa: "Forbes!" [Laughter] Oh, well. And when he died, as I said, he asked as his last request to be buried next to his son John.

Paul Stillwell: Did he help you to get a good assignment after that duty?

Admiral Forbes: He let me return to flying. No, he was like that. If you wanted him to, he would. I'm sure he'd help. But I said, "Let me apply and see what I can get." I was ordered back to VA-15 as executive officer. It was an attack squadron in Jacksonville, and we went back there for that tour.

Paul Stillwell: So it had been seven years since you'd been in an attack squadron, hadn't it?

Admiral Forbes: Yes.

Paul Stillwell: Did you have to do some catching up?

Admiral Forbes: I left there in '55. I'd been flying ADs then. But to go back to a squadron—

Paul Stillwell: Which is different from being an instructor.

Admiral Forbes: That's right, considering the carrier work, tactics, maintenance, squadron administration, plus your shipmates' welfare and morale. I had a good boss, and we started flying right off the bat. Actually, I had to go through a refresher course and carrier quals, and then I went to the squadron. They were just coming back from deployment.

Paul Stillwell: Who was your good boss?

Admiral Forbes: William J. Gray, class of '43.[*]

Paul Stillwell: Where did you operate?

---

[*] Lieutenant Commander William J. Gray, USN, commanded VA-15 from 10 December 1957 to 18 September 1959.

Admiral Forbes: In the Jacksonville op area. We did a Med deployment with USS *Shangri-La*.* I went there in '57, and in '59 I was yanked out of the squadron and sent to Stanford University, out of the clear blue sky.

Paul Stillwell: Well, let's talk some more about the squadron first, please. Did the *Shangri-La* also spend some time in the Pacific?

Admiral Forbes: No, no. These were strictly Atlantic operations. We operated out of Jacksonville proper and deployed to the Med. That was a routine squadron syllabus and schedule in those days. There was nothing unusual about it. We did all of our work-ups and practice bombing with VA-15. We used our "shapes" in the operating areas.

Paul Stillwell: Well, that's something that you remember and you take for granted, but the people who are interested in your career don't know that, so please tell that story.

Admiral Forbes: What story is that now?

Paul Stillwell: Well, about your work with the nuclear weapons and that training.

Admiral Forbes: Oh, well, this is later on in my own squadron.

Paul Stillwell: Oh, you didn't do this in the *Shangri-La*?

Admiral Forbes: No, sir. That was later on, when I had command of VA-176. No, we were just a regular attack squadron. Nothing sensational. Just work, work, work. These workups in VA-15 were designed to keep the planes on the line and ready materially.

---

* The aircraft carrier *Shangri-La* (CV-38) was commissioned 15 September 1944. *Shangri-La* was decommissioned and placed in the Reserve Fleet at San Francisco on 7 November 1947. She was recommissioned on 10 May 1951. Reclassified an attack aircraft carrier, CVA-38, in 1952, she returned to Puget Sound that fall and decommissioned again on 14 November, this time for modernization at Puget Sound Naval Shipyard. During the next two years, she received an angled flight deck, twin steam catapults, and her aircraft elevators and arresting gear were overhauled.

Paul Stillwell: What do you remember about the Med cruise?

Admiral Forbes: Well, we visited all the usual ports, which included Naples and Monaco. The Spanish ports were popular, and occasionally we went into Malta. Malta was the most memorable liberty port because of all the historic structures and the history. Malta's leaders later changed their political way of thinking, and that prevented our visiting that wonderful port. Istanbul was also popular. We would fly, fly, fly and then enter port for several days and then fly, fly, fly again. We would operate heavily at sea and then have a port of call. The objective was to get everyone qualified.

Paul Stillwell: What kinds of missions were you prepared to do?

Admiral Forbes: Bombing missions were primary for the attack squadrons. We all had pre-planned, designated targets which we knew about and planners back in Washington knew about but no one else. The captain of the carrier and the aviation squadron skipper were not informed about individual targets.

Paul Stillwell: That's a surprise.

Admiral Forbes: That was just one of those things. Each pilot knew how long it would take to get to the target. He'd tell the skipper and then be launched. That determined the flight schedule. We would launch off the carrier with both tanks filled and the bomb shape. We'd fly as long as it would take to arrive on target and then return and land on board the carrier. It was a good 150 feet off the water. We weren't permitted to approach any landfall or navigation aids. You could see them, but you couldn't fly over them. Understandable. There was no argument about that.

Paul Stillwell: So for however many pilots in the squadron there'd be that many different targets?

Admiral Forbes: Yes, sir. Some of the targets may have been duplicates. We didn't know the assignments of our squadron mates.

Paul Stillwell: Where was yours?

Admiral Forbes: My target was in Central Russia. I couldn't even find it on the chart now, it's been so long. I remember it was a big industrial complex.

Paul Stillwell: That seems like really excessive compartmentation to me.

Admiral Forbes: Well, it was very effective, though. We all had special clearances in the squadron. We had to have this special clearance, and they really kept track of you. Our conduct ashore was important. Boy, if anyone ever stepped out of line, he was canned right on the spot.

Paul Stillwell: Well, if everybody was flying separately, how did you and the CO have a way of measuring the performance of those in the squadron?

Admiral Forbes: Sometimes we flew as a squadron, but most of the time we just took off and went one by one. What the aviator did on the carrier determined his status and rating. We'd fly as a group once in a while. We were one of those independent outfits. Just the Spads operated that way.

Paul Stillwell: Was this when you had that loft technique for dropping the weapon?*

Admiral Forbes: Yes.

Paul Stillwell: How did that work?

---

* The loft bombing method was designed as a tactic to prevent airplanes from being damaged by their own nuclear bombs. The method called for the pilot to make a low-altitude approach to the target and pull up into the first part of a Cuban 8. The bomb would be released as the aircraft reached about 45-degree angle during the climb. The pilot then completed the half of the Cuban 8 and flew back in the direction from which he had made his approach.

Admiral Forbes: It was quite accurate, much to everyone's surprise. We practiced in Florida so much that we became proficient. We had those little shapes. We'd watch that shape as we pulled out, and we watched the G's on the meter. At the right spot we would trigger it; it would go off! We could see where it hit by the little puff of smoke. It was quite accurate. I was pleasantly surprised.

Paul Stillwell: Were you already onto your back when you released?

Admiral Forbes: The pilot was almost vertical at that point. The bomb went off when he was straight up. Then we rolled right over on our backs and left the scene. We flew the exact reverse track of the route we came in to escape the blast.

Paul Stillwell: How did you as the exec administer the individual departments in the squadron when you had not had many of these jobs yourself?

Admiral Forbes: I just did the best I could. I had to have faith in the various department heads. They were good shipmates. They were good aviators. We were very, very closely knit. We have maintained those friendships over the years.

Paul Stillwell: Any highlights in particular that you remember from then?

Admiral Forbes: Well, no. The skipper was Willie Gray. I'm the world's worst on names.

Paul Stillwell: No, you're not.

Admiral Forbes: We just had a good squadron. When I had my own squadron, we had people, as I say, like Chuck Larson. I can rattle them off forever from that tour.

Paul Stillwell: How well did the squadrons relate to the ship's company people?

Admiral Forbes: I thought very well. It was just one big team; that was what it boiled down to. We were a team, and we had to work with the air boss, who ran the operation and the flight deck crews. We did what they directed, which developed good teamwork. I had no complaint at all.

Paul Stillwell: How would you compare operations from an *Essex*-class ship to the bigger ones that you saw later?

Admiral Forbes: Well, just on a smaller scale was what it boiled down to. We didn't have the deck area, so we didn't carry so many aircraft. Your deck takeoffs had about the same distance to run. The living conditions weren't much different. As I said, it was just on a smaller scale.

Paul Stillwell: So you tended to do deck runs rather than catapult shots?

Admiral Forbes: Yes, we did with the Spads. A catapult shot was rare indeed. The plane went barreling down that deck, got that nose up, and away we went!

Paul Stillwell: What characteristics do you remember from that airplane?

Admiral Forbes: The power and the response. It was just a good, stable airplane. It was suited for its missions, no doubt about that.

Paul Stillwell: When the tape recorder wasn't running, you were telling me about some of the things you did to prepare for a long flight. Those are worth repeating.

Admiral Forbes: Well, we had a little rubber cushion that we sat on. It looked like a little inner tube. These cushions were for sale at any drugstore. We blew the cushion up to a certain pressure. And then, as we went on and the hours went by, we'd vent a little air off so it would change the pressure on your fanny. We made sure that our canteens were full. We made sure we had a little box lunch in the airplane. And then the doctor provided two pills to take before you took off and one to carry with you to take 15 minutes before your Charlie time when you landed. And we made sure we had our flashlights. And away we went. That was it.

Paul Stillwell: What were the pills?

Admiral Forbes: I don't know. I know one thing; they really hyped you up, because, as I mentioned, I've seen a few of the aviators whose planes went down before they could launch. They were just so hyper around the ready room that they were almost running around the room. It was just unbelievable. And whatever we took before we landed really perked us up. That pill put all our faculties right on the knife's edge, so to speak. Then we landed, and that was it. We got some sleep. It was interesting. We weren't like the fighter pilots who were used to going up for an hour and a half and come back.

Paul Stillwell: How long? What was a typical flight?

Admiral Forbes: The record in the squadron was 13.1 hours. We didn't count that because he got lost. But about 12 hours—anywhere from 10 to 12 hours, depending on where the target was and where we were when we launched.

Paul Stillwell: Did you feel any sense of letdown after dealing with all these world leaders and so forth? Now you were doing just regular Navy business.

Admiral Forbes: No, no. It was just a different Navy, a completely different Navy. It was back with the boys. I could relax and enjoy life and didn't have to be on the Q.T., listening for every little whim of someone's words or things of that nature. In that other job I had to keep my eyes open and remember what was said and the mood in which it was said, etc. etc. It was a very, very interesting and very responsible job.

Paul Stillwell: There are people who've described to me just the pure exhilaration of flying. Did you get that?

Admiral Forbes: Oh, yes. Some days I'd get airborne, and it would just be a beautiful day. I would just whip along and enjoy every minute of my flight time and regret having to land.

Paul Stillwell: On the other hand, there must have been some moments that weren't so pleasant.

Admiral Forbes: Yes. After nine hours of sitting there with a sore fanny and a dry canteen, I'd think, "Jeepers, creepers, another three hours to go." Oh, yes, sometimes it seemed to drag out forever. The beauty—I shouldn't use the word "beauty," but one of the most gratifying things about a squadron assignment was the people I associated with, my fellow aviators, and, by and large, they are a great bunch. I enjoyed working with about 99% of them. They were very good people.

Paul Stillwell: Well, I think you can account for that in that, first, it's an elite group and, second, you're all in the same business, so you have so much in common.

Admiral Forbes: Yes, that's true. That's true.

Paul Stillwell: Anything further on the tour in VA-15?

Admiral Forbes: No, I can't think of anything offhand. It was a good exec tour for me.

Paul Stillwell: What about disciplinary-type situations and administration of the enlisted people and officers?

Admiral Forbes: Well, I worked very closely with the enlisted people. I mustered the chiefs and had a little "Dutch Uncle" talk. Throwing your weight around was not the way to go but just saying, "Now we've got to do this. This is our mission. We've got to do that. And we've got to change this. Let's make this change. What do you think about doing it this way?" Conducting business like that produced results; it worked out very well.

Once I had the chiefs and the sailors behind me in the squadron, that was about 98% of the game. It really was. This included maintenance and everything. And I'd take care of my squadron mates. I've always said, and I know it's a cliché, but, "You take care of them, and they will take care of you." And this was the way it went. I truly enjoyed working with the enlisted people. They knew I always had an open door if they wanted to come see me and say anything. They used to come forth, and we'd get things squared away.

Paul Stillwell: Where to after that?

Admiral Forbes: Let's see. After VA-15 the Navy plucked me out. We were operating in the Med, and I was detached to attend Stanford University. I got back to the States, and we drove across country, which was an experience in itself. We found a nice little house to rent in Palo Alto, and I went down and checked in with the Navy; there was an NROTC there.[*] I had to report to them for duty. I went out to an airfield that's long since been closed. But there was a big naval air station near where I checked in, so I could get my flight time there. We were required to maintain our proficiency by logging flight time while we were going to school. So I became a student. I checked in with the NROTC staff. That was where I picked up my paycheck and administrative things like that. But, outside of that, I became a student in every sense of the world.

Paul Stillwell: Did you wear uniforms to class?

Admiral Forbes: No, sir. I went to see my professor, and I told him who I was and why I was there, taking these undergrad courses. They were all very nice, and I enjoyed them. I was assigned a desk in what was called the "stack" in the library. That's where I did all

---

[*] NROTC – Naval Reserve Officers' Training Corps.

my work. It was necessary to become totally involved in academics, particularly since I was working in a master's program. I had to make up and get the prerequisite undergrad requirements. That included what wasn't offered at the Naval Academy. Stanford was where I studied sociology and psychology, which I enjoyed very much.

I guess one of my greatest compliments or achievements was in that big class of undergrads in sociology. We submitted our term papers, and in due course they were graded. We were gathered in the little auditorium there, and the professor got up in front of the class and said, "Now, I have read and graded all the papers. I have awarded four A's and one 21-gun salute." That caught my attention. Then he looked at me, and he said, "Your paper was superb."

I said, "Even with my title?"

He said, "Who else but someone in the Navy would think of titling his paper in sociology 'Sex in the stacks'?" and laughed like mad. [Laughter] No, I very much enjoyed working there. It was hard, though. The study and all that library work really kept me busy—I mean, six days a week. I really went at it. And at night I'd work on my papers. I went through in a year, and at the end of the year that was it. Of course, I went to all the football games and enjoyed the university's extra activities. There was no Navy life there. I wasn't a freak, but they didn't know who I was or why I was there.

Paul Stillwell: How well did you relate to your classmates?

Admiral Forbes: I thought very well. They were all really sharp youngsters.

Paul Stillwell: Did you find that you had what is sometimes stereotyped as the military mind? Were you accused of that?

Admiral Forbes: Never. No, I was never accused of that. There was one other naval officer there, Paul Keenan.* He was going through another course. Paul was a submariner. We got to know him. We still keep in touch with him. We were the two Navy types that were going through there at the same time. It was a one-year course.

---

* Lieutenant Commander Paul C. Keenan, Jr., USN.

Paul Stillwell: Why had you been picked for personnel administration?

Admiral Forbes: I don't know. But I was really surprised when I got orders to that course. I thought, "Jeepers, creepers, this is something." But to go to Stanford—I couldn't argue with that. When I arrived there, I put in my comments sheet that there was no course in personnel administration. Stanford awarded a master's degree in education, and that was what mine ended up being, which paid off.

Paul Stillwell: Why did the Navy, in effect, want you to have a master's in education?

Admiral Forbes: Well, they thought it was personnel administration and training. I'm serious. That's what I ended up with—a master's in education. Since I was the only aviator they sent that year, I was really flattered.

Paul Stillwell: In what ways did that help you later?

Admiral Forbes: Well, the studying, the civilian approach to subjects, the research, the variety. At the Naval Academy everyone did exactly the same thing. Even the outside interests were uniform. I won't say fraternization but just the experience of being with younger people, as well as scholars who thought differently. I must admit that. While there wasn't that much difference, being with younger civilians who had their goals and their objectives was a good educational process in itself. I enjoyed that.

Paul Stillwell: What specific applications can you point to that you were able to achieve?

Admiral Forbes: Well, I learned how the academic civilians study. I learned how the courses were so different from the Naval Academy. It was also the discussions in class. At the Naval Academy we went to class and checked in. They made sure everyone was there. Then it was, "Gentlemen, man the boards." We went up to the blackboards, the prof came by with a sheaf of questions, and he gave each midshipman a slip of paper.

Maybe there were three questions. Another midshipman got three questions on something else. We wrote the answers in chalk on the blackboards. The prof graded the answers, and that was your participation in class. Whereas, at a civilian university they discussed things, and they talked back and forth and exchanged viewpoints. It was much different. I enjoyed that.

Paul Stillwell: I guess what I'm trying to get at is how did knowing that or that type of approach help you once you got back into the Navy way of doing things?

Admiral Forbes: I believe it gives you a broader approach to learning and developing your mind. It gives the student a different outlook on subjects and how things can be accomplished without this being such a cut-and-dried format all the time. It permits flexibility and the opportunity to change.

Paul Stillwell: So you're not so rigid as—

Admiral Forbes: That's right. I lost that—if you want to pardon the expression—military touch to everything. You can be much more relaxed and understanding.

Paul Stillwell: It was refreshing last year to hear a talk by Vice Admiral Boorda, the Chief of Naval Personnel.[*]

Admiral Forbes: Great man, isn't he?

Paul Stillwell: Yes, he is, and his approach seemed to be, "Let's always make common sense the first rule instead of whatever rule is printed in the book." And that was extremely refreshing.

---

[*] Vice Admiral Jeremy M. Boorda, USN, served as Chief of Naval Personnel from 9 August 1988 to 6 November 1991. He was later Chief of Naval Operations, 1994-96.

Admiral Forbes: That's right. I agree with him, and he did a superb job in the Bureau of Personnel, and now he has four stars. What is he, CinC—?

Paul Stillwell: CinCSouth.

Admiral Forbes: CinCSouth in Naples.* His secretary called me and told me he was going there. I gave him his first assignment as CinCSouth: "Check and see if Humpty-Dumpty's still on the wall."† Well, I'll get an answer someday.

Paul Stillwell: How much of an opportunity did you have for a family life with this demanding academic regimen?

Admiral Forbes: Well, we had the two small girls. Nell, my older daughter, went to first grade in the Palo Alto School. The neighbors in the next block and across the street from our house had a little daughter the same age, and they played together incessantly. However, family life was quite limited, because when I got home in the evening I studied. I had to hit those books, no getting around that. And then during the breaks we took the little girls to see snow for the first time. Betty and I took them up in the mountains to see snow. We did family things like that. We'd take three or four days and just travel around and visit that beautiful countryside there in the hills of California.

We went to numerous plays in San Francisco. My sweet wife couldn't get over San Francisco, where the ladies were always dressed properly and wore white gloves. They were dressed to go shopping. The ladies didn't go out in slacks or anything like that. That was just an education in itself. Of course, I didn't have much time to call my own, but it was a pleasant existence. I was home every night, and I didn't have to worry about some plane crashing or something like that or being gone for months at a time. So it went off, I thought, very well. We enjoyed it.

We drove back across country and went straight to Newport, Rhode Island. I don't know how the Navy works things. They sent me from Stanford to the senior course

---

* As a four-star admiral, Boorda served as Commander in Chief Allied Forces Southern Europe and Commander in Chief U.S. Naval Forces Europe from December 1991 to April 1994.
† "Humpty-Dumpty" was the nickname of a legendary Italian prostitute and madam.

at the Naval War College. And what broke me up at the Naval War College were the books and courses I had to study. I mean, I'd had the full-time, professional lifetime prof at Stanford. I enjoyed him very much. He and I got along wonderfully well. He was interested in the Navy.

Paul Stillwell: Who was he?

Admiral Forbes: Oh, I'm the world's worst on names. I've forgotten right now. But he was good. Very down to earth; I'll think of his name.

Paul Stillwell: Well, this is an interesting basis for comparison. How did the educational method at Stanford compare with that at the Naval War College?

Admiral Forbes: Completely different. At the Naval War College we attended lecture after lecture after lecture. It was much more concentrated. I'd put it that way. And more demanding. We all had desks. At Stanford we also had an assigned desk, which was in the stacks in the library. My individual desk was reserved for me, and that was where I kept my papers, did my work, and used the reference books. The big difference at the War College was that we had wonderful guest lecturers who would come visit. We learned a lot from them, whereas at Stanford University we had our prof and rarely had outsiders. This was the thing I liked about the War College.

Paul Stillwell: What examples do you remember of the outside lecturers?

Admiral Forbes: We saw and heard some well-known people who were experienced policymakers. Based on this exposure, we would choose a subject and submit a written paper that was judged by a board.

Paul Stillwell: What did you write about?

Admiral Forbes: Well, let's see. I've forgotten what it was at the War College, but it was on sea warfare. I remember that. But that was a good course up there.

Paul Stillwell: In what ways did it make you a better naval officer?

Admiral Forbes: It provided a broader education on the Navy and how it operated. We learned an appreciation for the naval service, what the Navy does for our country and has done in the past. We got a feel for the people of our generation, so to speak. That wasn't true at Stanford, which was understandable, as we had to take all those undergrad courses to learn the basics. At the War College we were working with shipmates, experienced naval officers, and new people with new ideas that we'd never seen before. They represented different fields and aired their views on various things. It was very educational. I enjoyed it. We worked hard. We didn't waste any time. It wasn't a place just to sit and read books.

Paul Stillwell: How much of a focus was there on the Cold War, which was really in full swing then?

Admiral Forbes: The Cold War wasn't a major factor. It was certainly addressed, especially when we had these outside speakers. I wish I could remember the title of that paper I wrote. I dug it out of the files just the other day when I was cleaning up and packing and repacking. We made some very good friends there; I'll say that.

Paul Stillwell: A number of individuals have cited War College experience as being useful later, just because they made contacts who were then in key positions that they could call on. Was that the case with you?

Admiral Forbes: Yes, and also we met people whom we were going to work with later on. We also had a feel for who they were, and when you met them quote professionally unquote you remembered how they were socially as students at the War College. This gave a better feel for the individual. We got to know each other quite well.

Paul Stillwell: Any of the faculty members that you especially remember?

Admiral Forbes: Well, I remember the head of the War College when I was there. He's dead now. We enjoyed the War College, including the drive back and forth every day to attend classes.

Paul Stillwell: Where did you live?

Admiral Forbes: We lived out in Middletown, that little town just north of Newport. We lived in a little house we rented up there on a back street. It was very nice, and we enjoyed it. We were there during a major hurricane. Our little garage blew down, and I put that back up. But we traveled every morning, back and forth in my Borg Ward. Then I sold it and bought a little Volkswagen. All in all, it was a good tour.

Then we left the War College and came south. I remember that very well. I was ordered to my squadron, VA-176.* I was back in Jacksonville, Florida, where I went through the indoctrination course at what was then known as VA-44. I relieved the VA-176 commanding officer, who was a senior gent. It became my own squadron, and we had a ball. We were the special weapons squadron, and we really worked.

Paul Stillwell: Please tell me about it.

Admiral Forbes: Well, I'll brag about it a little bit.

Paul Stillwell: All right.

Admiral Forbes: VA-176 won the E that year and received quite a pat on the back from the powers that be.† We won the E for the Atlantic Fleet in tactical aviation, and we made a Med cruise in the *Shangri-La*, which in itself was an experience. Good old

---

* VA-176 – Attack Squadron 176.
† An "E," for excellence, is generally awarded to a ship or component of a ship as a result of top performance in competition with other ships during a given time period.

CVA-38, an old bucket. The skipper of the *Shangri-La* was married to the ex-wife of the gent I relieved as the aide and flag lieutenant in CinCPacFlt years before—small world. I assumed command of the squadron in Jacksonville, and this was during the Cuban Missile Crisis.* We were alerted for that.

And I'll never forget—we were told, "Go," and each one of us in the squadron had a target in Cuba. Mine was a napalm target. I had these three big wing tanks full of petrol, and what I had to do when launched was to go out with my crew and dump all this napalm mixture in the wing tanks. By the time I would arrive, it would be just the right consistency. So I'll never forget when we got the real word, "Go." We all hurried out and dumped that stuff in the tanks, and we were just turning up the engines when the duty officer came out screaming and waving his hands violently. It was a cancellation; somewhere in Washington they changed their minds. As you can imagine, it was an interesting, interesting tour.

I lost one of my young officers who was a Naval Academy graduate. He took off one night in quote my unquote aircraft, 02, and that was the last we ever saw of him. We never heard a word from him, so he was presumed dead. He must have crashed at sea. He was a sharp, sharp pilot, and he was good. That was one of those very difficult duties. I returned to the States and paid a call on his sweet wife to tell her the sad news. That's a task that really gets to you.

Paul Stillwell: What can you say in a situation like that?

Admiral Forbes: One just has to tell the truth. We never knew. He just disappeared. We never heard a word from him. He just launched, and his takeoff was normal, as was everything in his initial flight. He had those little children who wanted to know, "Where's my daddy? Where's my daddy?" That really is most difficult and gets to the pit of your stomach; I can tell you that. But that happens in naval aviation. We had a good squadron; we had a good group.

---

* The Cuban Missile Crisis was triggered in mid-October 1962, when a U.S. reconnaissance plane photographed a Soviet nuclear missile site in Cuba and the presence of Soviet bombers. On 22 October President John F. Kennedy went on national television to announce a naval quarantine of Cuba, to be implemented on 24 October. On 28 October Premier Nikita Khrushchev of the Soviet Union notified President Kennedy that he was ordering the withdrawal of Soviet bombers and missiles from Cuba.

Paul Stillwell: When you went to the Med, did you still have the same format as for VA-15, that everybody had different targets?

Paul Stillwell: Yes, sir. We had the charts provided by Washington, which were kept locked in the safe. There was a series of lock boxes, to which only the individual had the combination. We kept our charts in there. Somebody back in Washington knew exactly where the target was, and the individual aviator knew where it was. We had little work booths where privacy was primary. All of us were honest about this. Nobody tried to be nosy. I would work in my private booth on my chart, as to where I was located. In the Med I would have to get my target, flying this and that distance, at what speed, on what course, and to navigate to points there. All of this was kept up to date all the time. This was not for publication, but in those days there were two aircraft of our 12 that were in that hangar bay loaded for bear at all times. They were ready birds, and, boy, I can tell you that the security around them was very strict and serious. That was something else. Of course, these were the duty pilots for each day.

Paul Stillwell: Did you sit in the aircraft?

Admiral Forbes: No. We would have enough warning to man the aircraft. It was realistic, but we didn't go overboard. There was no particular crisis going on then.

Paul Stillwell: Well, was it part of the deterrent force?

Admiral Forbes: Yes. That's right.

Paul Stillwell: Well, you talked about these flights over water. Did you also do flights over land to practice low-level navigation.

Admiral Forbes: Oh, yes. Spain was our favorite country for low-levels. That is the most fantastic country to fly over in the beautiful green topography with these little towns every so often. And every little town has its bullring, which broke us up. We'd see these little round white walls. That was the little bullring outside the town. The Spaniards were most cooperative and understanding, and we went out of our way to express our appreciation. Why have a big airplane come roaring over a house at 150 feet? We tried to stay out in the boonies, so to speak, so we wouldn't bother people. Never go over a town and hopefully not near many houses.

Paul Stillwell: What were the challenges of navigating at 150 feet, as opposed to higher?

Admiral Forbes: Well, we were down so low that we weren't picked up on radar. That was the idea of the whole thing.

Paul Stillwell: Well, that's the advantage, but what makes it hard for you to try to find your way that way?

Admiral Forbes: Because you can't see that far ahead. We were right down, almost on the deck. It's like driving on the road, and we had to make sure we had a good road map, so to speak, and know and see where we were going. Of course, as we climbed higher, we could see out to the horizon: see the topography and obstacles. You can't do that when you're right down near the ground. And on the water we were right down there too. It didn't make much difference over the open water. We made sure that we knew what the flight plan was, and we followed it. That's why I say the airborne record in the squadron was 13.1 hours. One of our youngsters got lost and had to find his way back. It was interesting.

Paul Stillwell: Well, please tell me about Chuck Larson in that squadron.*

Admiral Forbes: Well, oh, I could tell you stories about Chuck. I had quite a few young ensigns, and Chuck was out of the Naval Academy class of 1958. He was just out of flight training, and this was his first squadron. We were stationed in Jacksonville, and

---

* Lieutenant (junior grade) Charles R. Larson, USN, who later became a four-star admiral.

Chuck married the daughter of Commander Fleet Air Wing Jacksonville—the admiral's daughter, Sally.* Chuck was an outstanding young man who had buddies in the squadron. They formed a trio. One of them played a guitar, and they would sing, even though we never knew what they were going to sing. They were popular at all the smokers that we had, especially during deployment. They would gather up in the ready room. They would sing at the little picnics that we had every now and then, and they would always put on a little act. They were good and well-liked. Chuck was a very proficient young pilot. Let me add that. They all were.

When we returned after the six-month deployment, a good homecoming party was held at Cecil Field in Jacksonville for the entire air wing. Chuck came up to me and said, "Skipper, do you think we could get up Saturday night and do a couple of numbers?"

I answered, "Let me clear it with CAG." Howard Greer was the CAG, and I went to him and said, "CAG, my little trio—"†

He knew all about it, because they'd appeared and played on the ship. He said, "Beetle, that'll really kick things off. By all means."

So I gave them, "Okay." That night we were all there with our wives, as well as everyone else who was just right back from the Med. I was sitting next to my classmate Joe Moorer, who commanded VF-32, and his wife Eleanor.‡ It came time. I introduced Chuck and the rest of my little VA-176 singers, and they got up. We never knew what they were going to do. It was always extemporaneous. And Chuck said, "Now, ladies and gentlemen, it's so good to be home, and tonight we would like to dedicate an individual song to each one of our commanding officers." And since I was their commanding officer, they got off on me first about wearing my midshipman blues with no pockets on the sides. It was hilarious, and, the place was just clapping and cheering and carrying on.

But I'll never forget their lyrics when they got to Joe Moorer: "I am the fighter commander. I never go to sea. My brother is an admiral. He takes good care of me." It

---

* On 19 August 1961 Larson married Sally Craig, daughter of Rear Admiral Kenneth Craig, USN (Ret.), who had been stationed at Jacksonville until his retirement in May 1961.
† Commander Howard E. Greer, USN. CAG – commander of the carrier air group. In 1962 the terminology for a carrier's planes was changed to "air wing," but the abbreviation "CAG" still persists.
‡ Commander Joseph P. Moorer, USN, commanding officer of Fighter Squadron 32.

was so true, because Joe was always TAD.* Joe Moorer just turned apoplectic. His wife said, "Joe, laugh, laugh. They're looking at you." And he had this grin. Oh, he was furious.

So, year and years later, when Chuck was before the promotion board for flag rank, he was selected, of course. I picked up the phone and called him. I said, "Chuck Larson, you have my greatest admiration and congratulations on a well-deserved promotion. But do you know how lucky you are?" He was a submariner by then.

He said, "Sir?"

I said, "Do you know who the senior aviator was on the board?"

"No, sir. Who was it?"

I said, "It was one Joseph P. Moorer, and if he'd have remembered your name, you'd be dead." I thought he'd die.

He's a great young man. I was called several times about him. Once I was called about whom to get as aide to the President Nixon. I was a deputy director then in the Bureau of Naval Personnel, and I said, "Admiral, I know just the gent—Chuck Larson."

"Chuck Larson? I don't know anybody named Larson, Beetle." He gave me the names of two of his protégés, and then he said, "Well, it's a rainy old Monday afternoon. If you want to throw the other guy's name in, go ahead and throw it in the pot." So I sent all the records over to President Nixon. He had him over for an interview, and, sure enough, he chose Chuck Larson to become the naval aide at the White House. A few years later they called me and said, "Hey, Beetle, what do you know about this guy Chuck Larson? You know him. Do you think he'd make a good superintendent of the Naval Academy?"

I said, "I think you couldn't pick a better person than him. He'd do a superb job, in my estimation."

"Okay. If you like him, that's what we wanted to hear."

So he was assigned to the Naval Academy as superintendent and did a superb job.† He's a great guy, I tell you. When he came down here soon after he became superintendent—quick sea story—I said, "Chuck, how are you making it?"

---

* TAD – temporary additional duty.
† As a rear admiral Larson was superintendent from 1983 to 1986.

He said, "Boss, I had the worst experience. When I first got there, I tried to come in the gate and they said, 'Hey, you midshipmen are not supposed to be out here.'" They thought he was a midshipman he looked so young. He said, "They kept mistaking me for a midshipman and I said, 'Well, I'm the superintendent. Does that make any difference?'" I like Chuck Larson. He's good.

Paul Stillwell: How did he get out of aviation and into submarines?

Admiral Forbes: We were deployed, and one day he said, "Skipper, can I talk to you privately for a few minutes?"

I said, "Why, certainly, Chuck. What have you done now?" and laughed, because they were always into something.

He said, "No, seriously. Sir, you know, I just heard the news. We know now we're not going to get the A-4s. We're going to keep these Spads. I tell you, frankly, sir, I'd like to get into nuclear submarines. I think that has a better future than flying these things."[*]

I said, "Chuck, are you serious?"

He said, "Yes, sir, I'm serious."

I said, "Well, let's weigh the pros and cons. If you're really serious, let me write to my old academy roommate, Buzz Bessac, who's Admiral Rickover's right-hand man in Washington, and tell him about you and see what he has to say."[†]

So I did, and Buzz came back and said, "Beetle, what you say sounds great to me. How about sending him back here for an interview, and we'll make a decision."

I sent Chuck back, and when he returned from that interview he came in, and I said, "Chuck, how'd it go?"

"Captain, you know, he threw me out twice. The third time he had me in, he asked me, 'Larson, where did you stand in your academy class?' I told him, which was near the top. All he said to me was, 'You're in.'"

---

[*] The Douglas-built A-4 Skyhawk jet was a light aircraft capable of dropping both nuclear and conventional bombs.
[†] Commander Norman B. Bessac, USN, a nuclear submariner.

Then I talked to Buzz when I could get to the phone, and he told me about how the staff interviewed Chuck at length. They were so impressed that they recommended him to Admiral Rickover for acceptance. Then he said, "You know, he does this to all of our candidates. He has a little personal game plan. He will accept nine out of ten that we recommend, and on the tenth one if we've given the guy an up he'll give him a down, and vice versa. This was all just kind of his little formality with Chuck Larson." We sent him off to nuke sub school, and he became a nuke submariner and did extremely well.

Paul Stillwell: What was it about nuclear submarines that was more appealing than aviation? Why did it seem to have a brighter future?

Admiral Forbes: Well, aviation was still a bright picture, but he had two more years to go in our squadron, which was going to keep these old Spads, these prop planes, and this was the modern generation. Everyone was flying jets and all that, and he didn't think it was good for career purposes. He wanted to go into something more challenging than flying these old Spads, and that's what he did. He did extremely well in nuclear submarines.

Paul Stillwell: Obviously very versatile to be able to master both of those disciplines.

Admiral Forbes: That's right, and he is just one great individual. Very down to earth and very friendly, and he knows what he's doing. He was a sharp young man.

Paul Stillwell: Whom else did you have in the squadron?

Admiral Forbes: Oh, no one who went on to achieve the things that Chuck has. We were standard Navy types. They all went on to pretty good careers. Some of them dropped out of aviation later on. A lot were ex-NavCads, and they got good job offers from the outside, and away they'd go. They'd leave.

Paul Stillwell: Did you feel a sense of disappointment in that you still had these Spads and weren't moving along to an A-4?

Admiral Forbes: Yes, but I could see the reason that they couldn't change every Spad squadron, and we won the E. We were a crackerjack squadron, and we showed the Navy we could do what we had to do on our targets. Naval aviation had to keep somebody. Why not keep the best Spad squadron in the Navy? And, of course, while it didn't seem fair to get rid of the lesser ones, that's what they did. VA-176 today is flying A-6s, and there was an article in the paper this last week of this cutback now that Russia's fallen back into place, so to speak.* VA-176 will be decommissioned this spring. That's going to hurt.

Paul Stillwell: I can understand that.

Admiral Forbes: Yes.

Paul Stillwell: On the other hand, when the Vietnam War came along, the A-1 proved superior to the jets in some roles because it could go slower.†

Admiral Forbes: It could go slower, and I believe was more accurate—and it could go longer. That's another thing that counts so much. No, Spads were something else. Spad pilots had to be able to count to ten and all that sort of thing, but they were a good bird. Spads were good birds.

Paul Stillwell: What do you remember about Howard Greer?

Admiral Forbes: H. E. Greer, Howard Greer, Naval Academy class of '44. He was our CAG. Very friendly, very nice. I knew his wife. They were divorced when he got back.

---

* The Grumman-built A-6 Intruder was the Navy's principal carrier-based bomber from the early 1960s to the 1990s.
† In 1962 the AD Skyraider was reclassified A-1.

He remarried. He was later ComNavAirLant. I got to know him there. I always got along with Howard very well. And then he left the service.

Paul Stillwell: How much contact did you have with the skipper of the ship?

Admiral Forbes: Not much. He was polite and very nice, but he just couldn't have all the skippers up there on the bridge and in his cabin. We could get qualified on the bridge if you wanted to; he was good about that. We could handle the ship during replenishment and getting under way. I got fully qualified in that area, with all of it in writing. We could be the command duty officer in port. He was very good and helpful. That was an old ship, though, and she went by the board.

Paul Stillwell: I think she's since been scrapped.

Admiral Forbes: Oh, yes, I'm sure it has.* So many of the ships, like the *Barton*, my favorite destroyer, were sunk as target ships off the capes there, off Virginia Beach.† The charts are all marked. The location is on the chart where it is. That was one of my duties. I got a call from the wife of the communications officer, Frank Shorter. She said, "His last request was that his cremains [I learned that word for the first time] be scattered over where *Barton* is sunk." Frank was the *Barton* shipmate who started the reunions that we go to. What a great guy. I arranged the burial at sea. It was a very formal ceremony and a touching thing.

Paul Stillwell: Well, what happened after VA-176?

Admiral Forbes: I was detached and sent as air boss in USS *Franklin D. Roosevelt*, the

---

* The *Shangri-La* was decommissioned 30 July 1971. She remained in the reserve fleet for the next 11 years, and was stricken from the Naval Vessel Register on 15 July 1982. She was retained by the Maritime Administration until 9 August 1988, when she was sold for scrap and later towed to Taiwan.
† The decommissioned destroyer *Barton* was sunk as target off Virginia on 8 October 1969.

carrier, and that was the first time I learned about relief for cause.* On the way I went through all the little schools you had to go through about catapults, arresting gear, and all the associated equipment. I went aboard this carrier just at Christmastime, and I had no turnover. I was told, "Take over." The officer before me was fired, and I took over as air boss in the *Roosevelt*.

Talk about a demanding job! The air department on a carrier either makes it or breaks it. The air boss is fully responsible for the entire department. No passing the buck. We really worked on that bucket. We mustered my chiefs together and talked to them and the different officers working for and with me. We went over what we should try to do based on experience, etc., etc. It paid off, and I'll brag. We won—to everyone's surprise—the E and the Flatley Award for safety in *Roosevelt*. We proved she was a good bucket. Captain Jerry Miller was the skipper of the *Roosevelt*.† You've met him?

Paul Stillwell: Oh, yes. Wonderful person.

Admiral Forbes: I tell him to his face, and we laugh about this. [Laughter] The world's worst ship handler.

Paul Stillwell: I didn't realize that.

Admiral Forbes: Oh, I've worked with him several times. When we were on the bridge of the *Roosevelt*, he'd say, "Okay, Beetle, you take this damn thing in." This was when the ship came out of the yard and during other special sea details. He was a great man to work for. A carrier commanding officer is a very demanding job: Med deployments, shipyard overhauls. It takes something special to complete an overhaul.

---

* USS *Franklin D. Roosevelt*, a *Midway*-class aircraft carrier, was commissioned as CVB-42 on 27 October 1945. She was reclassified CVA-42 on 1 October 1952 and extensively modernized from 1954 to 1956. Among other changes, she received an enclosed hurricane bow and angled flight deck. Following the modernization she was 974 feet long, 110 feet in the beam, extreme flight deck width of 210 feet, maximum draft of 36 feet, full-load displacement of 62,000 tons, and rated speed of 33 knots. She could accommodate 70-plus aircraft.
† Captain Gerald E. Miller, USN, commanded the USS *Franklin D. Roosevelt* (CVA-42) from July 1963 to July 1964.

We had a yard period in the naval shipyard in Brooklyn. An officer there in New York was in charge of the Navy's big movie center. He and I had worked together before, and I went over to visit him. I said, "You know, the FDR is here in the yard. It costs a mint for the crew. How about some really good movies?" Soon we were getting brand-new movies just released by Hollywood. He'd give me one copy per day to show on the ship, which we did in the hangar bay. You talk about morale! These kids flocked to see these brand-new movies. They became big hits, and it provided our crew with an incentive to stay on board.

Also, we had trouble with people getting back to the ship when they were ashore in New York City. We were in Brooklyn, and we put one or two Marines per block between the subway station and the ship's entrance to the naval shipyard. The local police got the word, and they came to us and said, "If you feel that strongly about security, we'll beef things up around here."

We said, "We've had so many muggings and with the Marines there we haven't had any." So we worked that out. It went off very well.

Paul Stillwell: What more can you say about Miller? I have seldom met an individual with more enthusiasm than he has.

Admiral Forbes: Well, that's right. He is great. Jerry Miller is just one of those outstanding individuals. I worked for him twice. Later on, when I was chief of staff of Sixth Fleet, Admiral Miller reported as Commander Sixth Fleet.[*] The flagship was the old *Springfield*. Admiral Miller was true to his aviation background. He spent as much time as he could aboard the carrier. He'd leave the staff to run the show for him. We kept in touch with him, of course, and kept him informed so could make the decisions. Jerry Miller thoroughly trusted his subordinates and showed great confidence in them. I really enjoyed working for him. He gave us full responsibility; he never hovered over his subordinates. He was very pleasant and had a great sense of humor. Nice wife.

---

[*] Vice Admiral Gerald E. Miller, USN, commanded the Sixth Fleet from October 1971 to June 1973. His oral history is in the Naval Institute collection.

Paul Stillwell: Well, that sense of responsibility, that's a great thing about him, that he does not try to micro-manage people.

Admiral Forbes: That's right. He didn't, and he doesn't. He permitted me to operate the air department on that ship, and he was pleased with it. He never bothered us, which made us work harder to please him. We used to pull his leg once in a while, and that's when his great sense of humor kicked in.

Paul Stillwell: He told me he had learned his leadership style from Admiral Holloway when he was in BuPers. Admiral Holloway really believed those words in the officer's commission, "special trust and confidence," and he bestowed that on his juniors. Miller then did that with those who worked for him.

Admiral Forbes: Well, he was a great man to work for. He was a good skipper.

Paul Stillwell: What makes the air officer's job so difficult?

Admiral Forbes: Personnel. The whole area of responsibility is so widespread. The air boss has the hangar bays to worry about. He has the elevators to worry about. He has the flight deck to worry about. Add all the arresting gear, the catapults. Everything that makes a carrier operate is the air boss's responsibility. And I tell you, I had to really work with all the people to keep everything operating properly and safely. And, of course, the air boss is responsible for flight operations and the launches and the landings. It's *the* job on a carrier. There's no getting around it. And it requires long, long days.

Paul Stillwell: What kind of hours did you put in?

Admiral Forbes: Well, we used to fly until midnight and start the next day's preparations at first light in the morning. You eat all your meals topside. They were brought up on a tray. We'd get the last planes on board at midnight, the last recovery. Then, when everything was stowed away and secured, we'd go below and grab about six hours' sleep, if we were lucky. Then we were back up there, bang, going again, day after day. The carrier entered port every so often for ten days. Then it was time to make repairs and redo the flight deck and conduct required tests to ensure readiness. The air boss is responsible and depends heavily on his people to get everything accomplished. It's quite a job.

Paul Stillwell: Where did your deployment take you?

Admiral Forbes: All over the Med. That was the standard if you were in the Atlantic Fleet. Oh, once in a while we'd steam around Cuba for a short training exercise before deploying to the Med. We also operated off the East Coast for maybe a week of air ops, carrier qualifications, and other operational training requirements.

Paul Stillwell: Did you get as much satisfaction from a job like that as you did from flying?

Admiral Forbes: I believe so, because it provides that sense of accomplishment if it is done correctly. When all those planes return safely and no one is hurt, this is important.

Paul Stillwell: Did you have any especially difficult moments you remember from that tour?

Admiral Forbes: I'm just trying to think. You sweat out every launch. You watch with great care and get them on those catapults just right and ensure the arresting gear is ready. You make sure those wires are there at the right time and the right place, and the handling of the aircraft is safe, and who's walking around the flight deck. There's just so much about it that it's mind-boggling.

Paul Stillwell: There's a lot of potential for disaster.

Admiral Forbes: Oh, is there ever. Errors and mistakes could eliminate the crew and the carrier. Loading all these live weapons, launching and recovering the bombing missions that carry live ammunition, plus handling that ammo in the elevators up and down require the crew's full attention and utmost respect for safety. Yet the work has to be done quickly and smartly. This is where it takes the training and real teamwork of everyone concerned. It's teamwork that makes those carriers. If you don't have teamwork, forget it. You're not going to do anything.

Paul Stillwell: You've got those young enlisted men down on the flight deck, and their jobs really almost amount to cruel and unusual punishment.

Admiral Forbes: That's right.

Paul Stillwell: How did you keep them motivated?

Admiral Forbes: Every night at the end of flight ops I provided movies only for the airdales in the forward hangar bay. We spotted the aircraft and then put up a big movie screen. The airdales had their own movie. And, as I have said, with my contacts I used to get the very best movies. We had special rations and made sure they could eat without standing in line forever. Just little things like that indicated to them that we were taking care of them. I was able to do much more when I was air boss and then when I commanded my own carrier. I'll go into that later on. We did a lot of things on there that were different. We just took care of our people.

Paul Stillwell: Were you able to do extra things for them on liberty time when they weren't handling the planes?

Admiral Forbes: No, because there are set liberty hours. Everyone abided by that. But we'd get as many as possible off the ship. We did that by having a very small duty section. Why have a great big duty section if not needed? We were not flying airplanes.

Let them go. They'd get more liberty in that sense. We could let three sections out of four go. None of this port-and-starboard stuff.*

Paul Stillwell: Well, one thing I've heard over and over in connection with Med cruises is venereal disease. How your people try to cope with that?

Admiral Forbes: We had good doctors, and they'd talk to the crew. Must them in small groups and get down to plain Dutch Uncle talk. None of that huge hangar bay full of people; that doesn't pay off. We conducted the medical education in small groups. We'd get all the arresting gear people and all the catapult people together. We mustered these small groups and briefed them on what the facts were, what had to be done, and how it must be accomplished. This education included venereal disease ashore or any subject that needed attention. It made the sailors know that we were talking to them directly—and that we cared. And it paid off, I think. It paid off.

Jerry Miller left us pretty much alone. He permitted us to run that ship, and he was a very good skipper. He was well-liked. He was extremely well-liked.

Paul Stillwell: Did you have other skippers in that ship also?

Admiral Forbes: Jerry Miller's predecessor was Wally Clarke.† He was a good man. I didn't know him well. I'd known Jerry Miller. Then, I'll never forget, when he got married for the second time around. What was he, 65, when he had that little baby? Something like that. The last time I saw him, he wasn't in too good health. When did you see him last?

Paul Stillwell: It's been a while.

Admiral Forbes: Admiral Miller is quite a gentleman—class of '42.

---

* In this sense, port and starboard means having the duty one day in two. Four-section liberty provides the chance to go ashore three nights of four.
† Captain Walter E. Clarke, USN, commanded the USS *Franklin D. Roosevelt* (CVA-42) from June 1962 to July 1963.

Paul Stillwell: Were you still there when his successor came aboard?

Admiral Forbes: No. I detached from FDR before Jerry did.

Paul Stillwell: What else about that job do you remember? Any other specifics?

Admiral Forbes: Well, being the command duty officer and doing a lot of ship handling, because I was the only destroyer sailor on board among the heads of department. Captain Miller was very frank about that: "You take her alongside; you take her in." I remember right after our yard trials, when we came out of Brooklyn. The skipper called me to the bridge and said, "Beetle, you take her back in so that the pilot can take over." The pilot took the ship up that river, and he was good. The pilot worked with me and the OOD. He relied on my knowledge of the ship and any talents I might have had. We got along very well, and I enjoyed the learning experience.

Paul Stillwell: What was involved in being command duty officer?

Admiral Forbes: The CDO acted as the skipper after working hours; it boiled down to that. The CDO took care of all the problems that came up. He made the decisions. The CDO was the boss. The command duty officer worked with the civilians regarding liberty violations. He worked with the security in the shipyard. He worked with the yard personnel about fire hazards. It was a 24-hour duty assignment. The CDO kept busy doing what had to and should be done. The CDO held the sack, so to speak.

Paul Stillwell: Well, that time in the yard is not pleasant. That's about the unhappiest time in the life cycle of a ship.

Admiral Forbes: Oh, yes. Living conditions can be extremely poor, depending on the work being done.

Paul Stillwell: The noise and the dirt.

Admiral Forbes: The noise and trying to feed your crew and maintain the ship's cleanliness and smartness. And the weather. When the weather was bad, oooh, there's nothing more miserable than to be on a carrier's flight deck, trying to get things done on the superstructure. We came through well. *Roosevelt* was a good ship.

Paul Stillwell: What do you remember about the morale and ship spirit?

Admiral Forbes: It was excellent. We had a good group on board. The crew was also good ashore. We had very, very few problems. Oh, there are always going to be one or two; that's human nature. Basically, they were a well-behaved group. And we, as I say, had the movies for them. We tried to do everything we could to keep morale high because steaming is hard life. It is a hard life when you are out there operating. It never ends. The maintenance and movement of aircraft and trying to fix this, fix that, and the airplanes are in the way with no space to spare. It's not like shown in the movies, I can tell you that. We enjoyed it.

On *Roosevelt* we won the Flatley Safety Award, and, boy, the captain was happy about that. FDR made a comeback from zilch to winning this award. FDR was the best of all carriers on aircraft maintenance, and she was accident free. It was like when we won the E in VA-176. Work with your people; that's the secret that a lot of people know now. Work with your enlisted people and never fraternize. Don't do that. That's the worst thing you can do. If you're the boss, you keep it on the proper level, but you work with them and recognize their abilities and their dedication. Then you've got it made. The crew just knocks themselves out. The sailors know they're being respected and appreciated. Those are the big things I learned early on in the Navy, and it certainly paid off. That's what I think was responsible for winning so many awards. But when *Roosevelt* won that E for the best carrier in the Atlantic Fleet, we really cheered like mad, because we thought we were.

Paul Stillwell: Well, where from there?

Admiral Forbes: From FDR I was ordered to Washington. That was in '64. My job was in OP-103. I worked up there for two years in the manpower programs, and that was in itself a fascinating job. I had a fantastic job there in OpNav. I worked for Admiral B. J. Semmes.* I liked him. I got along with him very well.

Paul Stillwell: A real southern gentleman.

Admiral Forbes: In every sense of the word.

Paul Stillwell: What qualities in him did you admire?

Admiral Forbes: Well, his forthrightness, his sense of humor, and his southern gentlemanliness, as you call it. He was approachable, and he was a reasonable person to work for or work with. I enjoyed it. When he was Second Fleet Commander, he was the same great person: down to earth and a pleasure to work with.

Paul Stillwell: What especially did your job entail?

Admiral Forbes: I was head of the Manpower Program Branch in OpNav. It was from June of '64 to July of '66. That was when we worked so closely and carefully with Secretary McNamara in building up the Navy, which required getting the manpower necessary to do this.† Everything had to be validated. We "worker bees" had to brief him personally or brief his little inner staff on exactly what we wanted and why we wanted it. He would ask questions; we had to verify everything. We were expanding personnel numbers to get the proper number of people. I believe that was where I made my reputation.

I really worked hard one weekend at the office in the Pentagon. I put down every billet that we needed and detailed their functions. For instance, I wrote "ship's cook,"

---

* Vice Admiral Benedict J. Semmes, Jr., USN, served as Chief of Naval Personnel from 1 April 1964 to 31 March 1968. His oral history is in the Naval Institute collection.
† Robert S. McNamara served as Secretary of Defense from 21 January 1961 to 29 February 1968.

then placed a dash, explaining, "to prepare breakfast, lunch, and dinner for so many people." I mean, I put in minutiae; I did it kind of tongue in cheek. However, the list was long and overwhelming since Mr. McNamara was refusing these briefs and turning them back. I wanted to go down fighting. The standard phrase of the SecDef crowd was, "It doesn't tell me enough."

I approached my boss, and said, "Sir, I'm not going to show you this, because you'll throw me out of the building, but I want to try something on my own, and I'll take full responsibility."

"Okay, Beetle."

When I sent this request to SecDef, with all the verification, the details, the minutiae, it was because McNamara wanted details. Lo and behold, this request came back with his personal signature, stating, "Approved." Mr. McNamara asked, "Who in the world is this in the Navy who knows exactly what the Navy needs and why it needs it?" [Laughter] Trying to get people in those days and the justification and the money—oh, it was out of this world.

Paul Stillwell: Well, what you did was put yourself into his way of thinking, and that satisfied him.

Admiral Forbes: Yes, even though it was tongue in cheek.

Paul Stillwell: Yes, but that's the way he thought, so that appealed to him.

Admiral Forbes: Yes, that's the way he thought, and we got the people. So we did very well. I earned the Navy Commendation Medal out of that one. [Laughter]

Paul Stillwell: Was this part of the buildup for Vietnam?

Admiral Forbes: Yes, it was. We were putting ships back in commission, which, of course, required people and money. We were responsible for the people end of it.

Paul Stillwell: What about training? Certainly there were different missions in Vietnam than some of the traditional ones. How did you get people prepared for those things?

Admiral Forbes: We had schools. I was not that familiar with them. The Navy assigned the training to the type commanders, and they tailored the training to the operators' requirements.

Paul Stillwell: Were you more concerned then with numbers and billets?

Admiral Forbes: Numbers and billets, yes.

Paul Stillwell: What about the job of selling this program on the Hill?[*] Was that Admiral Semmes?

Admiral Forbes: Yes, along with Secretary McNamara. That was their charge, as long as we verified what we needed, and I believe we did. We didn't ask for anything we didn't need. We didn't pad the numbers.

Paul Stillwell: Well, the other part of it was that at that period the Vietnam War was still considered winnable and relatively popular, so Congress was more inclined to go along with the program than it was later.

Admiral Forbes: Oh, once we received the approval of the Secretary of Defense, it was almost assured of being granted. The challenge was getting it by him. He was the one who was really a detail person and a micromanager. I won't say he was a nitpicker; he just wanted facts and figures. You had to prove everything.

Paul Stillwell: Do you have other examples of working with McNamara?

---

[*] "The Hill" refers to Capitol Hill in Washington, D.C., that is, the U.S. Congress.

Admiral Forbes: No. That's the only time I ever had personal contact. I briefed what we required. He'd listen and ask questions. His staff would summon us to brief them on our needs and what ships we wanted to put back in commission for the buildup and why we needed this many people here and that many people there and be able to answer the questions from his staff. Of course, we also kept the CNO informed. It was a very interesting assignment, and the hours were long, unbelievable. We never knew what he would say. He'd just say, "I need umpty-ump by umpty-ump," which meant we would sometimes stay in our offices and work an entire weekend. We worked till 10:00 o'clock at night every night, Saturday and Sundays, all day Sunday and just go, go, go. It didn't do much for family life; I can tell you that.

Paul Stillwell: Well, you've described several successive tours that had that characteristic. You obviously have a very loyal and supporting family.

Admiral Forbes: Oh, yes. The most wonderful wife, who understood what we had to do. Betty would pick these things up when we had these little social affairs.

Paul Stillwell: Did you get into the business of detailing and detailing policy during this period?

Admiral Forbes: No, I didn't. I was involved strictly with manpower. We were a branch of the Bureau of Naval Personnel, but we had nothing to do with the personnel side, as far as assigning and managing over there. Our responsibility was numbers.

Paul Stillwell: One of the issues back then was proficiency pay. Were you involved in getting that passed?

Admiral Forbes: No, that was the policy and money people.

Paul Stillwell: What else about that job do you recall?

Admiral Forbes: Just the educational value. It was in that job that I met Commander Winifred Love.* Now, Commander Winnie Love had been in the first class of WAVE officers back when the WAVES became part of the Navy. She was a spinster by choice. Winnie was at Mary Baldwin, where she was an instructor until she entered the WAVES. She was one sharp lady and an English major. In the Naval Academy you'd say a bull major. Her mastery of the English language and poetry is to this day unbelievable. You could start any poem that you might know, and she'd finish it for you.

Paul Stillwell: From memory.

Admiral Forbes: From memory. My wife Betty and I see her still to this day. We think the world of Winnie. She was the only child of two medical doctors from West Virginia. She was attractive and sharp and a wonderful, wonderful lady. I tell you that when I returned from Vietnam I called her, and I said, "Home is the sailor, home from the sea," and she went on and finished the entire poem. We chatted. In fact, Betty and I saw her up in Newport this fall and had dinner with her. She is truly a great lady, I tell you.

Paul Stillwell: There's another Winifred who was in BuPers around then—Winifred Quick Collins. Did you know her?

Admiral Forbes: Yes, I met Winnie Collins.† I remember her. Not well, however; I talked to her a few times. We worked with the WAVES quite closely.

Paul Stillwell: But at that point they were still a very, very minor factor in the manpower situation.

Admiral Forbes: Oh, yes, they were. Winnie Love did a lot of this work in OP-103. She did a lot of the numbers and people work. It didn't involve detailing; again, it was just numbers.

---

* Commander Winifred Love, USN, who had entered the Naval Reserve in August 1942 and later transferred to the regular Navy.
† Captain Winifred Quick Collins, USN.

Paul Stillwell: So this was strictly under the OpNav hat rather than BuPers.

Admiral Crowe: Yes, exactly. We worked for Admiral W. V. Combs.* What a great gentleman he was. We worked directly for him. It was called OP-103, and it certainly was an introduction to duty in Washington, D.C.; I can tell you that. We had a house in Alexandria that was close to the Pentagon. I could get on that little back Army-Navy Drive and come down and scoot over to the Pentagon. It took me about ten minutes max. And in the Pentagon parking lot it took longer to find a place to park than it did to get there. I never had to get on Shirley Highway or anything like that. Just get on this little back road, which was very good. We enjoyed it.

Paul Stillwell: How much was the Naval Reserve a factor in your planning?

Admiral Forbes: None. This was all active duty. I never dealt with the Naval Reserve.

Paul Stillwell: Well, anything else about that tour?

Admiral Forbes: No. It was an education and a wonderful introduction to Washington. We stood the CNO command duty in the Pentagon every so often. We stood the watch at night and answered all phone calls and responded to this, that, and the other from congressmen. It was a very interesting tour. It was my first Washington tour and away from the fleet, and it was just an eye-opener in every respect. I enjoyed it.

Paul Stillwell: Well, actually, you were kind of lucky to have waited that late in your career to get to Washington for the first time. [Laughter]

Admiral Forbes: I'd been lucky. I had made the command list during the Washington tour, so I was waiting. I had been promised this, that, and the other as to what orders I

---

* Rear Admiral Walter V. Combs, Jr., USN.

would get when I left there. And, as you would know, one of the fair-haired boys came in and was given what I was supposed to get.

Paul Stillwell: Which was that?

Admiral Forbes: It was one of the big new support ships.

Paul Stillwell: Like the *Sylvania* or the *Mars*?

Admiral Forbes: Yes, it was the *Sylvania*. Anyway, I had said, "I'd like something that goes to sea." So someone called me in and said, "Well, you've got your wish at last. So-and-so [and I won't mention any names] wants the *Sylvania*, and you know how he stands with the CNO."

I said, "I understand." I was ordered to USS *Shasta* (AE-6), a former commercial ship that the Navy acquired and converted to an ammunition ship.* When World War II was over, USS *Shasta* was decommissioned and later brought back. I can talk about the USS *Shasta* for hours.

I left OpNav and went to Norfolk, where we were assigned quarters. However, I left Betty and the girls in Alexandria, because I knew we were going to sea. I reported to the ship, which was in the Norfolk Naval Shipyard in Portsmouth. The people called it the Portsmouth yard. I was relieving a gent—again no names—who was getting a carrier, and he could not give me the time of day. He was senior to me. My predecessor conducted the change of command in the shipyard cafeteria between shifts. Well, that was the first mistake he made, because the guest speaker had his sword stolen; the guest speaker subsequently wrote his fitness report.

In any event, I took command, and I got to see the ship for the first time; it was one of those deals. I went aboard and observed everyone working away in the yard. *Shasta* had one of the first master chief boatswain's mates in the Navy. I'll never forget

---

* USS *Shasta* (AE-6), an ammunition ship, was acquired by the Navy on 16 April 1941 and commissioned on 20 January 1942. She displaced 13,000 tons, was 459 feet long, 63 feet in the beam, and had a maximum draft of 23 feet. Her top speed was 15.5 knots. She was originally armed with one 5-inch gun and four 3-inch guns. She was decommissioned in 1946 and recommissioned in 1953.

him: Chief Sandover, 6-feet-6, a great big gent, to whom I said, "Master Chief, have the crew fall in so I'll see them, and they'll see that they have a new skipper."

Yes, sir, Captain."

The crew mustered, and I looked out at that crew. I turned to him and said, "Master Chief, did a dark cloud just pass over this ship?"

"You from the South, Captain?" the master chief replied.

"Yes, I am."

"I am too," he said. "We don't know how it happened, but we have 40% darkies in this crew." Now, this was in the Navy when there were perhaps one or two blacks in the officers' mess. Blacks weren't in the general crew. I knew, having come from the bureau, that everyone in the Navy had a personnel card, an individual card, with his name and other information. We were race-coded. Someone in BuPers pressed the wrong button, and I had a large number of black crewmen. Most of them were reservists. I mustered my chiefs and the wardroom, which was still being formed. I said to them, "We have our work cut out for us. It's going to be an entirely different situation than—" And, just by sheer coincidence, every one of those chiefs was from the South. A chief said, "Captain, we've got our hands full, and we'll do the very best we can."

When we started off, we redid all the bunks. We cleaned up that ship and made it spotless. My chief cook came to me and said, "Now, Captain, don't get mad at me. I want to try something."

I said, "What's that?"

He said, "We're going to have soul food." And we did.

Well, to make a long story short, not a one of them had ever been on an ammunition ship. Of the officers assigned, some of them were rejects. They were just killing time. I used to get angry. None of them had any experience. I had a good chief engineer who was an old mustang; he went back to year one, and he was good. He was just a good old snipe. We started to work on that ship. How do you handle ammunition when no one has ever operated a winch? So we worked and trained, worked and trained, and we worked and trained some more.

We then steamed to Yorktown, where we loaded ammunition. That was the first time we were under way, and the evolution went well. Oh, when we backed out of the yard for the first time, it was to leave the dry dock. The pilot was on board, the tugs made up, and as the *Shasta* maneuvered out of the dry dock, the pilot said, "All engines back one-third." Now, this ship had old Nordberg diesels, for which the United States Navy had no spare parts at all. When the engine room answered the bell, the ship started to move forward. We stopped everything. He tried again, and again *Shasta* moved ahead. I said, "Let's try going forward and see what happens." I meant, "Let's try reversing and see what happens." The ship went forward again, and we entered the dry dock, where we moored again. The shipyard people discovered that someone had put the screw—it had one screw—on backwards. The single screw had to be turned around, and that fixed the problem.

As I said, we steamed to Yorktown, where we loaded ammunition; it was a fairly good-sized load. We loaded old dummy shapes when we first started to work. We learned how to handle the winches and how to lift cargo and how to make the booms work. And, I'm telling you, we worked our fannies off on that equipment. Then we returned to the piers there in Norfolk. We were moored at pier two while we finished the last of the work.

To illustrate how things happen, I received a message on the back channel, which was a very closely held coded circuit. I received a personal message from the President of the United States, who wanted to know why I was violating federal order umpty-ump by taking John B. Dennison into a combat zone. He was a sole surviving son. Well, I got the master chief in, and I said, "Master Chief, John B. Dennison?" I'd only been in the ship for about three or four days.

He said, "Oh, Captain, that's the Blue-Eyed Coon." Well, this was when I was learning that every one of my black shipmates had a self-given nickname by which he went.

I said, "The Blue-Eyed Coon?"

He said, "That's what he calls himself, and that's what his buddies call him."

I said, "Let's get him up here." I got out his record in the meantime. I studied his record. He was a reserve. He came from a well-to-do black family in Detroit. He'd been to a private boys' school; he'd had a good education. He had four sisters and a brother. So when he came into the cabin and introduced himself, I said, "Excuse me." I had to go out in the passageway to break up. John Dennison had two of the biggest, bluest eyes I had ever seen. I went back in, and I said, "Dennison, I have a message here. Where are we?"

"We're in Norfolk, Captain."

I said, "We're not in a combat zone."

He said, "No, sir." He looked at me like I was losing my mind.

I said, "And don't you have four sisters and a brother?"

"Yes, sir."

And I said, "Then you're not a sole son."

He said, "Captain, has my mother been writing to President Johnson again?"

I said, "Apparently she has, and I got this message that I have to answer." Then I said, "Thank you very much. It is nice meeting you, and good luck on the ship."

I replied to the President on his own private channel: "Your umpty-ump not understood. One of [and I gave the number of] children. Ship alongside pier two, Norfolk, Virginia." That was the last we ever heard of that.

But my biggest problem was not to call and address my black shipmates by their self-given nicknames. I had "Sly Fox," "Slick Charles," "Sweet Willie from South Philly," "Big Daddy," "Big Money," the "Blue-Eyed Coon"—I could go on forever. As I learned, they all had these self-given nicknames.

We worked like mad to get under way and then steamed to the Panama Canal.* After we went through the canal, we went to San Diego, where we loaded ammunition, all the time working the booms and trying to make the shapes work. In the engine room it was a nightmare. Go, go, go. Upon departure from San Diego we steamed to Pearl. Then at Pearl we loaded ammunition on the decks. Ammo was just stacked up, and off we went.

Paul Stillwell: Were you satisfied with the material condition of the ship at that point?

---

* The *Shasta*'s deployment began with her departure from Norfolk on 14 September 1966; she went through the canal on 20 September.

Admiral Forbes: It was old, and there was nothing we could do about that. I'd published my formal message report stating that this didn't work, that didn't work, and we were fixing this—and the various and sundry things that we learned. The equipment was so antiquated. That was the biggest problem. And spare parts—jeepers, creepers.

Well, I worked out a deal. We arrived in Subic Bay on our transit to Vietnam.[*] Fortunately, the officer who operated the whole big movie complex there in Subic Bay was an old shipmate of mine. I got him aside and said, "We'll be coming in here about once every month and load ammunition, then go back on the line. The only recreation we have on that bucket are movies. What can you do?"

He replied, "Beetle, I get four brand-new movies a week in here. Sometimes I get three or four shipments a week but never less in a week. I'll save you one copy of each brand-new movie that comes in. When you come in, you can have them." So every time we'd come into port, we'd get all these brand-new movies that hadn't been seen. Then we used to use those to get other things. I'd see if other ships on the line wanted to swap for such and such. "Well, what can we do for you?" the carrier would ask when we were alongside for replenishment.

I'd say, How about two barrels of lube oil?" or something like that, because we were underfunded, and that's how we had to operate. We worked very hard, but we had the best food, clean bunks, and good movies. That was how we took care of our crew.

They appreciated it, and we broke the record for total amount of ammunition transferred by any ship. We received a message stating that we'd been judged—and I'm bragging now, but it's a fact, it's all in writing—the best of the 21 ammunition heavy support ships in the fleet and so forth and so on.

Once we got a call that the other ammunition ship on the line had suffered a casualty. The *Enterprise* had to be loaded up for these special strikes on North Vietnam. We were asked if we were ready and if we could get up there to provide the ammunition. Well, I looked at our position and measured the distance we had to steam to get there by a certain time. It was a greater distance than we could cover at the specified max speed for that bucket.

---

[*] The arrival at Subic Bay in the Philippines was on 26 October 1966.

I called my old chief engineer to the bridge and asked, "Chief, what do you think? We'll have to make 17 knots."

"Seventeen, Captain?"

I said, "Seventeen."

He replied, "Captain, you ring it up, and you've got it." That's what he said, "You ring it up, and you've got it."

So I went back to my seniors and said, "We'll make every effort." Away we went, and we made it. When the replenishment was completed, we passed 340 tons on that occasion.

After it was all over, I asked the chief engineer, "How did we do that?"

He explained, "Very simple, Captain. I put a youngster on the over-speed trip switch, and he held it down so it wouldn't trip." We just operated the plant beyond specifications. Of course, we couldn't get spare parts. It was a challenge to operate *Shasta*.

Paul Stillwell: So he was taking a risk.

Admiral Forbes: Yes, but he was an old-timer, and he knew more about these diesels than anybody else. So he did it, and we did it.

Paul Stillwell: What do you recall about the replenishment itself?

Admiral Forbes: We were alongside, and, as always, they rigged the telephone line over, and then-Captain Jimmy Holloway, later Chief of Naval Operations, was skipper of *Enterprise*.[*] I'd met him before, and he called over and he said, "Beetle, thank you for coming to our help on this ammunition. Is there anything we can do for you?"

I said, "Yes, sir. Could we get about ten pounds of popcorn from you? I want to give the crew some popcorn."

---

[*] Captain James L. Holloway III, USN, commanded the aircraft carrier *Enterprise* (CVAN-65) from 17 July 1965 to 11 July 1967. He later served as Chief of Naval Operations, 1974-78.

"No problem." We kept on rearming, and just towards the end of the rearming period, as the line came back, it had a great big canvas sack like a mail sack almost, and it was filled with popped popcorn. And he sent me back ten sacks of that stuff and said, "Beetle, there's your popcorn." And we had popcorn all over that ship. I learned my lesson then. From then on it was always unpopped.

Then we went to Hong Kong, where we won the award for best conduct ashore. We visited Hong Kong twice in the nine months we were over there on the line. Much of our morale was due to all these movies and then swapping them. *Shasta* had a good crew that we really worked with.

When we were getting near the end of our deployment, I sent a message back to ComServLant in Norfok and said, "We came out here via the Panama Canal, and it's just as close to come back via the Suez Canal. This would give these kids the break they need to see some of the world. Request permission."*

The answer was, "Do it. Sounds good to us." We departed the coast of Vietnam and started our trek west with a port call at Penang, Malaysia, where we refueled. I wanted to off-load the mail, but the Brits ran the place, and they said, "Oh, no, no, no. We cannot touch your mail."

But I saw that this one British official kept looking over at our magazines. There was a copy of *Esquire* on the wardroom table. I asked, "Would you like to see it?"

"Oh, yes, sir. You know, we're not allowed to have this magazine over here. It's banned."

I got to thinking. I conferred with my chief, and I said, "We've got those devilish *Esquire*s all over this ship." He went out and rounded up 40 of them. I invited the Brits back the next day, and when they arrived I had the magazines stacked up. I said, "Would you gentlemen care to have them?"

"Oh, sir, can we? Oh, may we, may we?" They went over and grabbed them. Of course, being British gentlemen, they had to say, "What can we do for you, sir?"

I said, "You can certainly send our mail."

"Okay, okay. Let us have your mail." So that's how we got the mail off the ship.

---

* ComServLant – Commander Service Force Atlantic Fleet was the type commander for replenishment ships such as the *Shasta*.

Then we prepared to transit the Suez Canal. We had to anchor, because all transits had to occur during daytime. While we were at anchor I observed a barge and a boat approaching the ship. It was the U.S. Consul General. He came aboard, and we went up to the cabin, where I asked, "Sir, what may I do for you?"

He said, "We understand that Egypt may attack Israel. I have orders. We've got to see what we can find out in the way of any indications. Do you have anybody on board who can take pictures as you go through the canal tomorrow? I'd like you to take picture, observe, and then give me a report when you arrive at the north end of the canal."

I said, "Yes, sir. We have some sharp youngsters on here." So I got them down and told them privately what to do with all these cameras that we brought with us. We started through the canal the next day. The Egyptians were doing just that, and sometimes they had to pause while their little boats went across. The trucks were broken down on both sides of the canal with the hoods up and guys asleep on the ground. I thought, "Boy, if they're going to fight the Israelis, they haven't got a prayer."

Well, we got all these pictures and counted the number of troops we saw. When we arrived at the north end of the canal, our consulate personnel were right there and took all the details down. They thanked us very much and sent us on our way. Then we visited Malta, with the next port of call at Barcelona, Spain. We finally arrived at our homeport of Norfolk on time, which surprised everyone, including myself.[*] We were right on the dot. We'd been deployed almost nine months.

Paul Stillwell: The Six-Day War was in June of 1967, so your trip through the canal must have been shortly before that.[†]

Admiral Forbes: I think so, yes. It was just before, because the Egyptians were all forming across there. They were really a lousy-looking bunch, if I do say so. It was unbelievable for a military outfit to look like that.

---

[*] The *Shasta* returned to Norfolk on 8 June 1967.
[†] The Six-Day War of June 1967 grew out of Egypt's action in closing the Gulf of Aqaba and moving troops into the Sinai Peninsula. Israel initiated the war on 5 June with air attacks on airbases in Syria, Jordan, and Egypt. In the days that followed Israeli forces completely defeated their Arab opponents and occupied the Golan Heights, West Bank of the Jordan River, the Sinai, and the east bank of the Suez Canal.

But, now, one more thing about that. Having gone to the Naval Academy and then to the fleet myself, I went through all these personnel records so I'd know whom we had on board. This one youngster whom I'd watched, Eugene Lovely, was a quartermaster striker who worked on the bridge. He was a sharp young black, a hard worker, and he did a good job. I reviewed his jacket and saw that he stood at the top of his class in high school. One day I called him to my cabin and said, "Lovely, I've been watching you in the months we've been deployed here. You're a sharp young man. I've been very much impressed. Would you like to apply to the Naval Academy Prep School and then go on to the Naval Academy?"

"Sir?"

I said, "Well, think about it."

About a day later, he said, "Captain, if you think I should try, I'll try."

I said, "Okay." We sent for the exams, which he took, and he was accepted for the Naval Academy Prep School with no problem. Just before we arrived in Norfolk, I sent him off to the Naval Academy Prep School.

When I brought the ship home, I was relieved almost immediately. I had commanded the *Shasta* for just about a year and had been gone a long time. My next assignment was to the Bureau of Naval Personnel for duty. This was in '67; I was the assistant detailer.

One day I received a call from the Naval Academy Preparatory School, which was in Bainbridge, Maryland. They said, "Captain, one of our young students here, Eugene Lovely, wanted me to call to tell you that he was being discharged from the prep school."

I said, "Discharged? He's smart as a whip."

"Oh, no, no, no, no, sir. Medically. He's got—" And he gave me a medical term that long.

I said, "Doctor, what does that mean in layman's language?"

"He's got flat feet."

I said, "You redneck. All darkies have flat feet. Give him a waiver."

"Oh, I can't give him a waiver for that, sir."

I said, "It will be a lot easier, Doctor, for you to give him a waiver for that in Bainbridge, Maryland, than to think why you couldn't when you're up in Alaska."

"What do you mean, sir?"

I said, "I'm your detailer, and we're short of doctors in Alaska."

Petty Officer Lovely got his waiver, and my sweet wife, Betty, and I went down on a day in June, and I personally swore in Quartermaster Third Class Eugene Lovely as a midshipman in the United States Naval Academy. He graduated in the class of 1972, and I was very proud of him. He did very well, and then he wrote me a note to tell me that he'd left the service on a medical discharge.* He attended graduate school and settled in Atlanta, where he's making a mint.

That was really a great, great tour in the *Shasta*. I really enjoyed it: working and meeting all the challenges you had with that old bucket and all of the cumshaw and those engineering things we accomplished. I look back on it now, and I'm just glad to be here. It went off very well. We were awarded the Bronze Star for the deployment, and we won the award as the best ammunition ship in the fleet and a couple of other honors.

Paul Stillwell: You must have won the confidence of the crew to get them to perform that well.

Admiral Forbes: They knew that I cared for them and that I was doing everything I could for them to make life better. We just worked hard and gave them responsible jobs. The crew gave their allegiance and loyalty and just knocked themselves out. People not assigned to the *Shasta* would say, "Look at all the blacks you have on that ship."

I'd say, "We were the first. They were one great crew, and they did a wonderful job." My shipmates were big black boatswain's mates, the "Blue-Eyed Coon," who was something else, as were "Sly Fox" and "Slick Charles." And to hear their sea stories when they were there talking and loading ammunition. I had to fight to keep a straight face on the bridge. But they were the best, and all of the experiences are a most pleasant memory.

---

* Eugene Lovely was released from active duty in July 1974.

Paul Stillwell: Well, please tell about what the pace of operations was like over off Vietnam.

Admiral Forbes: We worked our fannies off. We would go alongside the carrier and give them their entire load of ammunition, and then we'd go alongside another carrier. As I said, *Shasta* set the Navy record with 340 tons of ammunition transferred in 24 hours. Now, this takes teamwork and skill, and those kids were good, and we never—knock on wood—it's too late now, but we never had one single mishap or injury. Our chief electrician was an old chief who could work and fix everything. He would say, "Just don't look, Captain."

I said, "I'm not. I'm looking the other way."

He'd say, "I've got a jury rig. That'll make that winch work." The crew did things like that, because so many times we couldn't get spare parts. She was so old. She was like an old car. *Shasta* burned so much lube oil, which we couldn't afford, so I'd swap movies for a couple of barrels of lube oil. We just kept her going by sheer effort and ingenuity and all those jury rigs. And when we got back, the chain of command in Norfolk just shook their heads. They marveled at how we brought the old bucket home, as well as winning all the marbles. Of course, it was the crew. They did everything. Yes, the crew did a fine job.

Paul Stillwell: I daresay you were kind of short on sleep during that deployment.

Admiral Forbes: Oh, yes. I had a quartermaster chief, poor soul, who suddenly died after our return. He was superb. I tell you that I had every confidence in him and, as I say, my master chief boatswain's mate and the chief engineer, who led all those snipes. Those shipmates were the old school, and we looked the other way on a lot of regulations about how to run things. We had to. If we went by the book on an old ship like that, along with the lack of spare parts that were not available—we had to make our own or improvise or do this, that, or the other. And it worked. We were on the fortunate side, and it worked.

Making fresh water was always a challenge. And we fed well. Boy, did we eat. We had good cooks on board, and we ate like kings. That makes a big difference in a ship. When the crew likes and appreciates the food and they eat it in large amounts, they realized we just took good care of them. As I said, their conduct on liberty ashore in Hong Kong was superb. After the second time, they said, "What in the world? This is an all-time record for a ship to come here twice and not have one incident ashore." I explained to them I had a great crew, and they were a great bunch of youngsters—and that was it.

Paul Stillwell: How much did you get into serving the soul food?

Admiral Forbes: Well, I talked to the chiefs. I'd been raised in the South, so I knew what it was. We just wrote different menus, and the crew liked them. We had a good variety in our general mess. Our chief engineer would eat down in the general mess, or he ate with the chiefs half the time. He was good. He was an old, old-timer.

They were good chiefs who worked their fannies off. They'd grin and do this, that, and the other. No, there was just teamwork everywhere. But to never experience a single failure in operating all those old winches and cranes was miraculous. Those shipmates just kept everything operating. They knocked themselves out. Some of those jury rigs we did in *Shasta* would defy description and probably cause safety inspectors to jump over the side. However, they all worked, and they proved safe.

Paul Stillwell: The ship's boatswain is a key man in that operation, making sure that your people are well trained and so forth.

Admiral Forbes: Yes, and he was a crackerjack. An old-timer chief like my chief engineer, the old warrant officer. The chief quartermaster was a great guy. They were all good. I had no complaints. We didn't have any deadwood on there. They were just all good, hard-working old-timers. An old ship like USS *Shasta* was not considered a choice bit of duty.

Paul Stillwell: What about the junior officers? How capable were they?

Admiral Forbes: Oh, we got them right out of the ROTC. They did a good job—no complaints.

Paul Stillwell: What do you remember about ship handling once you got the propeller turned around?

Admiral Forbes: Well, the ships being supplied had to come alongside us to replenish. All we had to do was steer a straight course. But it was an interesting ship to handle with that one screw and those diesel engines.

Paul Stillwell: Well, you still had to take it alongside a pier to take on ammunition.

Admiral Forbes: That's right. And I did very carefully. It was "Back down" and "Go ahead."

Paul Stillwell: Where did you get the ammo, at Subic?

Admiral Forbes: Yes, on an average of once a month we went in, and that was another benefit we had over the other ships. The Filipinos would arrive with these mountains of ammunition to load. Well, the other ships filed complaints about being robbed and items being stolen. The Filipinos were hungry. I mustered my people together before we moored in Subic, and I said, "Okay, now let's set up a lot of food, edibles, up on that forward cargo deck with soft drinks and make it available to the Filipinos."

The workers cleaned that out, and we never had one bit of pilferage in *Shasta*. They say that was all they wanted, something to eat. We fed them. It didn't cost us anything to speak of, and it paid off, because they liked to steal ammunition. Well, I saw one worker right from the ammunition dump take this bomb out. Just by coincidence, the next day, when we departed, we saw this same worker in a little boat. The boat crew dumped this bomb over the side. It exploded, and fish were killed by the concussion and floated to the surface. The boat came around, and the crew scooped up the fish in their nets.

Paul Stillwell: You seemed to have a real facility for doing what it took to get the job done.

Admiral Forbes: Well, I enjoyed it. I tell you, that was challenge in itself. In fact, we had people who laughed at the fact that we even got out there and got back, which was a miracle in itself in that bucket. She was old. I mean, that was a 1940 model ship. And we chugged along at our 12 knots en route. And we got back on time. That was another thing our Navy friends laughed about, because you could never tell what was going to happen. Every day it was something. But she was a good ship. I enjoyed it.

Paul Stillwell: Well, Admiral, we're right at the end of the tape to wind up this session. I certainly have enjoyed it and look forward to the next meeting and the rest of your career.

Interview Number 2 with Vice Admiral Bernard B. Forbes, Jr., U.S. Navy (Retired)
Place: U.S. Naval Institute, Annapolis, Maryland
Date: Friday, 7 February 1992
Interviewer: Paul Stillwell

Paul Stillwell: Admiral, just to kick off this second session, you were mentioning some things that you'd been reminded to include that we didn't talk about the first time. And one would be your experience with Admiral Stump going to Korea. If you could start with that, please.

Admiral Forbes: That was in 1955. We traveled a great deal. The job required that in those days. He was head of the Southeast Asia Treaty Organization, which has now gone by the board. And he corresponded directly with the President of the United States on several occasions, either by phone call or by back-channel message. He received orders, so to speak, to go to Korea to see personally what the situation was there. We went to the front line with the North Koreans on one side, the South Koreans on the other side, and watched several skirmishes. They weren't put on for our benefit but just occurred by sheer coincidence. And it was very interesting to see that type of exchange.

Paul Stillwell: That was a couple of years after the armistice, so they were still hassling then.

Admiral Forbes: Yes, they were. That was why Admiral Stump was sent out there, I'm sure.

Paul Stillwell: And you mentioned also that you'd had some experiences with NBC when you were serving in the *Franklin D. Roosevelt*. What were those?

Admiral Forbes: Well, I was the "air boss," which is the nickname for the air officer. He runs the flight deck, as well as everything else. NBC came aboard to do TV coverage of actual aircraft carrier flight deck operations. They shot countless feet of film, and they were all over the ship. It all had to be correlated at the end, so I was sent from the ship—we'd come back to the States then—to NBC in New York City. I worked with the NBC personnel for a month as their consultant and helped to edit and to put out the film, which later became known as "Flight Deck." It was shown on national TV and demonstrated what went on on a carrier flight deck. It was an absolutely educational experience.

Paul Stillwell: And I think you mentioned that the Navy sent you TAD during this period, so that's how much it meant to the Navy.

Admiral Forbes: Yes, they did. I was TAD, but NBC covered most of the personal expenses up there.

Paul Stillwell: Who did the air boss job while you were gone?

Admiral Forbes: Oh, we were back in port then.

Paul Stillwell: I see.

Admiral Forbes: Oh, I can tell you who did it was my assistant air boss, Deaker Dauer, referred to as the "Mini-Boss."[*] A real character. [Laughter]

Paul Stillwell: Anything else to catch up on from the *Shasta*? We talked about that in some detail and your deployment and so forth last time.

Admiral Forbes: Well, I think I mentioned the message after I'd had *Shasta* just a matter of a couple of days from President Johnson, a personal message. She was quite a ship, quite a ship.

---

[*] Commander Frank H. Dauer, USN.

Paul Stillwell: Well, one of the purposes of sending you to the *Shasta* was to get you qualified for a carrier command.

Admiral Forbes: Yes. We had to have what was called in those days a deep-draft command before you could go to a carrier. Well, when I left *Shasta* the change of command was in July of '67. Then I was ordered up to the Bureau of Naval Personnel for duty, and I served there until '69. I was the assistant director for officer distribution control. I was called the "assistant daddy detailer" in the Navy.

Paul Stillwell: Well, this was probably something of a payback tour for your postgraduate school.

Admiral Forbes: Oh, it was, yes. They made no bones about that.

Paul Stillwell: What did it involve in that tour of duty?

Admiral Forbes: Well, I worked with the assignment of officers to various duties, which kept me very closely involved; I enjoyed it very much.

Paul Stillwell: What are some of the specifics you remember?

Admiral Forbes: Well, later on I can better cover it, because when I went back the second time I was *the* daddy detailer.

Paul Stillwell: Who were some of the people you worked with in this particular tour?

Admiral Forbes: Oh, Admiral Weisner, Mickey Weisner, who is now in the Naval Aviation Museum in Pensacola. Oh, what a wonderful gentleman. And he was a character who smoked cigars, practically chain-smoked cigars if you can imagine that.

One day he said to me, "Beetle, I'm going to give up these cigars. They're not good for your health, they tell me."*

He stopped smoking, and after about a week I went in and I said, "Admiral, would you please start smoking cigars again?"

"Why?"

I said, "Because you've become insufferable." I thought he'd die laughing, and he started smoking again. To the best of my knowledge, he probably still is.† I haven't seen him in years, but he is a great gentleman.

Paul Stillwell: What else do you recall about him?

Admiral Forbes: Just a fine, very dedicated, very efficient person.

Oh, I remember one thing that happened when I was the daddy detailer. We got a letter one day sent to the Navy Department from the Dallas Cowboys, words to the effect, "Dear Navy, where is Roger Staubach? You told us we could have him after four years. Four years have come, and now we've been paying him a $25,000 retainer fee each year, yet he cannot get out of the service. What gives?"‡

So I sat down and wrote them a nice letter back about Vietnam and the fact we'd extended the obligated service of all Naval Academy graduates to five years instead of four. And, lo and behold, in due course we got a letter from the White House to the effect, "Dear Navy, What's this about Roger Staubach? Let's get it squared away."

I was sent over to see Admiral Zumwalt. We sat down, and I said, "Sir, this is what the situation is." I gave him copies of the letter. I said, "We have, in my humble opinion, two options. We can either let Roger Staubach go—" And Roger Staubach, let me hasten to add, never asked for a thing. He is one fine, fine individual. I know him personally now, and he'd never ask for a thing for himself. With his eyesight he couldn't get a line commission. He was in the Supply Corps in Vietnam. I said, "Either let Roger Staubach go and hold the rest, or let them all go."

---

* Rear Admiral Maurice F. Weisner, USN.
† Weisner, who retired as a four-star admiral, died 15 October 2006 at age 88.
‡ Roger Staubach, who won the Heisman Trophy in 1963 and graduated from the Naval Academy in 1965, played professional football for the Dallas Cowboys from 1969 to 1979.

"Beetle, you give me these decisions to make, etc., etc." So I went on back to the office, and in about ten minutes the phone rang. "Let them all go, Beetle." So we changed the rules again, and Roger Staubach went to the Dallas Cowboys.

Paul Stillwell: What was Zumwalt's position then?

Admiral Forbes: He was Chief of Naval Operations, CNO.[*]

Paul Stillwell: Well, Staubach was in the class of '65, and the four years would have ended in '69, which was a year earlier than Zumwalt became CNO. He became CNO in July 1970 when he relieved Moorer.

Admiral Forbes: Well I'll be dogged. It wasn't Admiral Moorer. I never worked with Admiral Moorer.

Paul Stillwell: In fact, Zumwalt was over in Vietnam till the spring of '70.

Admiral Forbes: Well, I'm in error then, but I could have sworn it was Admiral Zumwalt. The newspaper said that Roger Staubach, day before yesterday, was 50 years old. That was in our Norfolk paper.

Paul Stillwell: I wonder if it was the VCNO. That sounds like the kind of thing a VCNO would handle.

Admiral Forbes: No. When the White House gets into things, it is the CNO. Well, I'm in error then, but I could have sworn it was Admiral Zumwalt, because I worked with him on several decisions. So '65, '69. Well, maybe this had gone in to the—no, it wouldn't. They wouldn't be writing that late. When did you say he became CNO?

---

[*] Admiral Elmo R. Zumwalt, Jr., USN, served as Chief of Naval Operations from 1 July 1970 to 29 June 1974. His oral history is in the Naval Institute collection.

Paul Stillwell: July 1970.

Admiral Forbes: And Roger Staubach would have been eligible to get out in—

Paul Stillwell: He was in the class of '65, so he would have got out in '69 if it hadn't been for the extension.

Admiral Forbes: Then he'd have had four years' service in '69.

Paul Stillwell: Well, that's a mystery.

Admiral Forbes: Yes, that is. I'll go back and review the bidding on that one.

Paul Stillwell: What do you remember about the bureau chief, Admiral Duncan?

Admiral Forbes: Well, Admiral Duncan was a very fine person.[*] I saw very little of him. Only at the morning briefs. I mean, as far as any personal relationship or on problems, no. I went to my boss, and I worked for John Dandridge Henley Kane, Jr.[†] I can't forget that name.

Paul Stillwell: Well, please tell me about him.

Admiral Forbes: Oh, another great gentleman. John Dandridge Henley Kane, Jr.

Paul Stillwell: I just had another thought and this may have been after you left there, but in the spring of '69 that's when I remember the extension for people because my roommate in the *New Jersey* was an NROTC graduate and he got extended at that point. And then in the fall of '69 they had project 703, or something like that, when there was a

---

[*] Vice Admiral Charles K. Duncan, USN, served as Chief of Naval Personnel from 5 April 1968 to 21 August 1970. The oral history of Duncan, who retired as a four-star admiral, is in the Naval Institute collection.
[†] Kane was then a rear admiral.

big budget cutback and a resulting end strength cutback. And so I think those extensions went away at that point, and then it was a case of letting people out early. I don't know at what point in '69 you left and whether that would have affected you.

Admiral Forbes: I left there on 13 June 1969. That was the exact date.

Paul Stillwell: Well, this was in about September 1969 when the Navy announced the early outs.

Admiral Forbes: No, I hadn't heard anything about that.

Paul Stillwell: What were some of the mechanics involved in detailing? We still had a large force over in Vietnam and a lot of ships to keep filled up. How did you go about matching requirements to available bodies?

Admiral Forbes: We just did the very best we could with what we had; that is what it really boiled down to. Now, the ships had priority, keeping them manned, to the detriment in some cases of your shore commands, but we did it. You have to make some decisions that are not in the best interests sometimes of the individual concerned. We would get congressional letters about, "Why have you got so and so? His mother's sick and this and that," and things of that nature, which is understandable. But it's just one of those tasks that had to be done, and some of us didn't brag too much about the fact that we were detailers in the Bureau of Naval Personnel.

Well, requests would come in sometimes, and oftentimes we'd see persons to talk about what they wanted to do and what they didn't want to do and so forth and so on. And we tried—I'm quite serious—conscientiously to accommodate the individual to what his desires were. But the needs of the service had to come first, understandably, and the person making the request bought that eventually.

Paul Stillwell: Well, the individual's view of the detailer really is directly related to how well his desires are being met.

Admiral Forbes: That's right.

Paul Stillwell: If he gets what he wants, he thinks the detailer's a great guy.

Admiral Forbes: Oh, my.

Paul Stillwell: What about things like training and PG education and so forth? Was there a need to skimp on some of that just to keep these shipboard billets filled?

Admiral Forbes: No. The PG we didn't touch. The shore stations were the ones that paid, as far as any shortages. They were the ones that had to take that into account. But keep those ships filled. They needed full complements.

Paul Stillwell: And especially the nuclear submariners. They were always in short supply.

Admiral Forbes: My Naval Academy roommate was a nuclear submariner.

Paul Stillwell: Which one was that?

Admiral Forbes: Norman Bagnall Bessac, better known as Buzz Bessac. A-Number-One-Crackerjack individual. In fact, he was one of the first submariners to be—I use the term perhaps correctly—drafted by Admiral Rickover to work directly for him in his office. And he would interview candidates for the nuclear program. When we were eligible for selection for captain—this was back in '64, my first tour in Washington—I had a phone call from Buzz, who was in New London: "Beetle, we're going up for captain, and being my old wife, I wanted you to be the first to know, I'm not going to stand for captain."

I said, "Oh, come off it Buzz. You're a shoo-in."

He said, "Well, thank you, but I've been driving boats for that man now for ten straight years. There's no light at the end of the tunnel. My family life's going to hell in a hand basket, and I'm getting out." And he put in his retirement papers, and he got out.*

Well, just to backtrack for a minute, I was in the War College, and he was in New London then. He had one of the nuclear submarines, and he invited us to New London for the weekend. We were having dinner at his home on a Saturday night, and halfway through the meal, as soon as the main course was over, Buzz excused himself and left the table. I didn't think anything of it. He came back in about ten minutes, dressed in his uniform, and I said, "Buzz, you don't have to go formal for us."

He laughed, and he said, "Beetle, I'm not going formal for my old wife, but that man's in town. He comes up only on the weekends. He has all the submarine skippers in to a meeting, and he tells us this, that and the other and how lousy we are. He just chews us all out. Then he goes back in his little private room we have for him there, and he has you back, each skipper, one by one, and he goes over your boat with him." He said, "That's where I'm off to tonight. It's always on the weekend. Saturday or Sunday." Buzz is now out in Walnut Creek, California.

Paul Stillwell: What sort of work did he go into after he left the Navy?

Admiral Forbes: He went into a nuclear program. I don't know the exact details of it, but he did very well. Well, he was a star man in the class. He was sharp as a tack and a great guy.

Paul Stillwell: And he had all that nuclear training from the Navy.

Admiral Forbes: Oh, yes, did he ever. He was one of the wives who got married when we graduated.

Paul Stillwell: How did your family enjoy living in Washington there during the late '60s?

---

* Bessac retired 1 January 1965.

Admiral Forbes: Well, we were, if you'll pardon the term, lucky. I found a nice house in Alexandria on Norwood Place, and all I had to do was go down to the corner, turn left, and get on the little back street. I could get right down and never had to get on the beltway there and could get right to the office. The girls enjoyed it very much. We kept that house for years. It was really pretty nice. And my sweet wife enjoyed it very much. There was a lot to do and you know how shopping is, as well as all those other things. The schools were good, and our children enjoyed going to school there. We enjoyed it, but we wouldn't retire up there.

Paul Stillwell: Well, anything else you remember from that tour of duty?

Admiral Forbes: No, it was just the regular long-day type tour. Very interesting, because I worked with individuals from whom I received a lot of phone calls, including some from congressmen and parents. We were the Navy front for many things, and we tried to do it conscientiously. We tried to do the very best job we could to meet their needs with what we had. That's what it really boiled down to. And I'll say there was no favoritism shown. It was all above board, to the best of my knowledge—at least as far as I was concerned.

Paul Stillwell: Was there a reasonably good match between the available bodies and the billets to be filled?

Admiral Forbes: Yes.

Paul Stillwell: Well, that's quite a chore making that match-up.

Admiral Forbes: Oh, yes, well, it is. The requirements we had to have this for that, and we got some irate commanding officers calling and saying, "I need So-and-so to do this and this." We tried to match their needs. As I say, the seagoing Navy came first—as it should, I think.

Then I left the Bureau. I remember the date, 13 June 1969. I was ordered to the carrier *Independence* as commanding officer and that was a wonderful, wonderful tour.* I commanded Indy exactly one year and five days, I remember, 14 August 1969 to 19 August 1970.

Paul Stillwell: Where were you between June and August in '69? Was that a pipeline training course?

Admiral Forbes: Oh, yes. Carrier COs went to AirLant. I went up to Philadelphia, where I learned about catapults. I went through all the indoctrination, which was excellent, so I'd have a basic understanding of what gives, and it was good. Ship handling courses and other things like that were useful preparation.

Paul Stillwell: Did you need any additional indoctrination on nuclear weapons, or was that covered previously from your time in the Spads?

Admiral Forbes: That had been covered thoroughly in the Spads. It was a very closely held capability that the Navy never talked about. I was thinking the other night how each of us had a target in Russia which we knew about and someone back in Washington knew about it, and no one else did. And we had our tracking charts and everything for our checkpoints. These documents were locked up in a safe on the ship, and only the responsible individual had access to them. We had to go down and give our names, and then a custodian opened the safe and handed you your material. Those were very interesting times.

Paul Stillwell: Was it essentially still that way when you became skipper of the *Independence*?

---

* USS *Independence* (CVA-62), a *Forrestal*-class aircraft carrier, was commissioned 10 January 1959. She had a standard displacement of 56,300 tons, was 1,046 feet long, 130 feet in the beam, and had an extreme width of 252 feet. Her top speed was 34 knots. She was originally armed with eight 5-inch guns and could accommodate approximately 70-90 aircraft.

Admiral Forbes: No.

Paul Stillwell: How was it done then?

Admiral Forbes: It was never discussed. It was never discussed. I know we had no special weapons squadrons on board as such. And it was a fine, fine command.

Paul Stillwell: What made it a fine command?

Admiral Forbes: Well, when I had commanded the ship just one day, we were alongside pier seven in Norfolk, and we were getting ready to get under way. ComNavAirLant, Admiral Townsend, was on board.* He wanted to look the ship over, so I'd been showing him around, and we were up on the bridge. All of a sudden, out of a clear blue sky, the ship got under way on its own. I ran into the pilothouse and yelled, "What's going on?" They all had their hands up in the air.

    Mooring lines were snapping—bang, bang—and the brow fell in the water. Then everything stopped, and we couldn't figure what in the world had happened. We later found out that there'd been a malfunction in the engine room. When the engineers were checking out the system down in their spaces, one of the valves stuck open and let the steam go right to the screws, so the ship started to move forward. Fortunately, I had a sharp chief engineer, best in the Navy, and he caught it. It was a malfunction, and he fixed that. That was my first experience in getting the *Independence* under way.

Paul Stillwell: Nothing like having the boss there to see it happen. [Laughter]

Admiral Forbes: Well, we didn't have to explain anything, because Admiral Townsend was right there on the scene. We restored power and soon had all the equipment on line.

Paul Stillwell: What do you remember about your turnover from Captain Matthews?

---

* Vice Admiral Robert L. Townsend, USN, served as Commander Naval Air Force Atlantic Fleet from 1 March 1969 to 29 February 1972.

Admiral Forbes: Spence Matthews.* He talked about channel 10, and I'm not speaking in a derogatory fashion now. Everyone to his own choice. His change of command speech was Channel 10, Channel 10, Channel 10, which was a TV channel there in the Norfolk area. Spence had great empathy with those people. He turned the ship over to me, and that was it. It was very, very simple.

Paul Stillwell: Well, I don't understand what you mean about Channel 10.

Admiral Forbes: I mean that in his change of command speech, he didn't talk about the ship. He talked about, "Channel 10 does this and this wonderful TV coverage and so forth and so on." It was all about Channel 10. People asked, "What in the world is he talking about?" But he was very close to that TV community down there.

Paul Stillwell: Well, your style strikes me as very different from his. I expect it took some adjustment for the crew.

Admiral Forbes: It did. I can tell you that right now.

Paul Stillwell: In what ways?

Admiral Forbes: Well, having been a crew member on a carrier myself as an enlisted men, I knew how things happened and what occurred. We got under way and then returned to port to have the ship's bottom scraped and get repainted before we went to the Med for our six-month deployment; the weather was miserable. And I told the exec, who was, I might add, a Spence Matthews man, "Now, you know, this is going to be an all-hands job. We have to get all the ammunition off the ship before we go in the yard, and the weather's miserable. Let's take care of this crew."

"What do you mean, sir?"

---

* Captain Herbert Spencer Matthews, Jr., USN, commanded USS *Independence* (CVA-62) from 2 September 1968 to 14 August 1969.

I said, "Well, let's set some booths up around the hangar bay. We'll have five colors of the bug juice we drink." What did we call it? Kool Aid. Different colors. It all tastes the same to me, but they're different colors and different names. And then I said, "Let's see. Why don't we put some doughnuts down there as a treat for the crew?"

"Doughnuts?"

I said, "Yes. Everyone likes doughnuts. That would be a little break for them."

"Aye, aye, sir. And how many doughnuts do you think we're going to have to have?"

I said, "Well, we've got 4,000 youngsters on this ship. Let's get 4,000 dozen." In those days, and I think still to this day, we put in what was called a logreq, a logistics requisition, by message while the ship was at sea. The logreq lists everything needed and wanted to load upon return to port. So I put on my logreq 4,000 dozen doughnuts, pier umpty-ump, morning of umpty-ump.

We submitted the logreq, and I got the rest of the story secondhand. The storekeeper at ComNavAirLant there in Norfolk read it and called Krispy Kreme, which had the contract. On Friday afternoon he told Krispy Kreme, "I want 4,000 dozen doughnuts for the USS *Independence* on Monday morning at umpty-ump," and got an aye-aye. Then the supply officer the next day was going over the logreqs, and he came across mine and said, "*Independence* said 4,000 dozen doughnuts? Either Forbes has lost his mind, or that's a garble. That should have been 400. He meant 400 dozen. You call Krispy Kreme and tell them to make that 400 dozen."

The staff member called Krispy Kreme, and Krispy Kreme came back and said, "Hey, Navy, we've had every subcontractor in Tidewater making doughnuts for that ship, and they're getting 4,000 dozen on Monday morning." And, sure enough, we moored, and here came the lighter right alongside with 4,000 boxes of doughnuts. Well, we off-loaded the doughnuts first, and then we off-loaded the ammunition. The crew ate them all up in the first day, so I ordered 4,000 dozen more. Later on in the day, or the next morning, I got a message to report to ComNavAirLant immediately.

We'd finished all the work then, and I jumped in the gig and reported to ComNavAirLant. The admiral had me in his office, and he said, "Beetle, what in hell is this about 8,000 dozen doughnuts?"

I said, "Sir, I'm within my budget. They have all been or are just about completely consumed by now, and the crew enjoyed them."

He said, laughing, "That's not what I got you over here for, really. I just wanted to tell you that you all have set a Navy record in off-loading ammunition."

I said, "Admiral, you take care of them. They care of you."

He said, "I know, I know. Well done."

So I went back to the ship. My supply officer was Jim Lynn, who's a Naval Academy graduate also, class of '50.* I said, "You know, Jim, if we could get a doughnut-making machine we wouldn't have to go through all this folderol every time."

He said, "You're right." And nothing else was said, and we went on. While we were in the yard one day he called me and he said, "Skipper, I want to show you something." I went down to the hangar bay, and there was this great big commercial doughnut machine and I mean the kind that has fingers that go through the dough like that—a big, long thing that still had the Krispy Kreme insignia on the side. I said, "Jim Lynn, where did you get this?"

"Don't ask."

I didn't inquire further. The doughnut machine was moved down below to the galley, welded in fore and aft so the grease wouldn't spill when the ship rolled. We started making doughnuts and seriously, Paul, when you put a tray of hot doughnuts up on that flight deck at 1:00 o'clock in the morning, you talk about morale. Well, I'll brag. When we deployed the *Independence* still holds the Navy record for the lowest number of unauthorized absentees. We had 17 during our six-month deployment. Some carriers had as many 300 and something. Fifteen of the 17 were bums, and I cheered privately. The other two couldn't leave their girlfriends.

We cranked out doughnuts all the time. Just by coincidence, about a month ago we were at the Naval Academy for some affair. Jim Lynn was there also. We were chatting, and I said, "Jim, it's been, let's see, '69 to '92—23 years. Will you tell me now where you got that doughnut machine?"

"No way, boss. No way." [Laughter] Indy had the doughnut machine until she had her big operational readiness inspection just before we left the ship. I think it was

---

* Commander James W. Lynn, Supply Corps, USN.

Admiral Bulkeley who said, "Get rid of that. It's not Navy issue. It's an unauthorized piece of equipment."* So my successor had to get rid of the doughnut machine. But now all ships have doughnut-making machines, so to speak. It's great.

Paul Stillwell: What do you remember about the operations in that ship?

Admiral Forbes: Well, we won the Flatley Award for safety. And that's one good thing I'll say. Serving as skipper after having been an air boss on a carrier, I had an appreciation for flight ops, and we just did well. I'll brag. We did well. The best in the West. We completed months over in the Med and had a good air group. Things went well.

Paul Stillwell: Well, please describe some of the things you did in the Med.

Admiral Forbes: That's long ago. We conducted fleet operations, followed by port visits. We visited Cannes, France, and embarked a whole group of Naval Academy midshipmen on board for indoctrination. We arranged with the local French authorities for what they call, a hop, a dance to be held in the hangar bay. We had the young French girls as guests.

Our U.S. Consulate people assembled a nice group of young ladies, all well dressed. And our midshipmen were in their good uniforms. We had the band. Everybody was just having a great time when somebody turned on the sprinkler system. As I look back on it, I laugh, but then it was almost tragic. From then on, whenever we had anything on that ship, we put a guard on the valve that activated the sprinkler system on the hangar deck.

Paul Stillwell: Was that a deliberate prank or what?

---

* Rear Admiral John D. Bulkeley, USN, began serving as president of the Board of Inspection and Survey in 1967, continued after his age-mandated retirement in 1974, and remained until he finally left active duty in 1988.

Admiral Forbes: Yes, it was just a deliberate prank. And I wouldn't be at all surprised if some midshipman didn't do it, but I'll never know. We were able to cut it off right away. I mean, a sailor ran right there and cut it off, but someone else had cut the thing on. And, you know, you couldn't see where it was done. The system control was down below deck; it wasn't up on the hangar deck. But it sprinkled on them a little bit.

Paul Stillwell: Please describe what it's like to handle a ship that big.

Admiral Forbes: You've got to have a feel for it.

Paul Stillwell: Well, how did you get that feel? The *Independence* was a lot bigger than the *Shasta*.

Admiral Forbes: Oh, yes. Well, she's also a lot more powerful than the *Shasta* and has four screws. I didn't have just one screw, and I didn't have to stop the engines and start them again every time I backed down. One just got a feel for the ship. It's seamanship, I guess. But coming alongside was a real test of ship handling. Well, one thing I did, I had my supply officers, who were great guys, up on the bridge, and I let them handle the ship. I showed them and worked with them—we had a happy ship, I'll say that—in how to conn the carrier alongside of an oiler or an ammunition ship when we were transferring. We got so the supply officers could stand officer-of-the-deck watches. They could give conning orders—left one degree and all these maneuvers—and they went off very well. We enjoyed it. We really had a good wardroom, a good group.

Paul Stillwell: Did you experience a sense of fatigue in that job after a while?

Admiral Forbes: No. I was much younger then. I slept up in my little sea cabin right behind the bridge all the time we were under way. I had a good group of OODs. We really worked with our people in *Independence*, and they would call me if they had to. They knew what their responsibilities were and what my responsibilities were. It went off very well.

Paul Stillwell: So the *Shasta* was probably a lot more demanding in that respect.

Admiral Forbes: Oh, was it ever. Yes.

Paul Stillwell: That's the difference, I guess, between a combat deployment and an essentially peacetime deployment.

Admiral Forbes: That's right. And I had people like Jerry Skoning.* We had crackerjack young ensigns. Ensigns and jaygees were assistant OODs and junior officers of the deck. We just had a good group of people. I enjoyed working with them.

Paul Stillwell: What do you remember about the engineering plant?

Admiral Forbes: One day my great chief engineer, Jim Hamel, came up to the bridge to look around and see how the rest of the Navy was running, and we were launching aircraft in afterburner.† I turned to him and said, "Chief, just think of the fuel those things burn getting up to altitude."

He said, "Yes, sir. That's one thing I'd like to discuss with you, Captain, if I may."

I said, "What's that, Jim?"

He said, "You know, could we burn some of the JP-5 down below?"‡

I said, "What do you mean?"

He said, "I'd like to burn JP-5 in the boilers one day a week."§

And I said, "Well, I have absolute faith in your decision," but I said, "You're not going to blow me up, are you?"

---

* Ensign Gerald D. Skoning, USNR.
† Lieutenant Commander James K. Hamel, USN.
‡ JP-5 is a type of fuel for jet aircraft. It was developed in 1952 and is notable for its high flash point, designed to minimize the risk of fire on board aircraft carriers.
§ The normal practice at that time was to burn a viscous black fuel known as Navy special fuel oil (NFSO). Later the Navy switched to lighter distillate fuels for its steam-powered ships.

He said, "No. I want to try something." And his senior chief was there and shook his head knowingly, and I admired that chief. He was a great gentleman, knew his work.

I said, "Okay, go ahead and do it."

So we burned JP-5 one day a week while we were under way, and we came back to Norfolk after our six-month deployment in the Med and had our operational readiness inspection. And after it was over, several days later, I got this call from Commander Air Force Atlantic Fleet to come up and see him. I did, and he wanted to discuss the ORI. Towards the end he said, "Beetle, I want to perhaps caution you about one thing."

I said, "What's that, Admiral?"

He said, "My people tell me you've got the cleanest firesides they have ever seen in the Navy. You must be working your snipes to death." Because in those days to clean your firesides people had to get inside the boilers and just brush, brush, brush, brush, brush to get all that debris off.

I said, "No, sir. I don't think so. Admiral, if I may, I'd like to tell you what we're doing, which may be the cause of it."

"What's that?" And I told him of our burning JP-5 one day a week. He said, "You do?"

I said, "Yes, sir." Nothing else was said, but now they looked into it, and that's what kept the firesides so clean. And now all carriers burn something like that same type of fuel to keep those firesides clean.

Paul Stillwell: How was it determined that one day a week was a good period of time?

Admiral Forbes: Well, they just wanted to try it as an experiment. And he was a great chief engineer and had great chiefs down there. My snipes.

Paul Stillwell: Did you have a division commander embarked?

Admiral Forbes: Yes. On several occasions.

Paul Stillwell: Who were they?

Admiral Forbes: Frankly, I've forgotten now, but I remember we did. And they didn't bother me. They were very polite, and they just used Indy as a flagship and a communications base.

Paul Stillwell: Well, that often depends on the admiral. Sometimes some admirals are more demanding and more intrusive.

Admiral Forbes: Oh, yes. I know having been on the other side of the fence myself on that job. I was Carrier Group Six and Carrier Group Two. You can make yourself absolutely obnoxious and ruin everything if you don't do it right, I think. My memory fails me on what their names were. On two occasions I remember we had flags on board.

Paul Stillwell: How much competitiveness was there with other ships in the Med, in terms of smartness and speed of operation and so forth?

Admiral Forbes: Very much so. You prided yourself on your appearance. We were assessed on our operations: being on time and doing things correctly. The only disappointment I had is we didn't win the Ney Award for being the best feeding ship. We were a top contender, but in the final run we didn't make it. But no one could tell my crew that, because we ate like kings on there. I spent a lot of time down on the mess decks. I'll never forget. I went down in the general mess one day after I first took over. I talked to the cooks and the supply officer, this same Jim Lynn. We went over the menu, and I said, "Now, we've got these devilish turkey rolls on here several places." And I don't know if you're familiar with those.

Paul Stillwell: Sure.

Admiral Forbes: I said, "Look at all these ovens we've got on this ship." That particular class carrier had a whole bulkhead of little ovens and good-sized ovens—like 60 ovens. I said, "We can get two turkeys in each one of those ovens—120 turkeys. Why don't we have regular whole turkeys?"

"Oh, Captain, that—"

I said, "Let's try it once." They tried it, and I went down to the mess decks for the trial. The cooks didn't know I was there. Those youngsters started coming through the chow line to eat. On a carrier you feed—I'm serious—22 hours a day. We got breakfast, dinner, supper, and then you have midnight rats and all that. Then two hours a day are for cleanup. But to watch the sailors come through, and they had that whole turkey and the cook out there slicing that breast and putting it on the plate. A little fellow came back and said, "Hey, Cookie, that's the best meal we've ever had—that turkey." That convinced the cooks that we were right, so we really improved that general mess in Indy. I spent a lot of time. I went and ate with them several times, and it paid off. You take care of your crew, and as Admiral Townsend told me, they take care of you. He was absolutely correct.

Paul Stillwell: What was the cooks' objection to the whole turkeys?

Admiral Forbes: Well, they're so much more trouble. You've got to take them out. You've got to put them in there, and you've got to take them out. You've got to skin and then slice them. With the turkey roll you just sit there and put it through a machine that slices it. I didn't think it was fit to eat personally. So we had whole turkeys as well as several other things. We tried different menus that were not exactly in keeping with what the Navy puts out, but they were good.

Paul Stillwell: What do you remember about the disciplinary situation on board?

Admiral Forbes: I inherited 73 mast cases from Spence Matthews. He never even mentioned that. I went through all of these cases, and I dismissed them. They weren't for anything serious. So I got the exec up there, and we went over them very carefully, and we agreed, "That's it. Forget those." We gave several talks on conduct and worked with them. And I had very, very few captain's masts. I'll brag about that. But one I did have.

Oh, that wonderful chaplain—I'm embarrassed; I can't remember his name at the moment, but he was a Catholic chaplain, and he was character. I really liked him. But we had very few disciplinary problems. I was very proud of that.

Paul Stillwell: Well, on these 73 cases. Were they trumped-up charges or what?

Admiral Forbes: I don't know what they were. At the time they were minor things that should have been handled at the scene and not by captain's mast. Also, how could I as a commanding officer hold mast for something that I didn't charge the man with?

Paul Stillwell: So you were just starting with a clean slate.

Admiral Forbes: I started with a clean slate, is what it boiled down to.

Paul Stillwell: I've talked to any number of flag officers, and a lot of them remember the greatest satisfaction from a big ship command. Would you say that was the case with you?

Admiral Forbes: The great satisfaction was a happy crew, a very efficient crew that won all the marbles, and they had a good time. They enjoyed it.

Paul Stillwell: Well, for you personally was that a very satisfying tour of duty.

Admiral Forbes: Yes. I enjoyed it. I'm trying to think of a famous captain's mast case we had and who the sailor was. I remember that the young man's parents were there.

Paul Stillwell: For mast?

Admiral Forbes: Oh, yes. Just some minor case and to make sure this was—what was it? One of the disadvantages of getting old is you forget some of these names, but I do remember that wonderful Catholic chaplain was at mast. The mast started with the sailor's division officer giving me the young man's credentials, including the fact that he went to Mass regularly. I turned to the chaplain, and I said, "Now, Father, he is one of your young men. What do you have to say for him?"

"Hang the bastard!" [Laughter] I almost dropped my—that broke up the mast.

Paul Stillwell: I'll bet his parents were thrilled.

Admiral Forbes: Yes, they were. So that was the *Independence*.

Paul Stillwell: How much contact did you have with the air wing commander?

Admiral Forbes: Oh, quite a bit. I worked closely with the CAG and his staff. The aircraft carrier was there to support the air wing, so that was our job. We did the very best we could, and that's how we won the Flatley—I mean helped to win the Flatley. I was very proud of that, because we won it in *Roosevelt*, too, when I was air boss.

Paul Stillwell: Your personal property there. You just kept it coming back.

Admiral Forbes: Well, you take care of your people. There are lot of things you can do on a carrier: the way you run it and the air wing, the working hours and consideration. Taking care of that crew. I mean, you take care of them, and as I again say, they take care of you. It went off very well.

Paul Stillwell: Were you disappointed that you had only a year and five days in command?

Admiral Forbes: Yes, and the reason was that they wanted me to become chief of staff of Second Fleet, and I was told that before I went to *Independence*. So everything was programmed. Then the incumbent chief of staff retired, and the admiral had to get a new one, so there was no billet for me. But the whole chain had been set up, including my relief as captain of the carrier, so when my year was up I had to get off. I've been back to her several times. Right now she's out in Japan. She's the home-ported carrier out there. And I always write a little Christmas card to the commanding officers and ask them how things are going. Yes, she's a good ship.*

Paul Stillwell: Since your Second Fleet billet fell through, what did you get as an alternative?

Admiral Forbes: Well, the Navy being what it is, I was sent to be chief of staff of Sixth Fleet out of the clear blue sky.

Paul Stillwell: An even better job.

Admiral Forbes: Yes. I went over there to work for one Admiral Isaac Campbell Kidd, Jr., who was Commander Sixth Fleet, and that was an experience in itself.†

Paul Stillwell: Please describe it. What kind of guy is he?

Admiral Forbes: Interesting. He had a wonderful family, and we were on a cruiser, *Springfield*, which was home-ported in Gaeta, Italy.‡ I don't know whether you know where that is or not, but it's about 60 miles north of Naples. During World War II it was the Italian submarine base. Now, we never moored to a pier. We anchored 99% of the time. It was a very interesting staff.

Admiral Kidd lived in Gaeta in one of those little houses down there on a little point of land. And our staff people who were married and had their families with them lived over there in Gaeta. High school children had to go to a boarding school in

---

* The *Independence* (CV-62) was decommissioned on 30 September 1998 at the Puget Sound Naval Shipyard, Bremerton, Washington.
† Vice Admiral Isaac C. Kidd, Jr., USN, commanded the Sixth Fleet from 29 August 1970 to 1 October 1971.
‡ The guided missile light cruiser *Springfield* (CLG-7) was Sixth Fleet flagship, 1970-73.

Northern Italy, at one of the U.S. bases up there. Then there was a little elementary school right there in Gaeta. It was an interesting tour. My family didn't come with me. My wife's an only child, and her mother was in terminal cancer at the time, and she wanted to stay with her. I understood that. She had to take care of her back here in the States. So I lived on board ship.

Admiral Kidd is an interesting individual.

Paul Stillwell: Well, please give me some specifics. You worked closely with him.

Admiral Forbes: Twice. I worked for him again. He's a very robust gentleman, and I'm being polite there. He told me his philosophy of life was, "Beetle, never stand when you can sit. Never walk when you can ride."

"Aye, aye, sir." [Laughter]

I used to argue with him about some things, and we got along pretty well. I don't want to go into any personal details, but he's just one interesting individual. Well, on the humorous side, on the few occasions when we moored at the pier, he would use his barge. He'd come out of his cabin and go down the accommodation ladder. He'd depart the ship in his barge, go to the head of the pier, get out of the barge, get in his car, and drive home. He wouldn't walk the length of the pier. No, he was a very interesting individual to work for, and I like him. I got along with him very well. We won't go into personalities, if you don't mind.

Paul Stillwell: Well, I do mind. I mean, this is going to be more useful for historians and so forth if you talk about the man. The more you can say, the better. The Kidd personality is one of a kind. He's the boss. There's no question about that, and I'm just interested in how you observed that style, the types of decisions he made, the way he operated.

Admiral Forbes: Well, I think the reason I got along with him so well, I was not afraid to stand up to him and argue with him on some of the decisions he would make, and he would listen. He'd day, "Okay, Beetle, we'll do it your way," and things like that. So we got along, I think, very well together. But not socially inclined.

I'll never forget when we went to Monaco in the cruiser. I handled all the social details. We invited the Prince and Princess, Grace Kelly, aboard *Springfield* for dinner. I'll never forget that as long as I live. I sat on Princess's left, and she is, or was—she's dead now, poor soul—one absolutely magnificent lady.* But as she sat there, I caught out of the corner of my eye that she worked her hands under that table as if she was a nervous wreck the entire time when we were just chatting. Her husband is one of those outgoing gents, and what did he call the one son?† Oh, the "garbage bag," because he ate so much and went to school and all this and that. The prince has a sense of humor, and he just carried the conversation in that flag mess that night. We were invited to tour around in the municipality and things of that nature. It was a great honor to get that particular social affair.

Paul Stillwell: Would you say that Admiral Kidd intimidated the staff?

Admiral Forbes: Yes.

Paul Stillwell: That's a tough job for you, getting them to put forth their efforts when the boss is like that. How did you go about that?

Admiral Forbes: Well, I worked with him, and I'd argue with him. I wasn't afraid to argue with him, and I think he respected me for it. And we used to argue about certain decisions and do this, do that, and he ended up by kind of letting me run things, run the staff. As to the social thing, Admiral Kidd was required, just by virtue of his job, to do so much. We had all the congressmen who would come aboard to observe, and this and that. I'll never forget we had a female congress lady come aboard once who was going to spend the night, so I gave her my cabin. I moved out and that was fine. Groups like that

---

* Princess Grace died 14 September 1982, at Monte Carlo, Monaco, a day after suffering a stroke and being involved in an auto accident.
† Her husband was Prince Rainier, who was succeeded as monarch upon his death in 2005 by their son, Prince Albert.

would come aboard and talk and observe. It was a very, very interesting tour. And when I leave here, I'll think of all the sea stories I'm sure but—

Paul Stillwell: Well, let's see if we can think of them now. What were some of the operations that the fleet was involved in? The Soviet Navy was certainly becoming more prominent then than had been in years past.

Admiral Forbes: Oh, yes.

Paul Stillwell: How did you deal with that experience?

Admiral Forbes: We'd anchor, because the Soviet ships anchored. We would sometimes steam the flagship alongside the Soviet ship, just to see if they would render us honors, which they did. I'll never forget one particular time we were passing alongside, and the Soviets were having a formal inspection and they were all lined up at attention. Here came this one Soviet sailor down the back of the line, and I thought, "Now, what is he going to do?" As he went down he stopped and goosed one of the other sailors, and the guy jumped. They're human beings, typical sailors, and we laughed.

There always were a couple of Soviet destroyers nearby in any exercise we conducted. They stayed out of the way. They weren't going to cause any embarrassment as far as ship handling and operations of that nature, but they were there watching everything we did.

Well, I remember when I commanded *Independence*, the Soviet ships would always be right there, and I got my people aside one day and said, "Let's give this guy something to think about." So we got the great big 20-pound tins that coffee came in, the big square oblong cans. We placed them up on the bridge very quietly one afternoon and hooked them on the signal halyard. Just as the sun was going down and twilight made it difficult to see, I had the signalman hoist these large coffee cans up, and we were watching the Russians over there.

They got their binoculars, and they homed in on the halyard, and they were pointing. I thought, "Now you guys, you think that's some kind of a special weapon."

And the next morning just at sunrise, when you could just barely see, down it would come. We did this for about three days, and they went wild. They were out there every time, you know, out there watching those things. But they were observant, and they were trying to learn what they could about us and our operation.

Paul Stillwell: Well, it wasn't a real signal, was it? Just something you put up there to get their goat?

Admiral Forbes: Just empty cans, just to see what their reaction was. They were always looking for things. We just gave them a hard time. I'd like to know what kind of reports they sent back about the new special weapons the Americans have on that carrier they hoist up that they don't want us to see. [Laughter]

Paul Stillwell: How much emphasis was there on intelligence collection against the Soviets?

Admiral Forbes: Oh, we reported what we saw and what type of ship and what their tactics were. I must give them credit. They never tried, at least in my experience, to embarrass us by ship handling. But they were there.

Paul Stillwell: Well, there had been a number of incidents, and that's what led to the Incidents at Sea Agreement about that time between the U.S. and the Soviet Union, so maybe they were already backing off in the time you were speaking of.[*]

Admiral Forbes: I think they were. However, they were always there. They were ever present, but we had no particular problems with them.

---

[*] U.S. and Soviet officials signed the Incidents at Sea agreement in Moscow in May 1972. See John Erickson, "The Soviet Naval High Command," *U.S. Naval Institute Proceedings,* May 1973, pages 66-87, and David F. Winkler, *Cold War at Sea: High-Seas Confrontation Between the United States and the Soviet Union* (Annapolis: Naval Institute Press, 2000).

Paul Stillwell: What do you recall about the Jordanian crisis in the fall of 1970, when the carriers were massed over in the Eastern Mediterranean?*

Admiral Forbes: Just that. We were there. We were ready to react if they had to.

Paul Stillwell: I daresay there was a lot of high-level message traffic flying around.

Admiral Forbes: There was. All of those were back-channel messages and required a special little thing to decode them. No one else could copy and break the back-channel traffic.

Oh, we had several dignitaries who would come aboard. As I say, the congressmen visited to observe how the Navy operated in the Sixth Fleet. We hosted them and gave them an honest viewpoint and let them see what they wanted to see.

Paul Stillwell: Admiral Kidd was unusual in that that billet had been almost exclusively for aviators up to that point. He was a surface officer. Did he bring a different kind of agenda to the Sixth Fleet?

Admiral Forbes: Not to my knowledge. He counted on me for everything relating to aviation, and we worked together very closely. He is an interesting, interesting individual. I see he wrote an article for you all here recently in your *Institute Proceedings*.

Paul Stillwell: I guess I missed it then.

Admiral Forbes: It's the last one that has all the flag officers' pictures in the back. That one. I've got to pull your leg after this and show you where there's a grammatical error in there. [Laughter] That broke me up. No, he was a very dedicated family man, very

---

* In September 1970 commandos of the Popular Front for the Liberation of Palestine (PFLP) blew up three airliners—U.S., British, and Swiss—at Amman, Jordan and took the passengers as hostages. On 18 September the Pentagon announced that additional ships and aircraft had been ordered to the eastern Mediterranean because of U.S. concern for the safety of an estimated 450 Jordanians threatened by fighting there.

much so. And a good host. Just most, most interesting. He's a different cut of cloth. Let me put it that way.

Paul Stillwell: Well, that's what I'm trying to get from you. In what ways was he different?

Admiral Forbes: Well, his relief for example. We went back to aviators with Vice Admiral Jerry Miller, Naval Academy—as I recall, class of '42—and that was like night is from day.*

Paul Stillwell: In what ways?

Admiral Forbes: Well, quick sea story. [Laughter] Jerry came aboard the flagship, and when we got under way, I went below, and he sitting there in the cabin in his chair with his head in his hands, and I thought, "Well, I won't bother him. He's thinking about something." I came back a little bit later, and he was still sitting there with his head in his hands. Finally I said, "Admiral, is there anything I can help you with?"

"This damn thing rolls." That was when I learned that he had chronic seasickness. And from then on every time that cruiser got under way—and we did roll—he would fly over to the carrier and ride the carrier and leave me on the cruiser. He was quite a gentleman, and he still is. He lives in the Washington area somewhere.

Paul Stillwell: Yes. Falls Church, I believe, or somewhere around there.

Admiral Forbes: And he has a little boy. He got married a second time. I remember that.

Paul Stillwell: Well, did Admiral Kidd seem to have a specific agenda that he wanted to implement as fleet commander? He's always been very big on readiness.

---

* Vice Admiral Gerald E. Miller, USN, commanded the Sixth Fleet from October 1971 to June 1973. His oral history is in the Naval Institute collection.

Admiral Forbes: Yes, and he was then. We operated that fleet. He's a hard worker. He spent a lot of time at his desk, and he kept his finger on the pulse of everything. He wasn't the most popular flag officer in the world over there. Just interesting—a unique personality, I would say.

Paul Stillwell: Did you have any NATO exercises during that period?

Admiral Forbes: Oh, yes.

Paul Stillwell: What do you recall about those?

Admiral Forbes: They went off very well. We worked with the NATO navies and then conducted the critiques. Admiral Kidd would attend the critiques and make his comments. Of course, we had staff personnel aboard the flagship.

When I commanded the carrier *Independence*, we had 12 German generals on board. I invited them to the bridge, and I couldn't resist. I brought up the subject. I asked, "Now, where were you in World War II?" Of the 12 generals on board, every one was on the Eastern front, and I thought, "Egad, how you guys can lie." [Laughter] Every one had fought only on the Eastern front. That really broke me up.

The NATO exercises went well, and we worked well with those foreign navies. The ones that, in all due respect, that we had—I shouldn't say trouble but—the most interesting ones, in an adverse way, were the French. Those Frogs. They would do things such as sending a message, "We have a submarine contact umpty-ump umpty-ump umpty-ump umpty-ump." They were trying to find our submerged nuke submarines over there, and they'd use these various little ways of seeing if they could get us to say, "Oh, no, no, no. That's, you now, one of ours. It's not a Russian," and all that. We didn't fall for that. We had to be very careful when we were working with the French Navy.

Paul Stillwell: Well, a few years before that, they had pulled out of the NATO military structure, so they were still being difficult.

Admiral Forbes: Yes, that's right.

Paul Stillwell: What recollections do you have of Italy as a homeport and as essentially a base for the flagship?

Admiral Forbes: Yes. Gaeta. We never had one single incident of trouble with the civilians in Gaeta. I mean, there was no petty robbery. U.S. Navy personnel could walk anywhere they wanted on the streets, any hour of the day and night. The little school for the dependents operated very nicely. Everything went very smoothly.

Admiral Kidd would leave the flagship in the afternoon and get in his car. He always carried two briefcases home with him. One of the cases carried a loaded .45. He was always apprehensive of being stopped, and he lived, oh, several miles from the flagship. His quarters were down south. I've forgotten the Italian name of the town where he lived in a nice little home.

I went there several times to have dinner with him, and it always amused me. Everything was always very formal. He had three children living at home with him at that time, and one was at the Naval Academy, I might add. The table would be all set, and there was always this one chair for the miniature dachshund. That little dachshund would sit up in that chair and just be as good as gold. [Laughter] So he was a great dachshund fancier. Quite a gentleman to work for, I tell you.

He wanted me to be very frank with him, so when we discussed things I wouldn't mind arguing with him about certain things, and we got along very well.

Paul Stillwell: How much contact was there between the Sixth Fleet Commander and CinCSouth?

Admiral Forbes: Oh, considerable. I'm embarrassed about names.

Paul Stillwell: Was Admiral Rivero in that job then?

Admiral Forbes: Rivets Rivero.* Yes, I think he was. We worked with all the flags over in the Med. There were several of them. Yes, Admiral Kidd worked with them quite closely.

Paul Stillwell: Well, particularly in that role there would be a lot of planning. What do you remember about the planning aspect of the Sixth Fleet staff? You've got more to do than just run the fleet today. You've got to think about a wartime contingency.

Admiral Forbes: Oh, yes. We worked on the plans and made recommendations. We were very realistic about the support we had and what we didn't have. We visited a lot of ports. I'll never forget Malta being one of the very interesting and strategic points in the Mediterranean, and we went down to the Suez Canal. He visited the ports and talked to the powers that be in each place. It went off well and contributed to a lot of planning. The Sixth Fleet was in good hands when Admiral Kidd commanded it.

Paul Stillwell: Why do you say that?

Admiral Forbes: Well, that was his only life, the Navy. He was dedicated to it. He had no serious outside interests. In all due respect, his social life was zilch. If he had to do something, he would do it as a duty but nothing voluntary.

Paul Stillwell: I would have guessed there was a fair amount of social life just connected with the job. Official social life.

Admiral Forbes: Oh, yes. When we visited ports he had to socialize, as he did, say, with Princess Grace and the Prince there and things of that nature. Com6thFlt had to entertain on board quite a bit. We had dinner parties in various ports and greet visiting principals on board.

---

* Admiral Horacio Rivero, USN, served as Commander in Chief Allied Forces Southern Europe from January 1968 to May 1972. His oral history is in the Naval Institute collection.

Paul Stillwell: How much interaction was there with the British?

Admiral Forbes: Oh, not excessive. We worked with them very well. They're good people to work with. We got along with them very well and worked well with the Italians. They were, again, interesting, interesting people. It was just busy, busy, busy all the time. And you had to work back with the Pentagon and the Navy Department—those back-channel messages back and forth about what was going on. The intelligence reports were very, very interesting.

Paul Stillwell: Did you sense a feeling of relief on the part of the staff when Admiral Miller came on board?

Admiral Forbes: Yes.

Paul Stillwell: How was that manifested?

Admiral Forbes: Everyone just kind of [sound of long sigh]. He was so different. He was still getting his flight time in, and he was very sociable, you know, hail fellow, well met, and all over the place. And he was an aviator's aviator. He didn't get all bogged down in all the details and technicalities. He was just an outgoing individual. Let's put it that way. Different personalities. Just completely different personalities.

Paul Stillwell: He's a very gregarious man, and also he believes the words on the officer's commission, special trust and confidence, and he leaves it to an individual to do his job rather than try to do it for him.

Admiral Forbes: That's right, and we got along wonderfully well. I enjoyed working with him.

Paul Stillwell: Well, it's customary not to have two brown shoes together in the top jobs, so you probably left fairly soon.*

Admiral Forbes: Oh, I did. Admiral Miller came aboard in October as I recall, and I left in January, as soon as a relief was designated.

Paul Stillwell: Do you remember any of the specific incidents that you worked on with Admiral Miller during those few months?

Admiral Forbes: No. No, as I say, he embarked in the carrier most of the time and still went flying. He enjoyed a nice family. The Millers had the same quarters as the Kidds. Jerry is just a nice individual. I've always liked him. Of course, I'd served with him before. He was the skipper of *Roosevelt* when I was air boss on FDR.

Paul Stillwell: Well, with him gone that left you in charge a lot of the time.

Admiral Forbes: Oh, yes. I carried the sack all the time. As I say, I'm not being derogatory. He's an aviator's aviator. He had to be over there on that carrier. He wasn't going to ride one of these devilish cruisers watching everything. He had to be over where the action was, and the carrier was a firmer platform. [Laughter] He's a great individual. I enjoyed Jerry Miller.

Paul Stillwell: Well, it's good that he's the kind of person he is because the skipper of the carrier probably wouldn't be too thrilled to have a fleet commander flag on board. Was there any problem with the communications in that he was in a different ship from his staff?

Admiral Forbes: No, we took care of that. That was a very interesting tour. I was virtually a bachelor over there. My wife came over to visit a couple of times. I lived on

---

* In the early days of naval aviation, the aviators wore brown shoes with their khaki uniforms and green uniforms. They thus acquired the nickname "brown shoes" to distinguish them from the traditional surface ship officers, who are known as "black shoes."

board, and I just worked, worked, worked. That's all I had to do. And go to the movies. We had the movies on board. That was about my only recreation. I enjoyed it.

Paul Stillwell: Well, you had these two high-profile sea jobs right in a row, the carrier command and then the fleet chief of staff. Did you face a letdown after two like that?

Admiral Forbes: No, I was ordered back to BuPers. I was *the* daddy detailer. I went back and got a fancy name, which I wrote down so I wouldn't forget it. I was the Assistant Chief of the Bureau of Naval Personnel for Officer Distribution Control, and I ran them all. That was an absolutely fascinating job. That was where and when I got mixed up with politicians and their pressure. They demanded personnel assignments: "I want so-and-so here," and "Now, why, Navy, are you doing this?" "I want so-and-so there." It was just a fascinating job in which we wanted to be fair and square to career development of all the officers in the Navy. We really worked with them. That was a fascinating job in Washington.

Paul Stillwell: What specifics do you recall? What congressional pressures, for example?

Admiral Forbes: Oh, just about individuals. "I want so-and-so to go here." or "Why can't he go there?" and "Why did he get passed over?" and so forth and so on.

I tell you, the one that hurt me the most concerned Admiral Stump's son, John Morgan Stump, Naval Academy class of '51. He went to one of the first jet squadrons and did quite well. He was doing wonderfully well. Then he went as aide to an admiral, no names, did a complete tour, two fitness report periods. Later he went to the training command. He came up for commander, and he didn't make it. Now, I was shocked because I liked him. He was a good aviator. He loved aviation. He was a personable person. Just a nice young man.

When I was there at BuPers in the early '70s, I got a call from a senator from West Virginia. He said he wanted to know why John Morgan Stump never made commander. Well, I had a kind of a Boy Scout code that I lived by up there. I never looked at anyone's fitness report who was senior to me or any personal friends or classmates. However, I drew his fitness report, which I was eligible to do, and I looked in there, and I went almost apoplectic. The admiral that had asked for John Morgan as his aide was someone I knew personally. I knew that he hated Admiral Stump's guts, so it puzzled me why he asked for the son as his aide. He gave him two deliberately unsat fitness reports.

Well, any selection board that meets and sees that an admiral gave a lieutenant an unsat report is not going to question it. He never was selected. Then John Morgan was in the training command and on a hop, making a radio approach. The youngster in the front seat tuned in the wrong radio station, unbeknownst to John Morgan. They were making a radio approach under the hood on Station A when they were actually tuned to Station B. The plane ran into the side of a mountain and killed John Morgan.[*] I never got over that. That really hurt me. His son's death really got to Admiral Stump too. It really broke him. I never told Admiral Stump about the fitness reports, but his son's death really hit him. John Morgan was a fine young man. It was Admiral Stump's last request that he be buried next to his son up in Arlington.

Paul Stillwell: Well, when you got these requests from congressmen, "Why was so-and-so passed over?" how did you respond to something like that?

Admiral Forbes: Well, I was honest. That's the epitome of doing a job. Don't try to falsify things or play games, because it's going to catch up with you eventually. One has to be absolutely honest. I mean, one never impinged on someone's personal secrets or life. There's a lot of material in those records that a detailer could pick out when he gets in that business. But I was honest with the inquiries I received and the questions of "Why didn't So-and-so?" "Why wasn't he selected?" Well, detailers know the selection board process. We had to explain to the people asking the questions how these things are done. And as long as we were frank and open, we didn't have any great problems. But it was a time-consuming job. Detailers just go, go, go all day long.

---

[*] Lieutenant Commander John Morgan Stump, USN, died 6 November 1970 near Monterey, California.

Paul Stillwell: Well, sometimes it just depends on the makeup of a particular board why an individual did or did not make it.

Admiral Forbes: That's right. That's right.

Paul Stillwell: It depends on what they're looking for, and the cut line has to be somewhere. And the bottom guy who makes it is not much better than the top guy who doesn't.

Admiral Forbes: That's right. You're absolutely right.

On the humorous side, one day I felt this burning sensation. I thought, "Jeepers, creepers, this coffee." I said, "I wonder how many cups of coffee I drink in this job a day." So the next day I kept track and didn't change anything—29 cups. People came in to visit, and one of us would say, "How about a cup of coffee?" We'd have one. I wouldn't drink the whole thing, but I'd have one with him. So I had all these visiting firemen and, boy, I had to change that.

Paul Stillwell: That gets to be a lot of caffeine intake. That was before decaffeinated coffee probably.

Admiral Forbes: We didn't even spell it much less have it. No, that was a job where integrity and being able to keep your mouth shut were important. You could not talk about some of the things that you learned in that job would make headlines. A detailer could really be the center point of attention of everyone if he wanted to talk about things he'd discovered. We had to be very close-mouthed and keep everything to ourselves and not talk about the job at home.

Paul Stillwell: One question, both from the period in the late '60s and then when you came back. What was the impact of the racial situation on the way you did business? They were having all those unpleasant things in carriers and the oiler *Hassayampa* and so forth in the early '70s.* The *Constellation, Kitty Hawk*—so-called mutinies and what have you. Did you have any special consciousness on detailing blacks?

Admiral Forbes: No. No, I think I mentioned on *Shasta* I sent one to the Naval Academy.

Paul Stillwell: Right. What do you remember about the impact of the Z-grams as they began hitting the fleet?

Admiral Forbes: The Z-grams caused a lot of eyebrows to be raised.† In my humble opinion, you don't try to run a ship from Washington with all of these details about do this, do that, you can't do this, you can't do that. They didn't go over well at all. They were a butt of a lot of jokes.

Paul Stillwell: Well, Admiral Matthews told me that he as a flag officer was summoned for some racial-awareness training, and it did not go well with him. He resented it. Were you also in that kind of a situation?

Admiral Forbes: No. We treated everyone fairly and squarely. As I say, I'm proud. I brag about the morale on *Independence*. We got good movies. When I commanded *Shasta* it was the same way. We showed movies for, for example, the flight deck crew. Those poor souls couldn't go attend a movie at 6:00, after the evening meal with the crew, because they were working on the flight deck. So I got with my air boss up, and we discussed a solution. At the end of flight ops at night we had a screen rigged up in hangar bay one and put all the chairs and benches up there. We'd have a movie if they

---

* Racial disturbances broke out in the carrier *Kitty Hawk* (CVA-63) on 12 October 1972; in the oiler *Hassayampa* (AO-145) on 16 October 1972; and in the carrier *Constellation* (CVA-64) on 3 November 1972. See Captain Paul B. Ryan, USN (Ret.), "USS Constellation Flare-up: Was it Mutiny?" *U.S. Naval Institute Proceedings*, January 1976, pages 46-53.

† Admiral Elmo R. Zumwalt, Jr., USN, served as Chief of Naval Operations from 1 July 1970 to 29 June 1974. Z-grams were consecutively numbered policy directives from Zumwalt's office that attempted to deal with such issues as enlisted rights and privileges, equal opportunity, and Navy families. Junior personnel viewed them much more favorably than did their seniors. See *U.S. Naval Institute Proceedings*, May 1971, pages 293-298.

wanted to go. And, boy, they ate that up. The flight deck crews lost a little sleep over that, but they got to see a movie if they wanted to. These little things build morale. Good food. You take care of them like you want to be taken care of, and they respond in kind.

Paul Stillwell: I've been aboard carriers in recent years, and they've got TV movies constantly.

Admiral Forbes: Yes, TV movies 24 hours a day and, oh yes, that's something else.

Paul Stillwell: And VCRs and tapes.

Admiral Forbes: Yes. But then it was just plain old movies and projectors.

Paul Stillwell: What satisfactions did you get as a daddy detailer when you were able to put the round peg in the round hole?

Admiral Forbes: Great.

Paul Stillwell: How often did you get that kind of a feeling—more often than not?

Admiral Forbes: More often than not, right. And the decisions I had to make on some detailing and the people that I knew from personal experience in the fleet or from things that I heard from good authoritative sources which caused changes to a person's career pattern or where he was going; it all paid off. Detailers have got to be conscientious and absolutely fair and square. Detailers are human beings, but they can't let personal likes affect their detailing.

Paul Stillwell: Back in the prewar or pre-World War II Navy it was still relatively small, and virtually everybody had a service reputation. Was that still the case when the Navy got so much larger?

Admiral Forbes: Yes. You still have a service reputation.

Paul Stillwell: Did it go beyond the fitness reports?

Admiral Forbes: In what sense?

Paul Stillwell: Well, I mean things that you hear at cocktail parties or chatting in the corridors of Main Navy?

Admiral Forbes: Oh, yes, yes. Very much so. And things you observe on your own and at social events and things of that nature. An observer gets a good all-around aspect. I enjoyed being a daddy detailer. I'll tell you whom I worked with very closely. Jim Watkins had the enlisted detailing when I had the officers.* I was B-1, he was B-2. We worked together very closely. He's a great gent.

Paul Stillwell: What do you remember specifically about him?

Admiral Forbes: I just like him. He's honest, straightforward. We got along well. Great gentleman. I was delighted to see him go on up the line.

Paul Stillwell: Well, you were in a job that had considerable power to it, because you could make or break careers of individuals.

Admiral Forbes: That's right. I could, and that's why I say the detailer had to be thoroughly objective. Well, I remember in certain cases there were people I knew whom I personally didn't care for, but they were professionally superb. I went ahead and gave them what they'd earned.

Paul Stillwell: And probably there were a few cases the other way, too, of people who were friends but not quite up to muster.

---

* Rear Admiral James D. Watkins, USN, later Chief of Naval Operations from 1982 to 1986.

Admiral Forbes: That's right. That's right. You're absolutely correct.

Paul Stillwell: Well, the detailer really can have as much impact as a selection board, because if there are two good people competing for one spot and you give it to man A, that gives him a leg up. Like a carrier command, for example, or what have you.

Admiral Forbes: That's right. It's a very responsible job, and the responsibility wears on you. You feel it later on. I mean, you have to be so involved and so close-mouthed and fair and square. It was quite an assignment.

Paul Stillwell: How much of a factor in your detailing decisions were combat experience and performance?

Admiral Forbes: Considerable. And I worked with those who had postgraduate training, which is a very broad field. I was involved in so many things and had to become aware of so many details. It was a full-time job. It was one of those where I never left the job. I may have gone home, but I didn't leave my work. The phone was ringing all the time about this, that, and the other. It was good.

Paul Stillwell: Were you able in those jobs to see a direct value of the postgraduate education you'd had? Could you apply it specifically?

Admiral Forbes: Not specifically, but I guess I had that background of personnel administration and training at Stanford. That paid off. We learned a lot of things at PG school that helped my general background but not in any particular case. It gave me a good broad feel, I think.

Paul Stillwell: Did you have contact with the bureau chief in that billet more so than when you'd been there before?

Admiral Forbes: Oh, as the daddy? Oh, yes, I worked with him. I worked with him in his office and in the case of Admiral Dave Bagley I sometimes went to his home.* He lived out here in a little farm. I've forgotten exactly the location now. It was in the suburbs in Virginia here. I'd go out there and sit down and discuss things. On the flag detailing I was involved in that very, very much with Admiral Bagley. That was a very responsible job.

Paul Stillwell: What do you remember of Bagley as someone to work with?

Admiral Forbes: Well, he would listen to you. He was a Zumwalt man, if you'll pardon the expression.

Paul Stillwell: Very much so.

Admiral Forbes: Very much so. But I used to argue with him about certain things that Admiral Zumwalt wanted to do and how they would adversely affect us—in my opinion, anyway—and he would listen to me. He was forthright.

Paul Stillwell: Do you remember any specifics in that regard?

Admiral Forbes: No, no specifics. I know that some of the things were so sensitive, though, that we went to his home to discuss because he didn't want anyone there in the office to possibly hear what was going on. Secretaries and BuPers staff personnel would come in all the time. He would have me in his office, the door was closed, and we went in a little cubbyhole. But sometimes he said, "You come on out to my place. We want to sit down and discuss this at length." And of course his brother, Worth Bagley, had a prominent position on the OpNav staff.†

---

* Vice Admiral David H. Bagley, USN, served as Chief of Naval Personnel from 1 February 1972 to 10 April 1975.
† Vice Admiral Worth H. Bagley, USN, served as Director of Navy Program Planning, OP-090, from May 1971 to April 1973.

Paul Stillwell: Well, I interviewed Admiral Zumwalt and he said that because he had been jumped over so many senior officers to become CNO, he wanted people whose personal loyalty he could count on. And he had known Bagley from a prep school, even before he went to the Naval Academy, so he knew he would be very solid for him.

Admiral Forbes: I didn't know that, but I knew they worked very closely together.

Paul Stillwell: Well, he was very close to Worth Bagley too. He was OP-090 for a while, for example.

Admiral Forbes: Oh, yes. Worth Bagley was the power behind the throne. But Admiral Zumwalt used to call on the phone direct: "Hey, Beetle, what in the hell's going on here? What are you going to do about that?" and things of that nature. This is—I shouldn't say off the record—but when you could get to Admiral Zumwalt personally, one on one, you could accomplish a lot of things. But when you had to go to that little inner staff he had, oh, jeepers, that was the world's worst. You never knew what was going to happen. But when you could talk to Admiral Zumwalt and explain to him why something in your opinion had to be done or was done, he was a very understanding person. He would say, "Okay. Cut it."

Paul Stillwell: Admiral Zumwalt is one of the most efficient people I've encountered. He doesn't waste any time on small talk. He's direct and businesslike and concise.

Admiral Forbes: That's right. What's he doing now, I wonder?

Paul Stillwell: Well, he's had his own outfit for a number of years, a consulting business in a number of areas. For a while he was out with American Medical Buildings in Milwaukee, but I think that's pretty well wrapped up now.[*]

Anything else to recall from that tour?

---

[*] Admiral Zumwalt died on 2 January 2000.

Admiral Forbes: No. It was just a very busy, very interesting, satisfying tour. I enjoyed it very much. And you worked with a lot of good people you got to know.

Paul Stillwell: Were you in that billet when you were selected for flag?

Admiral Forbes: No, I was selected for flag when I was the chief of staff, Sixth Fleet.*

Paul Stillwell: I see.

Admiral Forbes: I was one of the few who couldn't get frocked, because I was in a captain's billet. That was okay. It didn't bother me.

Paul Stillwell: Well, please tell me your reaction and how you found out the news that you were selected for flag?

Admiral Forbes: Well, let's see. I guess we just got a message over there with the names on it, and that was it. Ike Kidd had me in and congratulated me, and he was most gracious. He was A-Number-One in that sense. He and I got along very, very well.

I went from BuPers to be Commander Carrier Group Six.

Paul Stillwell: What was your flagship?

Admiral Forbes: We had various ones. We didn't have any fixed flagship. We rode them all.

Paul Stillwell: Was this again out of Norfolk?

Admiral Forbes: No, that was down at Mayport, Florida, near Jacksonville, '73 to '75. We moved down there. We had a little set of quarters down there on the Mayport base and enjoyed that. I had a good staff. We rode all the carriers.

---

* The selection was in the spring of 1971.

Paul Stillwell: *Forrestal* was one the carriers out of there, wasn't she?

Admiral Forbes: Yes, *Forrestal* was home-ported there, and so was *Kennedy*.[*] In fact, I was in *Kennedy* when I took command of the carrier group over in the Med. When I reported aboard, the staff was lined up. As I was going down to meet each one of them, I came to this commander who was absolutely egg bald, and I was told, "Sir, this is Commander Colbus."[†]

I shook hands with him, and I said, "Commander Colbus, nice to meet you. What is your job on the staff?"

He looked at me and he said, "I'm the staff maven, sir."

I said, "Maven? Maven? I've heard a lot of acronyms up in the Pentagon and the bureau, but maven, I don't connect with that."

He said, "That's not an acronym, sir. That's Yiddish."

I said, "What does it mean?'

"It means an avowed expert on a subject about which you know absolutely nothing." And that was when I first met Louie Colbus. And then he passed me his calling card, a formal calling card with, "Lou, the Jew," and later on I found he had two more sets of formal calling cards, "Lou, the Roué, from Altoona, Pa.," which was where he was from, and "Big Lou from the BOQ." And he was an absolute character whom I nicknamed "Head Hebe" on the staff, which had two other Jewish officers. They were nicknamed "Middle Hebe" and "Junior Hebe." This was during the Yom Kippur War and was very appropriate.[‡] Lou's a great guy. Still is.

---

[*] USS *John F. Kennedy* (CVA-67) was commissioned 7 September 1968. She was the last conventionally powered carrier built by the U.S. Navy. She has a standard displacement of 61,000 tons, is 1,048 feet long, 130 feet in the beam, and an extreme width of 268 feet. Her top speed is 30-plus knots. She can accommodate approximately 85 aircraft.

[†] Commander Louis Colbus, USN. The oral history of Colbus, who retired as a captain, is in the Naval Institute collection. His oral history contains a number of stories about Admiral Forbes.

[‡] The Yom Kippur War started on 6 October 1973. Egyptian and Syrian forces began major coordinated ground offensives against Israeli positions, seeking to improve territorial claims in the wake of the Six-Day War of 1967. Supported in part by weapons supplied by the United States, Israeli forces counterattacked and drove back the Arabs. A cease-fire finally took effect on 25 October.

Paul Stillwell: Well, please tell me more about him. What function did he carry out on the staff?

Admiral Forbes: I've forgotten exactly what his specific job was. They all worked very closely on everything. I've forgotten his official title now.

Paul Stillwell: Who was your chief of staff?

Admiral Forbes: It was Tom Porcari, another blackshoe on this mirror-image staff concept.*

Paul Stillwell: What do you remember about your flagship?

Admiral Forbes: It was during this period when the Navy had just gone through this fire prevention process that really changed everything. The wardrooms no longer had the nice wooden tables and chairs. The furnishings were glass with the metal legs, except in *Kennedy*. It broke me up. In the flag quarters there was a reception room that was much larger than the normal shipboard space. It was not a lounge but just a nice area. It was similar to a flag office. The Kennedy family stepped in and said, "Hey, Navy, you're not going to touch that. We decorated it the way we wanted, and it's going to stay that way." It had all the nice wooden chairs and the wooden tables and all that, so they had to put in this very sophisticated sprinkling system to protect it. [Laughter] But that was quite a bucket, that *Kennedy*.

Paul Stillwell: Well, please tell me your recollections of the Yom Kippur War.

Admiral Forbes: Well, we just did everything they told us to do. It was just a good operation, and the Russians observed us very carefully, everything we did.

Paul Stillwell: How much were you monitoring the battle ashore?

---
* Captain Thomas J. Porcari, USN.

Admiral Forbes: Just the intelligence reports we received. We had connection with that. We were just a kind of force in reserve, so to speak.

Paul Stillwell: Were you involved at all in the ferrying of planes and other war materials to the Israelis?

Admiral Forbes: No. We were the Med deployment force on the scene, so to speak. Just in the background.

Paul Stillwell: Was the atmosphere tense in the Eastern Mediterranean at that time?

Admiral Forbes: As I recall, yes, but not anything of really major concern, but everything was a little on the tense side. The liberty ports were carefully selected when we visited them the few times we ever got ashore. But I'll say this for our task force: we knew why we were there and everyone reacted accordingly. That was what we were paid for, and morale was good. We had no problems. Very little liberty, as I recall. We just were on the scene, just off the coast all the time with the power in reserve.

Paul Stillwell: Can you describe the difference it made for you being a carrier group commander, as opposed to the skipper of a single ship, as you had been before. How did the role differ?

Admiral Forbes: Well, you're the sea daddy. You oversee all the ships. Not only the carriers but your destroyers, the replenishment ships and all of that type of thing. If you're smart you do not get into the CO's business of how to run that carrier. I was very careful about that. Some things I didn't agree with personally. I thought to myself, "I didn't do it like that on Indy," but I never told him. But we used to chat, shoot the breeze just like buddy-buddy things. I'd bring up something, like, "Egad, I saw that So-and-so something," and he'd come back and, "Yes, what do you think we ought to do." It was just on a very low-key basis so I could get my point across, but I mean, not as some people I know who stepped in and said, "You stop that!" and things like that. I tried not to get into the ship's business, and it paid off, I think.

Paul Stillwell: It takes a good deal of self-restraint sometimes.

Admiral Forbes: It does. Oh, can you say that again. [Laughter]

Paul Stillwell: Do you remember any particular things that you wished you could change?

Admiral Forbes: No, offhand I don't. But, I used to think back, "Now, gee, when I had Indy, and I had that cargru on board he used to sit down there." So I thought, "Now, I'm not going to be like him."

Paul Stillwell: Which of your flag captains do you specifically recall?

Admiral Forbes: I'm the world's worst on names, and off the top of my head I can't tell you. We had some good skippers. I say we used to just shoot the breeze and work with them but never got into their business. I was very, very careful about that. I don't believe it pays off.

Paul Stillwell: Med deployments were probably a routine thing for you by now.

Admiral Forbes: Oh, yes. Med deployments were routine.

Back in Mayport I was tasked by ComNavAirLant himself when he called me and said, "Beetle, that *Saratoga*, that bucket—"* Oh, I could agree with him on that. Jeepers, creepers. Anyway, he said, "You get on there and relieve that commanding officer for cause." Well, I knew the fellow socially. We lived right there, three sets of quarters apart, in Mayport. So I went over and got him in the cabin and talked to him and told

---

* Vice Admiral Frederick H. Michaelis, USN, served as Commander Naval Air Force Atlantic Fleet from 29 February 1972 to 14 February 1975. Admiral Michaelis's oral history is in the Naval Institute collection.

him he was relieved and so forth and so on. ComNavAirLant thanked me, and that was that. Then he said, "Now, Beetle, who in the hell can we put on that bucket to get her squared away?"

I said, "I'll tell you who to put on there, Admiral. If I were back in my detailing days, I'd tell you whom I'd put on there."

"Who?"

I said, "Bob Dunn." Now, I knew Bob Dunn, because Bob Dunn had been my air wing commander on board *Independence*. And then I had worked with him again on the Sixth Fleet staff, and I said, "I'd put Bob Dunn, and I think he could do a superb job. He'll get that bucket squared away."

So he said, "Okay." And it happened. Bob Dunn became CO of *Saratoga*, and he got her squared away.* I'm a great admirer of Bob Dunn. I've liked him all along the way. He still runs strong.

Paul Stillwell: What qualities did you admire in him? Why did you think he would handle that job well?

Admiral Forbes: Well, let's put it this way. He was Forbes trained. He knew the things I liked to do, and he was a very observant type of individual. His aviation outfits were run well, and I thought, "He knows what has to be squared away on that thing." He and I had little chats, and he did extremely well.

Paul Stillwell: Well, another thing is he has a very positive outlook on things.

Admiral Forbes: Oh, he does, he does. I tell you, when his wife died, Annette, that really hurt us all. She was one wonderful, wonderful lady. Yes. So that was one job I remember as CarGru 6, having to relieve the skipper of *Saratoga* for cause. He didn't run the ship. His wife ran the ship. That was the standing knowledge down there in Mayport. Jeepers, creepers. She was into everything.

---

* Captain Robert F. Dunn, USN, commanded the USS *Saratoga* (CVA-60) from 12 September 1974 to 11 September 1976.

Paul Stillwell: I would think that that's quite rare, to relieve a carrier skipper for cause, isn't it?

Admiral Forbes: It is. It is.

Paul Stillwell: Do you remember, for example, doing that when you were in the bureau?

Admiral Forbes: No.

Paul Stillwell: Because presumably the system is going to send the best and the brightest to a job like that because it's so select.

Admiral Forbes: That's right, but mistakes are made. Personality clashes and personality changes happen, and that was the case there. At parties his wife would tell you what she was going to do with that ship dit, dit, dit, dit. And he didn't do anything. Nice guy, but that was it, and you can't run a carrier just by being a nice guy. Yes, I remember a lot about CarGru 6. That was one of the distasteful jobs.

Paul Stillwell: Was there any frustration that you didn't have the degree of control you had as a skipper?

Admiral Forbes: Well, there are those incidents, yes, when you say, "Boy, if I was running this ship, I'd do it this way," but you've got to bite your tongue and remember that you are not the commanding officer. That's the important thing.

Then I was yanked out of CarGru 6 and sent over to CarGru 2. I became Commander Carrier Group Two in the Mediterranean, because the wife of the admiral who was then ComCarGru 2 had to go into the hospital. They wanted to do that back in the States, and they were home-ported over there, as I recall, somewhere outside of Athens, Greece. They didn't want to break up the family, so I went over there and relieved him. Then he and his wife took 30 days' leave in Europe, which kind of irked me. I mean if she was that ill—anyway. So I had that job until a regular relief for him was detailed. We operated over there.

Paul Stillwell: How much does the admiral control the task group—or battle group, as it's now called—in running that entire show beyond just the carrier?

Admiral Forbes: You run the show. You're the carrier group commander. Of course, the black-shoe admirals were there, too, commanding the destroyer groups and things of that nature, and I worked with them. It depends on who is the senior, and most times the carrier group commander is. At least, that was my personal experience.

Paul Stillwell: This was about the time that the CVAs were getting phased into the CV role with the S-3s on board for ASW.[*] What do you recall of that transition?

Admiral Forbes: I don't.

Paul Stillwell: The CVSs had pretty well been phased out by then.[†]

Admiral Forbes: Oh, yes. We just had straight CVs. I mean like *Kennedy* and *Forrestal* and *Saratoga*, all of that class and the *Independence*. The old ones had gone.

Paul Stillwell: Were you involved when the *Kennedy* had her collision with the *Belknap* in '75?[‡]

Admiral Forbes: Yes.

---

[*] The S-3 Viking is a jet-powered, carrier-based antisubmarine aircraft with a four-person crew. Built by Lockheed, its first delivery to a fleet training squadron was in February 1974. The S-3A has a wingspan of 68 feet, 8 inches; length of 53 feet, 4 inches; maximum gross weight of 52,539 pounds, and a top speed of 514 miles per hour.

[†] The last of the ASW carriers, the *Intrepid* (CVS-11), was decommissioned on 15 March 1974.

[‡] During exercises in the Mediterranean Sea on 22 November 1975, the guided missile cruiser *Belknap* (CG-26) ran into the aircraft carrier *John F. Kennedy* (CV-67). All told, seven men were killed and another 24 injured seriously enough to require hospitalization. This was after Admiral Forbes's command tour.

Paul Stillwell: What do you remember of that?

Admiral Forbes: Now let's see. Yes, to my memory, I know we were very closely involved in that. How that happened is unclear; I don't recall the details. It has been so long.

Paul Stillwell: Were you in on the investigation at all?

Admiral Forbes: Yes. I'm just trying—my memory slips me. I've forgotten the details of that one.

Paul Stillwell: Bill Gureck was the skipper, and he did make flag.* I don't know if that impinged on him or not. I don't think it was the carrier's fault.

Admiral Forbes: I've forgotten now.

Paul Stillwell: How long did the assignment last in CarGru 2?

Admiral Forbes: I can tell you exactly, because it's a sore point—from 11 June 1975 to 14 July 1975. One month, three days. Then I went straight from there to be Chief of Staff and Deputy Commander in Chief, Atlantic Fleet and all that business back in Norfolk again under one Admiral Isaac Campbell Kidd, Jr.

Paul Stillwell: Did he ask for you specifically for that?

Admiral Forbes: Yes. I found out later he did.

Paul Stillwell: So you must have made a good impression in Sixth Fleet.

---

* Captain William Gureck, USN, commanded the aircraft carrier *John F. Kennedy* (CV-67) from 24 May 1974 to 29 November 1975.

Admiral Forbes: I must have. He and I could work together, which was kind of an exception to the rule. But, boy, I tell you down there in Norfolk, Admiral Kidd, in all due respect, except for movies, had no outside interests. He would come to work in the morning at 7:00 o'clock, and he'd have his official car take him down around the pier area. And if he saw anybody hitchhiking, he'd stop and pick him up and say, "Now, Son, what ship are you off of?" And the youngster would tell him. This happened on three occasions. I'll never forget because I was the recipient of all of this.

He'd say to the driver, "Find out where that is and take me down there." And they'd go to the ship. He'd take the young man and go aboard to the OOD. Now, here he was, a four-star admiral—this was early in the morning—and the CO in most cases was not on board. Admiral Kidd would say, "I want to see your commanding officer."

"Sir, he's not on board yet."

"Well, where in the hell is he?"

I got all this information in working with the people. The OOD's reply was often, "Well, sir, it's just not 8:00 o'clock yet."

"Well, this man was out on the street trying to hook a ride." He would do this, and then he'd call me in when he arrived at headquarters. He'd say, "Beetle, I want the commanding officer of such-and-such relieved for cause. He's doing a lousy job."

I'd argue with him. We never did relieve the skipper, let me put it that way, but I spent most of my time arguing with him on things like that. I was just trying to be the intermediary. And we worked at night. He'd always see callers; no one ever had any trouble with that. I'd go in and brief him, and there'd be so many things that had gone on during the day, then I'd ride home with him ofttimes. Now, I'll get back to why in a minute. And he'd walk in and there'd be something on this message: "Admiral, we've got so-and-so, and we've got to add this and what do you propose and we've got to answer that, you know."

"Okay, okay." And we'd go in to his quarters. He was about three sets of quarters up from where we lived. He lived in Virginia House. We lived in Missouri House. He had a little place where he parked the official car. We'd go in the back door, walk right in, and the stewards were waiting. They knew he was coming because we'd tell them on the car phone. His sweet wife would be there, and the table would be set, and the candles would be on. He'd walk right in and sit down at the table and start dinner. I mean, there was not a lost motion. Finish dinner, get up, and I was still there. And a couple of times I had to keep on briefing him.

He'd walk right from the dinner table into the lounge, where the movie screen and everything were all set up. He'd say, "Roll it," and the movie would start. Now, that was it. He'd watch a movie and go to bed. Then he was up in the morning before the crack of dawn. And on Sundays, lo and behold, that was his only exercise. I don't think he ever took off his uniform. He'd walk down to my quarters. I'd be out there in the backyard, because I like to garden. That's one of my hobbies, and we had these nice grounds there. I'd be working on my tomato patch, and he'd come walking, "Now, B, what are we going to do about such and such and such and such?" And he'd sit down there and shoot the breeze on Sunday afternoon and then get up and walk back home. When you talk about workaholic, he was it. There's just no getting around it.

Paul Stillwell: Consumed by his job.

Admiral Forbes: Right, and just call people. Most of my job was to say, "Admiral, you can't do that."

"No?"

I'd say, "You just can't."

Paul Stillwell: What would you have put the brakes on, for example?

Admiral Forbes: Oh, having people relieved for cause. He used to travel. He used to call me long distance. He did so much NATO business. "Now, B, we're going to dah, dah, dah, dah, dah, and I want you to do this."

"Well, Admiral, you can't do that."

"What do you mean, you can't?"

I'd say, "You can't—I'm not going to do it."

He'd slam the phone, and later he'd come back and say, "B, you saved my ass again." He'd make these snap decisions, but he fed them through me all the time. I was kind of the filter for him. But he just kept up; it was go, go, go. I never got one day off, and I worked all day Saturdays and on Sundays.

In that particular job I was one of the eight military personnel in the United States who had my finger on the nuclear trigger after the President. In case the President was killed in an attack, I was in the decision chain, and therefore I had to carry what we called a brick. It was the size and the shape of a brick. This communication thing with a little antenna on it went everywhere I went. I was not allowed to drive my own personal car. The Navy gave me about a '73 black Plymouth with regular Virginia license plates, but the whole trunk was filled with radio equipment. I had to travel in that car wherever I went. There were three antennas here in Norfolk at different strategic locations where I could maybe send these things through. And I had to carry that brick wherever I went, including to meals.

Well, the thing that broke me up about that car was that these drills were conducted all the time. I'd be at a stoplight there on Granby Street, with a red light, and all of a sudden the lights would come on, and the horn would start to blow. People would look at you and say, "There's a red light." The lights and horn were a signal to alert me. The beeper would go off too. In my social life I had to be where I could receive on that beeper 24 hours a day.

I'll never forget going to church. I always used to put it up in the little hymnal rack on the back of the pew. One day Ike Kidd got on that by mistake on the wrong channel and said, "I'd like to know where that son-of-a-bitch is today." His voice came out of my communications device in church. [Laughter] So from then on, I kept it down and just watched it. It had a little light that came on when it came on. Oh, jeepers, you talk about the congregation. I never got over that one. That broke me up.

But it was just go, go, go. We worked on Sundays, and they had these drills at night—1:00, 2:00, 3:00 o'clock in the morning. And Admiral Kidd would call me from overseas. He did all the traveling while I stayed home all the time. I'd say, "Admiral, do you know what time it is?"

"What time, B?"

I'd say, "It's 2:30 in the morning back here."

"Not that late over here."

I'd say, "No, I know that." [Laughter] But, anyway, he and I got along very well. But it was just work, work, work and then boom, I had that heart attack right on the job.

Paul Stillwell: When was that?

Admiral Forbes: I'll never forget. August 9, 1976. I'd just finished briefing. We had a group of reserve admirals coming on board in Norfolk for active duty. I had just finished briefing them, and this was on a Monday. I remember that on the previous Friday I got a call informing me that one of my young commanders who was on TAD had been stricken. I said, "Oh, well, tell him to take it easy, and we'll see him when he can get back."

Then I was called that night and told, "He just had a heart attack." The caller said, "He started feeling just a burning sensation and broke out in heavy perspiration--I was there, Admiral—and just felt awful, and all of a sudden that was it." So I was sitting at my desk after that briefing, and I suddenly had this burning sensation. I thought, "Jeepers, creepers, what's this?"

I remembered about the young commander, and I got my office mates to call the doctor. Sure enough, I'd had what the doctor called a myocardial infarction of the right [unclear] branch block or something. They whipped me over to the naval hospital in Portsmouth, and I was there in intensive care. In walked Admiral Kidd in his uniform, and the nurses started to fuss. But he had to have his briefing. He said, "Now, B, what are we going to do about this? What do you think we ought to do about so-and-so?" He started off with all these business matters, like he did every day up in the office.

Then Doctor Kevin came in and said, "Admiral, what are you doing here? What are you doing?"

"My boy runs the fleet for me, and we've got to make some decisions on some matters here."

The doctor said, "Admiral, he's in no condition for that."

And Admiral Kidd just looked at him and started up again, "Now, B—"

The doctor said, "You. Out." He actually almost physically threw him out. [Laughter] Admiral Kidd was back the next day with the same routine. This time the head of the hospital, whom I knew was a personal friend of Admiral Kidd, came down and said, "Ike, for heaven's sake, leave Beetle alone. You're the reason he's here now. Leave him alone." So that ended that.

Paul Stillwell: Well, was that literally true, that you were running the fleet?

Admiral Forbes: I guess it was really. He was up to his ears in NATO all the time and all the entertaining and meetings with those foreigners over here. We went to all those social events at night when they were held in Norfolk.

But one more thing about Admiral Kidd that was almost pathetic. As guests walked into his quarters in Virginia House, on the right there was this nice big oversized den, which had a fireplace. It was an extra room with a sofa and chairs. Very nice. Over the fireplace hung a life-sized oil portrait; it was tremendous. It was his father in his uniform, which was very touching.

In that job of his, of course, we had to work with the Japanese on certain occasions. Every time one of them came he'd call me and say, "B, you take that son-of-a-bitch. I'm not going to have him in here. I wouldn't touch him with a ten-foot pole." So I'd entertain. My sweet wife, Betty, and I would take care of the Japanese visitors. But one day the phone rang, and it was from the CNO: "Ike, the Japanese ambassador's coming down and wants to see you, etc., etc." And it was all over. And I looked at him and said, "Admiral, you can't shun, in all due respect, the Japanese Ambassador. This is going to reflect back up the line. I know how you feel, and I understand it, but you must entertain him."

"B, I guess you're right. Okay. Let him come." So he had Betty and me there for that dinner party, and I'll never forget there were three Japanese, and they were no one's dummies. They'd been briefed, too, very carefully.

Paul Stillwell: That the Japanese had killed his father.*

Admiral Forbes: Yes. When they walked in that front door, it was so obvious that they kind of turned with their backs so they never looked at that room the whole evening. They made a point of just avoiding that. He was a very interesting individual to work for like that.

Paul Stillwell: What were some of the things you did in running the fleet? What kinds of decisions would you make?

Admiral Forbes: Just the normal fleet operations. I did it all. I cleared it with him, of course, but he called on me. He expected me to do this. I used to go, when I could, for the noon meal. He was an eater. In the flag mess one never knew when noon meal was going to be. It could start at 11:00 o'clock in the morning, or we'd start at 2:00 in the afternoon. He'd always let us know when the meal would be. But I went in there, and he ate the works, I mean the whole nine yards. The stewards prepared everything they could in the way of food. While we were eating, he would talk shop. We got most of our business done at that noon meal. Then in the afternoon we carried out what he wanted done. It was very interesting the way he operated.

Paul Stillwell: Do you think it was a wise decision subsequently to separate off that SACLant role?†

Admiral Forbes: Yes. There was too much there for one person. There was just too much, because the job required working with those foreign navies. Then there were the

---

* Rear Admiral Isaac C. Kidd, USN, Commander Battleship Division One, was killed on board his flagship, the USS *Arizona* (BB-39), at Pearl Harbor on 7 December 1941.
† In 1985 the three-hatted command was split. One U.S. four-star admiral now serves as Supreme Allied Commander Transformation/Commander U.S. Joint Forces Command (the former SACLant/CinCLant; another serves as Commander U.S. Fleet Forces Command (the former CinCLantFlt).

personalities. It was a full-time job, and I might add that Bud Edney does a superb job down there now.* He and Paul Miller divided it.†

Paul Stillwell: What was it about these hitchhiking sailors that so infuriated Admiral Kidd?

Admiral Forbes: Oh, that was just not the Navy he'd been raised in. I mean, just the little things, most of them petty. He was nitpicking things all the time. He'd see different things he didn't like, and it was interesting. Talk about a 24-hour-a-day worker. That was Admiral Kidd. He had no outside interests, and his social schedule included only what he had to do, what was expected of the commander in chief. But as far as any other social life, none; that was it. He stayed in his quarters, and he stayed in that uniform. It was just work, work, work.

Paul Stillwell: Was he an imaginative individual?

Admiral Forbes: I don't think so. He would go to Washington when he was summoned. Ike Kidd was just a very dedicated, hard worker. That was his life, the Navy. And that wonderful family of his. They were delightful.

Paul Stillwell: Do you think it's literally true—this comment that the hospital commander made—that Admiral Kidd was responsible for your heart attack?

Admiral Forbes: Well, when you ask my sweet wife she'll tell you "Yes." I never had a moment to really call my own, because I was always on call, and most of the time the calls were coming with that beeper thing. We couldn't go to the plays in Norfolk when nice Broadway shows would come in, because my beeper could not receive in Chrysler Hall. That one whole section of my life was cut out. I had to be in communication—and

---

* Admiral Leon A. Edney, USN, served as Supreme Allied Commander Atlantic and Commander in Chief Atlantic Command from 18 May 1990 to 13 July 1992.
† Admiral Paul David Miller, USN, served as Commander in Chief Atlantic Fleet from 31 January 1991 to 13 July 1992.

understandably so. I can't fault that. I was just one of the eight. I had to be in communication with the quote White House unquote all the time, and that's the way it went.

Paul Stillwell: Were you linked directly with the strategic submarines? Was that part of this procedure for carrying out the order if it had to be?

Admiral Forbes: No. I think this was all done up the line somewhere. The decision whether to go nuclear had to be made and transmitted.

Paul Stillwell: I see.

Admiral Forbes: That was it, and that's why I had to be available.

Paul Stillwell: Were there any guidelines or parameters laid out on what kinds of things would lead to that decision?

Admiral Forbes: No.

Paul Stillwell: It was strictly a judgment call.

Admiral Forbes: Strictly a judgment call, and I was flabbergasted when I got that assignment.

Paul Stillwell: How much of all this could you share with your wife?

Admiral Forbes: Very little. No one knew except Ike Kidd and me.

Paul Stillwell: She must have thought it a bit strange that you had all this apparatus.

Admiral Forbes: I'd say, "I've got to be in touch with this job all the time," and she bought this.

Betty would say, "Gee, we can't go to this, can't do that." Well, she adapted to it. We had that nice set of quarters there.

Paul Stillwell: Well, you had lived that kind of life when you were with Admiral Stump, so she was at least used to it from then.

Admiral Forbes: Yes.

Paul Stillwell: I am curious how your duties got carried out during your convalescence from the heart attack.

Admiral Forbes: As soon as I had the heart attack and the powers that be found out I was going to be in the hospital, they called on different people. Howard Greer, who was ComNavAirLant, came over.[*] So did Rojo Adamson, who was SurfLant.[†] People like that had to sit there and cover the work until I returned. But then it was determined I couldn't go back on active duty. And that was it.

Paul Stillwell: When did you retire then?

Admiral Forbes: On 1 March 1977. And Admiral Kidd, being the gentleman that he is, when I was released from the hospital, he let me stay in those quarters until I fully recovered and we could find a place to live. My sweet wife found a lot out there on the water in Virginia Beach, and we liked it very much. A good builder was recommended to us, and we contracted with him. That was the smartest move we ever made. We had this nice little home built, and until it was ready to be moved into he let us stay in those

---

[*] Vice Admiral Howard E. Greer, USN, served as Commander Naval Air Force Atlantic Fleet from 14 February 1975 to 31 March 1978.
[†] Vice Admiral Robert E. Adamson, USN, served as Commander Naval Surface Force Atlantic Fleet from 1975 to 1977.

quarters. Well, we had to pay rent, which was okay, until we could move into our new home.

Paul Stillwell: This was even after you retired, you stayed on?

Admiral Forbes: Yes. While I was recovering the Navy wouldn't let me retire. I retired on 1 March. We moved into the house on eighth of April, 1977, so we lived in the quarters just for a little over a month because my relief didn't want to move down.

Paul Stillwell: Who was he?

Admiral Forbes: I never saw him. Who was it? It slips my mind for the moment.*

Paul Stillwell: Was there any discussion before the heart attack about what other jobs you might have been groomed for or considered for?

Admiral Forbes: No. I was going strong. It was really a challenging job. It was a 24-hour day, and most interesting. The contacts I had and the people I met made it a very, very interesting job. But as I look back on it, I should have been smart enough to know. I never got any exercise, and I never had a chance to do anything except work and be on that devilish phone.

Paul Stillwell: But you had no way or breaking out of that shell, did you?

Admiral Forbes: No. I mean, no leave. I never got any leave. I never got any time off at all. I was always on duty, and with Admiral Kidd traveling so much, that made it even more responsible all the time.

---

* The relief as Admiral Kidd's deputy was Vice Admiral Donald D. Engen, USN, whose oral history is in the Naval Institute collection.

Paul Stillwell: But he wasn't demanding of you anything he didn't do himself, it sounds like.

Admiral Forbes: Oh, no, that's right. He wasn't. No, he was a workaholic.

Paul Stillwell: Of course that makes it tough for the workaholic's subordinate.

Admiral Forbes: Yes. Trying to get him to write a fitness report was like pulling teeth. For some reason he just didn't like to write fitness reports. I'd say, "Sir, he works directly for you. You've got to write a fitness report."

"You write it."

I said, "I can't and I shouldn't and I won't. You write it."

"Okay." He always wrote them in ink. None of this typing. I'll give him credit for that.

Paul Stillwell: To an extent, it sounds as if you were his conscience.

Admiral Forbes: Well, you know, now that you put it that way, that was right. We did it the same way in the Sixth Fleet as we did in the Atlantic Fleet. We worked very closely together. He is quite a gentleman.

Paul Stillwell: How did you react emotionally to this sequence of events?

Admiral Forbes: I was crushed. The Navy was my life, and I enjoyed every minute of it. But it had to happen, so it happened, so once it did that was it.

Paul Stillwell: It was so abrupt you didn't get a chance to adjust psychologically.

Admiral Forbes: Well, that's true. And the Navy never lets you retire anyway. I'm serious. For a year after I retired, I was getting calls: "Now, B, you know him better than anybody else. We don't have a fitness report on so-and-so. Would you speak to Ike and see if you can get this? We've got to have it. We've got a selection board coming up."

I'd work on Ike and help Washington on fitness reports, and then the Bureau of Naval Personnel would call: "Now, you've been around. What do you think if we assign so-and-so to so-and-so job?" And I'd give an answer.

Paul Stillwell: Well, how did you adjust to his new life that you hadn't planned for? I mean, there were still the calls, but you had to do something else to get on with your life.

Admiral Forbes: Well, I got a call from the CNO, Admiral Holloway, who said, "Beetle, we understand you're not doing anything down there but sitting on your rear, and we want to start a naval museum. Would you be the director?" Coming from him I was a little bit taken aback.[*]

I said, "Well, if I just can do it physically, I'll check with my doctor. I'd be delighted." So I got that job, and took the old Pennsylvania House, we converted that into a naval museum and I was the director of the naval museum there from late '77, and it's still going strong. So I stayed busy with things like that. My official title was Director of the Hampton Roads Naval Historical Foundation. I was later relieved by Ralph Cousins.[†]

I got involved with the Red Cross, helping them, and did a lot of volunteer work. I stayed busy, because I remembered very well my favorite uncle, who was head of the Federal Reserve. That was his only job in life. I mean, he was completely immersed in the Federal Reserve and what he did 24 hours a day. When he finally had to retire because of age, he went back to the old family farm, which is a beautiful place near Kilmarnock. He sat down, no outside interests, and literally died of boredom. And I said, "That's not going to happen to me."

So I got involved and stayed busy, busy, busy on things like that. I became a member of Naval Academy Alumni Association board of directors. I'd come up to meetings in Annapolis, make the visits, and so forth. I've enjoyed it and stayed busy.

---

[*] Admiral James L. Holloway III, USN, served as Chief of Naval Operations, 29 June 1974 to 1 July 1978.
[†] Admiral Ralph W. Cousins, USN (Ret.), who had previously been Vice Chief of Naval Operations and SACLant/CinCLant/CinCLantFlt.

But, as I jokingly say, I hold my Naval Academy class record for the amount of money earned on the civilian economy: $14.00. That was before I went to the Naval Academy. In the good old days, you used to get two dollars during the harvest time for working on the farm. No, I've enjoyed it very much. Just stay busy, stay occupied. Don't sit around and look out the window.

Paul Stillwell: Or get your mind rotted by television.

Admiral Forbes: Oh, I watch very little. I watch the news and that's it. And "Larry King Live" once in a while when they've got a good person on there. And I have got my family enjoy our grandchildren. I just enjoy life. Just like we're here in Annapolis right now to visit our daughter and our son-in-law, who teaches at the Naval Academy, and our two grandchildren, Kelley and Bo. We'll see the midshipmen do *Hello, Dolly* tomorrow night. That should be very good. My children had four midshipmen over for dinner last night, including two female second classmen, and they were charming young ladies.

Paul Stillwell: Well, you've talked about your children when we haven't had the tape running. Please put that on the record as well, because that's part of the story.

Admiral Forbes: Well, we have two daughters, and they're charming young ladies. Both are now married. My older daughter and her husband Doug live in Virginia Beach. He is retired Navy and is with an airplane parts distributor that that is a big company in Norfolk.

Paul Stillwell: What's her name?

Admiral Forbes: She's Marian Nelson. My wife's mother's maiden name was Nelson, so we named her Marian Nelson. We've always called her Nell. Our other daughter, Sue, is married to Jim Snead, Naval Academy class of '73.[*] He's a fighter puke, and he's on duty over at the Naval Academy now. They have quarters on the academy grounds,

___
[*] Commander James C. Snead, USN.

and I've never seen a person—I must say—any more enthused about his job than he is. He works directly for the commandant. And he works with the midshipmen and that's one reason they invite the midshipmen to their quarters. Well, for the Super Bowl game the other night she called. They had ten plebes over. They fed them dinner and watched the game, and they got them all back on time. And they go by the book. No beer, nothing. As I said, they had the four over last night. They've done this several times.

Paul Stillwell: Well, she must have seen something in the Navy life-style that appealed to her to have married a Navy man.

Admiral Forbes: I guess so, and she was doing very well. She likes it up here very much. She really does.

Paul Stillwell: Well, are there any other holes to fill in, Admiral, or overall thoughts and conclusions to put a benediction on this story of your career?

Admiral Forbes: Well, I just look back in retrospect and think about my Uncle Francis on my mother's side of the family. He was in the Naval Academy class of 1922. And, as I understand, he was a soccer player. He had a bad accident on the soccer field here, and the doctors couldn't get it to heal properly. He had to leave the Naval Academy. Well, he had all these dress uniforms, and when we'd go to visit my grandmother up here in Maryland, what I call Windy Bottom, up in the attic was hanging this Naval Academy dress blue uniform and all the trimmings. I, being a youngster, that really intrigued me, and I got this feeling about wanting to go to the Naval Academy.

Well, my father was a Republican, and in the Democratic district there was no chance of getting an appointment, so when that recruiter came through high school talking during the Depression, talking about three square meals a day and the running water. And I thought, "Running water? We've got a nice stream behind the barn. What's he talking about?" When I say we lived on a farm, I mean we had nothing—no electric lights, no indoor plumbing, no anything. We were back in the good old days.

I wanted to try for that Naval Academy, so I did a little digging and found out about that Naval Academy Preparatory Class and how I could go out to the fleet, and gain entrance to the Naval Academy. That's why I joined the Navy. Ironically, that was on the 15th of August, 1938, and they sent me down from Baltimore to Norfolk on the old Bay Line. We went in the Navy style, first class, with your meals provided, and they gave me a dime. That was to get from the terminal there in Norfolk out to the naval base, where the recruit training was in those days.

When I got out there, I was walking in and met this other youngster named Chris Peterson. To this day we're still close personal friends. Chris was from Norfolk and still lives there. We went to the Naval Academy together, the whole nine yards. And I see him all the time. We're in the Rotary together. But to go into the Navy that way was interesting.

After I was in the old carrier *Yorktown*, I went to the Naval Academy Preparatory Class, one of the lucky few. And I entered the Naval Academy through that route. That was one smart thing to do, because then you know how the other half lives, which paid off in later days. In taking care of your crew and everyone on the ship, I remembered things that I didn't like and how they could be changed. And when you have that authority, you can do it. This provided a good career. I enjoyed every moment of it. I worked for and with some very interesting people. It was just good.

Paul Stillwell: Interesting to deal with such personalities as Stump and Kidd, and obviously what you did appealed to both of them for them to keep asking for you.

Admiral Forbes: Apparently so. We got along. Well, you have to be frank and tell them what you think. You can't be a yes-man. Not with people like that. No, I tell you that those tours with Admiral Stump were something else. I really learned a lot. He took me everywhere he went, so I got to meet Pope Pius and many others. I was always right there with him when he talked to these people. I was his walking recorder. I remembered what was said when we had to write the reports. I could put in my two cents' worth on what my opinions were, what you thought they said and so forth and so on. That was quite a job.

Paul Stillwell: Any final thoughts?

Admiral Forbes: No, except "Go Navy." [Laughter]

Paul Stillwell: Well, Admiral, on behalf of the Naval Institute and those dozens, hundreds of people who will be reading this in the future, I thank you very much for your contribution. We're grateful to get this on the record, and I'm sure it will be of great value.

Admiral Forbes: Well, I thank you. It's been a privilege and an honor.

Launched in 1969, the Naval Institute's oral history program is among the oldest in the country. Used in combination with documentary sources, oral histories offer a richer understanding of naval history. Often they contain candid recollections and explanations never entered into contemporary records. In addition, they can help depict the atmosphere of a particular event or era in a manner not available in official documents.

The Naval Institute gratefully accepts tax-deductible gifts to strengthen its oral history initiatives. This support allows the Institute to preserve the life experiences of today's service men and women so they may teach and inspire future generations.

For information about opportunities to underwrite Naval Institute oral history projects, please contact the Naval Institute Foundation at 291 Wood Road, Annapolis, Maryland 21402; by phone at (410) 295-1054; or by e-mail at foundation@usni.org.

Index to the Oral History of
Vice Admiral Bernard B. Forbes, Jr., U.S. Navy (Retired)

AD/A-1 Skyraider
    Flown in 1950 by squadron VC-33, 73-74, 79-80
    Flown by Marine Corps pilots in the early 1950s, 98-99
    Used by Attack Squadron 15 (VA-15) in the late 1950s, 118-125
    Used for training for nuclear weapons delivery missions in the late 1950s-early 1960s, 80, 120-122, 181
    Flown by Attack Squadron 176 (VA-176) in the early 1960s, 140-141
    Role in the Vietnam War, 141

Air Force Atlantic Fleet
    Vice Admiral Felix B. Stump as type commander in the early 1950s, 74-77, 82-89
    Vice Admiral Robert L. Townsend as type commander in 1969-70, 182-185, 189

Alcohol
    In the early 1940s a Naval Academy company officer found an empty whiskey bottle hidden in a midshipman room, 37-39
    Serving of unauthorized wine to Naval Academy midshipmen in 1943, 38
    In World War II crew members of the destroyer *Barton* (DD-722) drank torpedo alcohol, 51-52
    Beer for the crew of the *Barton* in 1945 after a long session of loading ammunition, 58-59
    Rum ration served to crew members of British warships in the early 1950s, 93-94
    In the mid-1950s Admiral Felix Stump objected to staff members bringing alcohol to Hawaii, 113

Alexander, Lieutenant William H. II, USN (USNA, 1944)
    Flight training in the late 1940s, 70
    Service in the early 1950s in squadron VC-33, 74-76

Ammunition
    Use of proximity fuzes on 5-inch projectiles fired by the destroyer *Barton* (DD-722) in 1944-45, 44, 60
    Explosion of a white phosphorus 5-inch projectile on board the *Barton* in March 1945, 54-55
    Replenishment of ammunition for the *Barton* at Kerama Retto in 1945, 58
    Handling of in the mid-1960s by the crew of the ammunition ship *Shasta* (AE-6), 158-163, 166-167, 169-170
    Off-loading of ammunition from the aircraft carrier *Independence* (CVA-62) in 1969, 183-185

Anderson, Admiral George W., Jr., USN (Ret.) (USNA, 1927)
In the mid-1950s was Deputy CinCPac, 115
Former Chief of Naval Operations who took care of funeral arrangements when Admiral Felix Stump died in 1972, 110

Antiair Warfare
The destroyer *Barton* (DD-722) fired her 5-inch guns against Japanese aircraft in 1944-45, 48-49, 51, 60

Army, U.S.
Some of General Douglas MacArthur's staff members rode the destroyer *Barton* (DD-722) in World War II, 49

Atlantic Fleet
Admiral Isaac C. Kidd, Jr., served as fleet commander in chief, 1975-78, 223-235

Attack Squadron 15 (VA-15)
Operations in the Atlantic and Mediterranean in the late 1950s, 118-126

Attack Squadron 176 (VA-176)
Operations in the Atlantic and Mediterranean in the early 1960s, 133-141
On alert during the Cuban Missile Crisis in 1962, 134

Australia
In the mid-1950s Admiral Felix Stump, CinCPac, visited Australia to commemorate the World War II Battle of the Coral Sea, 114

Bagley, Vice Admiral David H., USN (USNA, 1944)
Served as Chief of Naval Personnel in the early 1970s, 213-214

Bagley, Vice Admiral Worth H., USN (USNA, 1947)
Served as the Navy Director of Program Planning in the early 1970s, 213

Barnes, Midshipman Willis C., USN (USNA, 1945)
Served as a company commander at the Naval Academy in the early 1940s, 42

***Barton*, USS (DD-722)**
Damaged during the D-Day operation at Normandy in June 1944, 45
In 1944 Marian Forbes visited the ship at Boston, 26-27, 61
Quality officers on board in 1944-45, 45-46, 48
World War II combat duty in the Western Pacific, 1944-45, 47-55, 58-60
Enlisted crew members during World War II, 51-52, 54-55
Collision with the destroyer *Ingraham* (DD-694) on the night of 16 February 1945, 52-54
Explosion of a white phosphorus 5-inch projectile in March 1945, 54-55
Postwar service in 1945-46, 60-64

Transport of atomic bomb components to Bikini Atoll in 1946, 63-65
Decommissioning in January 1947, 66
Was sunk as a target ship in 1969, 142

Becker, Midshipman Merlin D., USN (USNA, 1945)
As a Naval Academy midshipman, 1941-44, 28-29, 37

Bessac, Commander Norman B., USN (Ret.) (USNA, 1945)
Nicknamed "Buzz" as a Naval Academy midshipman in the early 1940s, 37, 39
In the early 1960s served with Admiral Hyman Rickover in the nuclear power program, 139-140, 178-179
Retired in 1965 to seek civilian employment, 178-179

Bikini Atoll, Marshall Islands
Site of atomic bomb tests in 1946, 63-65

Bombs/Bombing
Atomic bomb tests at Bikini Atoll in 1946, 63-65
The AD/A-1 Skyraider was used for training for nuclear weapons delivery missions in the late 1950s-early 1960s, 80, 120-122, 181

Bonds, Midshipman Joseph E., USN (USNA, 1945)
At Naval Academy Prep School in 1941, 13-14
As a Naval Academy midshipman, 1941-44, 37

Boorda, Admiral Jeremy M., USN
Served 1988-91 as Chief of Naval Personnel and 1991-94 as CinCSouth, 129-130

Boston Navy Yard
Repaired the destroyer *Barton* (DD-722) after battle damage in 1944, 26-27, 45

Brown, Midshipman John Wilson IV, USN (USNA, 1945)
As a Naval Academy midshipman, 1941-44, 9-10

Bureau of Naval Personnel
Detailing of officers to various billets in the late 1960s, 173, 177-178, 180
Detailing of officers to various billets in the early 1970s, 206-215

Burke, Rear Admiral Arleigh A., USN (USNA, 1923)
As CNO designate in 1955 visited Admiral Felix Stump in Hawaii, 108-109

Carrier Group Six
Operations in the Atlantic and Mediterranean, 1973-75, 215-221
Staff officers in the early 1970s, 216-217
In 1974 the commanding officer of the aircraft carrier *Saratoga* (CVA-60) was relieved for cause, 219-221

Carter, Midshipman Robert Ross, USN (USNA, 1942)
  As a Naval Academy midshipman in the early 1940s, 21-23

Chiang Kai-shek
  As President of Nationalist China in the mid-1950s, conferred with Admiral Felix Stump through Madame Chiang, 102-104

Colbus, Commander Louis, USN
  Served on the Carrier Group Six staff in the early 1970s, 216-217

Collisions
  The destroyer *Barton* (DD-722) collided with the destroyer *Ingraham* (DD-694) on the night of 16 February 1945, 52-54

Combs, Rear Admiral Walter Vincent, Jr., USN (USNA, 1936)
  Headed OP-103, the Manpower Program Branch of the OpNav staff, in the mid-1960s, 156

Composite Squadron 33 (VC-33)
  Operations in 1949-50 centered mostly around antisubmarine warfare and attack against surface ships, 72-74, 79-82

Corpus Christi Naval Air Station, Cabaniss Field, Texas
  Site of naval aviation training in the mid-1950s, 97-98

Cuban Missile Crisis
  Attack Squadron 176 (VA-176) was on alert during the 1962 crisis, 134

Dement, Captain Donald E., Medical Corps, USN
  In the mid-1950s lived near Admiral Felix Stump while stationed in Hawaii, 112

Dexter, Commander Edwin B., USN (USNA, 1928)
  Commanded the destroyer *Barton* (DD-722) during World War II, 49-50, 67

Disciplinary Problems
  Captain's mast on board the aircraft carrier *Independence* (CVA-62) in 1969-70, 191-193

Dunn, Captain Robert F., USN (USNA, 1951)
  In 1974 became commanding officer of the aircraft carrier *Saratoga* (CVA-60) when his predecessor was relieved for cause, 219-221

Education
  Forbes's education in Virginia, Maryland, and Pennsylvania in the 1920s-30s, 1-8
  For Naval Academy midshipmen in the early 1940s, 27-30, 40-41
  Forbes received postgraduate education at Stanford University, 1959-60, 126-131

Egypt
    In the spring of 1967 the crew of the ammunition ship *Shasta* (AE-6) photographed Egyptian troops while passing through the Suez Canal, 164

Eisenhower, President Dwight D. (USMA, 1915)
    In the mid-1950s conferred with Admiral Felix Stump about U.S. relations with Taiwan, 102-105

Englehart, Midshipman Harry A., Jr., USN (USNA, 1945)
    As a Naval Academy midshipman, 1941-44, 30-31, 39

Enlisted Personnel
    Boot camp training at Norfolk, Virginia, in 1938, 7-8, 11-13
    On board the aircraft carrier *Yorktown* (CV-5) in the late 1930s, 8-9, 14-21
    In the crew of the destroyer *Barton* (DD-722) during World War II, 51-52, 54-55
    In Attack Squadron 15 (VA-15) in the late 1950s, 125-126
    In the crew of the aircraft carrier *Franklin D. Roosevelt* (CVA-42) in the early 1960s, 146-147
    In the crew of the ammunition ship *Shasta* (AE-6) in 1966-67, 157-160, 165-168
    Crew members of the aircraft carrier *Independence* (CVA-62) in 1969-70, 183-185, 190-193

Ennis, Midshipman Francis W., USN (USNA, 1927)
    Had to drop out of the Naval Academy in the 1920s because of a soccer injury, 4, 6, 237

***Enterprise*, USS (CVAN-65)**
    Replenished at sea during the Vietnam War by the ammunition ship *Shasta* (AE-6), 161-163

Estes, Commander Carl Lewis, USNR
    Newspaper publisher who received hospital treatment in Hawaii in 1945 after being injured when his airplane was shot down, 56-57

Fashbaugh, Lieutenant (junior grade) Howard, USNR
    Served in the engineering department of the destroyer *Barton* (DD-722) in World War II, 45, 61-63

Fay, Midshipman Richard C., USN (USNA, 1945)
    As a Naval Academy midshipman, 1941-44, 9-11, 21, 23-25, 30, 32, 36, 39
    Service during World War II in the light cruiser *Philadelphia* (CL-41), 25

Flight Training
    In Florida and Texas, 1947-49, 70-72, 78-79
    In Texas in the mid-1950s, 97-98

Food
    Doughnuts and turkey as morale boosters for the crew of the aircraft carrier *Independence* (CVA-62) in 1969-70, 184-186

Football
    Games involving Naval Academy midshipmen in the early 1940s, 42-43

Forbes, Vice Admiral Bernard B., Jr., USN (Ret.) (USNA, 1945)
    Ancestors, 1
    Parents, 1-4, 14, 237
    Sister Marian was a Naval Reserve officer in World War II, 26-27, 61
    Wife Betty, whom he married in November 1950, 85-86, 96, 106, 109-110, 116, 130, 154-155, 157, 180, 195, 205, 228, 230-232
    Daughters Nell and Susan, 100, 109, 116, 130, 157, 180, 236-237
    Boyhood and education in Virginia and Maryland in the 1920s and 1930s, 1-8
    Service as a Navy enlisted man, 1938-41, 4-9, 11-21
    As a Naval Academy midshipman, 1941-44, 9-11, 24-43
    Origin of nicknames "Beetle" and "Rabbit," 36, 60-61
    Service as a junior officer in the destroyer *Barton* (DD-722), 1944-47, 44-67
    Brief service in 1947 as commanding officer of the USS *PC-572*, 67-69
    Went through flight training in Florida and Texas, 1947-49, 70-72, 78-79
    Served in 1949-50 in Composite Squadron 33 (VC-33), 71-74, 79-82
    Duty 1950-53 as flag lieutenant to Vice Admiral Felix Stump, 74-77, 82-88
    Involved in flight training at Corpus Christi, Texas, 1953-55, 97
    Duty 1955 to 1957 as aide to Admiral Felix Stump, who was Commander in Chief Pacific/Commander in Chief Pacific Fleet, 100-118, 171, 238
    Served 1957-59 as executive officer of Attack Squadron 15 (VA-15), 118-126
    Postgraduate education at Stanford University, 1959-60, 126-131
    In 1960-61 attended the senior course at the Naval War College, 130-133, 178-179
    In 1961-62 commanded Attack Squadron 176 (VA-176), 133-141
    Served as air officer of the carrier *Franklin D. Roosevelt* (CVA-42) from 1962 to 1964, 142-149, 171-172
    From 1964 to 1966 served in the manpower section, OP-103, on the OpNav staff, 151-156
    Commanded the ammunition ship *Shasta* (AE-6) in 1966-67, 157-170
    From 1967 to 1969 was a detailer in the Bureau of Naval Personnel, 173-181
    Commanded the aircraft carrier *Independence* (CVA-62) in 1969-70, 181-193, 197-198, 201
    Served 1970-72 as chief of staff to Commander Sixth Fleet, 194-206
    In 1972-73 was head detailer in the Bureau of Naval Personnel, 206-215
    Commanded Carrier Group Six, 1973-75, 215-221
    Briefly commanded Carrier Group Two in 1975, 221-223
    Served in 1975-76 as Deputy Commander in Chief Atlantic/Deputy Commander in Chief Atlantic Fleet, 223-234
    Post-retirement activities, 232-236

Franklin D. Roosevelt, USS (CVA-42)
    Shipyard period in the early 1960s, 142-144
    Operations in the Atlantic and Mediterranean in the early 1960s, 145-149
    In the early 1960s NBC did a television program about the ship, 171-172

French Navy
    Involved in NATO exercises in the Mediterranean in the early 1970s, 201-202

Grace, Princess
    Former film actress who visited the Sixth Fleet flagship in the early 1970s, 196

Gray, Lieutenant Commander William J., USN (USNA, 1943)
    Commanded Attack Squadron 15 (VA-15) from 1957 to 1959, 118

Greer, Vice Admiral Howard E., USN (USNA, 1944)
    In the early 1960s commanded the air group based on board the carrier _Shangri-La_ (CVA-38), 137-138, 141-142
    In 1976 filled in temporarily as Deputy CinCLantFlt, 232

Gunnery – Naval
    Firing by the destroyer _Barton_ (DD-722) in the Western Pacific in 1944-45, 47-49, 54, 58-59

Halsey, Admiral William F., Jr., USN (USNA, 1904)
    In 1945 received medical treatment at hospital in Hawaii, 57

Hamel, Lieutenant Commander James K., USN
    Served in the late 1960s-early 1970s as chief engineer of the aircraft carrier _Independence_ (CVA-62), 188-189

Hawaii
    In the mid-1950s the headquarters of CinCPac/CinCPacFlt was near Pearl Harbor, 101, 105-106, 111-112, 115-116
    Vice President Richard Nixon visited Admiral Felix Stump in the mid-1950s, 106-108

Holloway, Vice Admiral James L., Jr., USN (USNA, 1919)
    Served in the mid-1950s as Chief of Naval Personnel, 88-89, 100, 117, 145

Holloway, Admiral James L. III, USN (USNA, 1943)
    Commanded the aircraft carrier _Enterprise_ (CVAN-65) during the Vietnam War, 161-163
    As CNO in the mid-1970s asked Forbes to head the Hampton Roads Naval Historical Foundation, 235

Independence, USS (CVA-62)
>Operations in the Atlantic and Mediterranean in 1969-70, 182-193, 197-198, 201
Enlisted crew members in 1969-70, 183-185, 190-193
Doughnuts and turkey as morale boosters for the crew in 1969-70, 184-186
Propulsion plant sometimes used JP-5 fuel in 1969-70, 188-189

Ingraham, USS (DD-694)
>Collided with the destroyer *Barton* (DD-722) the night of 16 February 1945, 52-54

Intelligence
>In the spring of 1967 the crew of the ammunition ship *Shasta* (AE-6) photographed Egyptian troops while passing through the Suez Canal, 164

Iowa, USS (BB-61)
>Served in the early 1950s as Second Fleet flagship, 91-94

Italy
>Pope Pius XII had an audience with Admiral Felix Stump in the mid-1950s, 104-105
In the early 1970s Gaeta was the homeport for the Sixth Fleet flagship, 194-195, 202

Iwo Jima
>Gunfire support provided in March 1945 by the destroyer *Barton* (DD-722), 54-55

Japan
>Visited by crew members of the destroyer *Barton* (DD-722) shortly after the end of World War II, 61-62

Japanese Navy
>In World War II the destroyer *Barton* (DD-722) fired proximity fuzes at Japanese suicide planes, 48-49, 51, 60

John F. Kennedy, USS (CVA-67)
>Served as flagship of Carrier Group Six in the early 1970s, 216-217

Kamikazes
>In World War II the destroyer *Barton* (DD-722) fired proximity fuzes at Japanese suicide planes, 48-49, 51, 60

Kidd, Admiral Isaac C., Jr., USN (USNA, 1942)
>Commanded the Sixth Fleet, 1970-71, 194-197, 199-203, 215
Served 1975-78 as Supreme Allied Commander Atlantic/Commander in Chief Atlantic/Commander in Chief Atlantic Fleet, 223-235

Kissling, Lieutenant Paul T., USN
>In the early 1950s served as aide to Admiral Felix B. Stump, 74-77

Koch, Midshipman Konrad K., USN (USNA, 1945)
As a Naval Academy midshipman during World War II, deliberately flunked out and joined the Army, 32-33

Korea
Visited by Admiral Felix Stump, CinCPac, in 1955, 171

Larson, Rear Admiral Charles R., USN (USNA, 1958)
In the early 1960s flew an AD as part of Attack Squadron 176 (VA-176), then switched to nuclear submarines, 136-138
Recommended by Forbes as President Nixon's naval aide and later to be Naval Academy superintendent, 138-139

Lederer, Captain William J., Jr., USN (USNA, 1936)
In the early 1950s served as public affairs officer on the staff of Admiral Felix Stump, CinCPac, 113-114

Lindsey, Commander Robin M., USN
In the early 1950s commanded Composite Squadron 33 (VC-33), 81-82

Love, Commander Winifred, USN
Served in the manpower section of OpNav in the mid-1960s, 155

Lovely, Midshipman Eugene, USN (USNA, 1972)
Enlisted crew member of the ammunition ship *Shasta* (AE-6) in the mid-1960s and later graduated from the Naval Academy, 165-166

Lynn, Commander James W., Supply Corps, USN (USNA, 1950)
Served in the late 1960s-early 1970s as supply officer of the aircraft carrier *Independence* (CVA-62), 184-186, 190-191

Manpower
Work of OP-103, the Manpower Program Branch of the OpNav staff, in the mid-1960s, 151-156

Marine Corps, U.S.
Learned flying proficiency from Corpus Christi, Texas, instructors in the mid-1950s, 98-99

Marschall, Midshipman Albert R., USN (USNA, 1945)
As a Naval Academy midshipman, 1941-44, 23, 28-30, 32, 34-36

Matthews, Captain Herbert Spencer, Jr., USN
Commanded the aircraft carrier *Independence* (CVA-62) in 1968-69, 183, 191

McIntire, Commander Harrison P., USN (USNA, 1935)
  Commanded the destroyer *Barton* (DD-722) during World War II, 49

McNamara, Robert S.
  As secretary of Defense in the 1960s was concerned about military manpower, 151-154

Medical Problems
  In 1945 Forbes was treated for wounds suffered when a 5-inch projectile exploded, 54-56
  In August 1976 Forbes had a heart attack that led to his being retired from active duty, 227-230

Mediterranean Sea
  In the early 1960s Attack Squadron 176 (VA-176) was deployed to the Sixth Fleet, 135-136
  In the late 1960s-early 1970s the aircraft carrier *Independence* (CVA-62) deployed to the Sixth Fleet, 186-187
  Soviet Navy operations in the Mediterranean in the early 1970s, 197-198, 217

Military Academy, West Point, New York
  Football games against the Naval Academy in the early 1940s, 43

Miller, Chief Fire Controlman George, USN
  Served in the crew of the destroyer *Barton* (DD-722) during World War II, later became a physician, 51

Miller, Vice Admiral Gerald E., USN (USNA, 1942)
  In 1963-64 commanded the aircraft carrier *Franklin D. Roosevelt* (CVA-42), 143, 148-149
  As Commander Sixth Fleet in 1971-73 used an aircraft carrier as flagship, 144-145, 200, 204-205

Montgomery, Lieutenant Commander Robert, USNR
  Movie star who served in the crew of the destroyer *Barton* (DD-722) in World War II, 45-46

Moorer, Commander Joseph P., USN (USNA, 1945)
  In the early 1960s commanded a fighter squadron based on board the carrier *Shangri-La* (CVA-38), 137-138

Movies
  Shown to the crew of the aircraft carrier *Franklin D. Roosevelt* (CVA-42) in the early 1960s, 144, 147

Shown to the crew of the ammunition ship *Shasta* (AE-6) in the mid-1960s, 161, 209-210

Shown to the crew of the aircraft carrier *Independence* (CVA-62) in 1969-70, 209-210

Naval Academy, Annapolis, Maryland
Midshipman activities in Bancroft Hall in the early 1940s, 9-11, 21-24, 28-33, 36-40
Social life for midshipmen in the early 1940s, 10-11, 34-36
Summer training cruises in the early 1940s, 25-26, 33-34
Academics in the early 1940s, 27-30, 40-41
Chapel services in the early 1940s, 28
Sailing in the early 1940s, 28-29
Football in the early 1940s, 42-43
The class of 1945 graduated in 1944, 43-44
Midshipman activities in the early 1990s, 236-237

Naval Academy Preparatory School, Norfolk, Virginia
Training of potential midshipmen in 1940-41, 9, 13

Naval Reserve, U.S.
Quality reserve officers in the crew of the destroyer *Barton* (DD-722) in World War II, 45-46, 48, 62

Naval War College, Newport, Rhode Island
Senior course in 1960-61 included many lectures, 130-133

New York Naval Shipyard
In the early 1960s did an overhaul on the aircraft carrier *Franklin D. Roosevelt* (CVA-42), 144

Nixon, Richard M.
As Vice President, visited Hawaii and Admiral Felix Stump in the mid-1950s, 106-108
In the late 1960s picked Charles Larson to be presidential naval aide, 138

Norfolk, Virginia
Site of Navy recruit training in the late 1930s, 7-8, 11-13
Naval Academy Preparatory School, 1940-41, 9

North Atlantic Treaty Organization
Conducted at-sea exercises in the early 1950s, 91-94
The U.S. Sixth Fleet was involved in NATO exercises in the Mediterranean in the early 1970s, 201-202

Norway
Visited by NATO warships during an exercise in the early 1950s, 94

Nuclear Weapons
    Atomic bomb tests at Bikini Atoll in 1946, 63-65
    The AD/A-1 Skyraider was used for training for nuclear weapons delivery missions in the late 1950s-early 1960s, 80, 120-122, 181
    In the mid-1970s Forbes had to be available for possible release of nuclear weapons, 226, 230-231

Okinawa
    In 1945 the destroyer *Barton* (DD-722) provided heavy gunfire support for the U.S. invasion of the island, 58-59, 61

***PC-572*, USS**
    Operations in the Caribbean in 1947, 67-69

Pay and Allowances
    For junior Navy enlisted personnel in the late 1930s-early 1940s, 13
    Limited spending money for Naval Academy midshipmen in the early 1940s, 34-36

Pearl Harbor, Hawaii
    Reaction at the Naval Academy to the December 1941 Japanese attack, 22-23

Personnel
    Work of OP-103, the Manpower Program Branch of the OpNav staff, in the mid-1960s, 151-156

Petersen, Midshipman Christian Charles, USN (USNA, 1945)
    As a Navy enlisted man and Naval Academy midshipman, 1938-44, 7, 9
    Resigned from the Navy as a lieutenant commander, 7

Philippine Islands
    In 1966-67 the ammunition ship *Shasta* (AE-6) took on ammo and supplies at Subic Bay, 161, 169-170

Pigott, Lieutenant John T., USNR
    Served as gunnery officer of the destroyer *Barton* (DD-722) in World War II, 48

Pius XII
    Pope who had an audience with Admiral Felix Stump in the mid-1950s, 104-105

Polhemus, Ensign William B., USN (USNA, 1946)
    Served in the destroyer *Barton* (DD-722) shortly after World War II, 63-64, 67

Propulsion Plants
    On board the ammunition ship *Shasta* (AE-6) in the mid-1960s, 158-160, 167
    On board the aircraft carrier *Independence* (CVA-62) in 1969-70, 188-189

Puerto Rico
    Base of operations for the patrol craft *PC-572* in 1947, 67-69

Pugh, Lieutenant Commander Donald E., USN (USNA, 1934)
    As a company officer at the Naval Academy in the early 1940s, inspected some of the Bancroft Hall hiding places he had known as a midshipman, 37-38

Racial Issues
    In the late 1930s Forbes had his first experience with integrated education, 4-5
    In the mid-1960s the ammunition ship *Shasta* (AE-6) had a high percentage of black sailors in the crew, 158-160, 165-166

Recruit Training
    At Norfolk, Virginia, in 1938, 7-8, 11-13

Replenishment at Sea
    By the ammunition ship *Shasta* (AE-6) in 1966-67, during the Vietnam War, 161-163, 166-167

Rickover, Rear Admiral Hyman G., USN (USNA, 1922)
    In the mid-1950s visited Admiral Felix Stump in Hawaii, 111-112
    Experiences in the early 1960s while running the nuclear power program, 139-140, 178-179

Robinson, Ensign Hugh M., USN (USNA, 1938)
    As a division officer on board the carrier *Yorktown* (CV-5) in the late 1930s, 8-9, 18, 21

Royal Navy
    Participation in NATO exercises in the early 1950s, 93-94

SNJ Texan
    Aircraft used for flight training in the late 1940s, 71, 78-79

Sailing
    By Naval Academy midshipmen in the early 1940s, 28-29

Saratoga, **USS (CVA-60)**
    In 1974 the ship's commanding officer was relieved for cause and Captain Robert Dunn became skipper, 219-221

Searls, Midshipman Henry H., Jr., USN (USNA, 1945)
    As a Naval Academy midshipman in the early 1940s, 31, 33

Second Fleet, U.S.
    Vice Admiral Felix B. Stump as fleet commander in the early 1950s, 83, 90-97
    Conducted NATO at-sea exercises in the early 1950s, 91-94

Semmes, Vice Admiral Benedict, J., Jr., USN (USNA, 1934)
    Served as Chief of Naval Personnel, 1964-68, 151-153

Shangri-La, **USS (CVA-38)**
    Operations in the Atlantic and Mediterranean in the early 1960s, 133-134, 142

Sharp, Captain Ulysses S. Grant, USN (USNA, 1927)
    In the early 1950s served on the staff of Commander Second Fleet, Vice Admiral Felix B. Stump, 83, 91
    In the mid-1950s served in Hawaii on Admiral Stump's CinCPac staff, 105-106, 114-115

Shasta, **USS (AE-6)**
    Enlisted crew members in the mid-1960s, 157-160, 165-168
    Propulsion plant, 158-162, 167
    Replenishment at sea during the Vietnam War, 161-163, 166-167
    Returned to the United States from Vietnam by going through the Mediterranean and Atlantic in the spring of 1967, 163-164

Six-Day War
    In the spring of 1967 the crew of the ammunition ship *Shasta* (AE-6) photographed Egyptian troops while passing through the canal, 164

Sixth Fleet, U.S.
    In the early 1960s Attack Squadron 176 (VA-176) was deployed to the Mediterranean Sea, 135-136
    In the late 1960s-early 1970s the aircraft carrier *Independence* (CVA-62) deployed to the Med, 186-187
    Involved in NATO exercises in the Mediterranean in the early 1970s, 201-202
    Vice Admiral Isaac C. Kidd, Jr., as fleet commander, 1970-71, 194-197, 199-203, 215
    Vice Admiral Gerald Miller as fleet commander, 1971-73, 144-145, 200, 204-205
    Sixth Fleet posture during the 1973 Yom Kippur War, 217-218

Snead, Commander James C., USN (USNA, 1973)
    Served on the Naval Academy staff in the early 1990s, 236-237

Soviet Navy
    Operations in the Mediterranean in the early 1970s, 197-198, 217

Spain
    In the early 1960s aircraft from Attack Squadron 176 (VA-176) flew over Spain during a deployment to the Sixth Fleet, 134-135

***Springfield*, USS (CLG-7)**
    Served as Sixth Fleet flagship in the early 1970s, 144, 194-196, 200

Stanford University, Palo Alto, California
    Forbes received postgraduate education at Stanford, 1959-60, 126-131

Staubach, Lieutenant Roger T., Supply Corps, USN (USNA, 1965)
    Resigned from the Navy in the late 1960s to play professional football, 174-175

Stump, Admiral Felix B., USN (USNA, 1917)
    Service in the early 1950s as Commander Air Force Atlantic Fleet, 74-77, 82-90, 96
    Service in the early 1950s as Commander Second Fleet, 83, 90-97
    Service in the 1950s as Commander in Chief Pacific/Pacific Fleet, 101-117, 171, 238
    His second wife was much younger than he, 84, 89-90, 106, 110-111
    Son John Morgan Stump was a naval officer, 84, 90, 110, 117, 206-207

Stump, Lieutenant Commander John Morgan (USNA, 1951)
    Naval aviator who was passed over for commander in the late 1960s and died in an air crash in 1970, 84, 90, 110, 117, 206-207

Suez Canal
    In the spring of 1967 the crew of the ammunition ship *Shasta* (AE-6) photographed Egyptian troops while passing through the canal, 164

Sylvester, Captain John, USN (USNA, 1926)
    In the early 1950s served on the staff of Commander Second Fleet, Vice Admiral Felix B. Stump, 83, 90-91
    In the mid-1950s served in Hawaii on Admiral Stump's CinCPac staff, 106

TBM Avenger
    Flown by squadron VC-33 in 1949-50, 72-73, 79

Taiwan
    As President of Nationalist China in the mid-1950s, Chiang Kai-shek conferred with Admiral Felix B. Stump, 102-104

Taylor, Midshipman Warren, USN (USNA, 1945)
    Stood high in his class at the Naval Academy in the early 1940s, 32

Television
    In the early 1960s NBC did a program about the aircraft carrier *Franklin D. Roosevelt* (CVA-42), 171-172
    Coverage of the change of command of the aircraft carrier *Independence* (CVA-62) in 1969, 183

Torpedoes
    In World War II crew members of the destroyer *Barton* (DD-722) drank torpedo alcohol, 51-52

Townsend, Vice Admiral Robert L., USN (USNA, 1934)
    Association with the aircraft carrier *Independence* (CVA-62) in 1969-70, while serving as ComNavAirLant, 182-185, 189

Training
    Boot camp at Norfolk, Virginia, in 1938, 7-8, 11-13
    Naval Academy summer training cruises in the early 1940s, 25-26, 33-34
    Instilling of standards at the Naval Academy in the early 1940s, 41-42
    Flight training in Florida and Texas, 1947-49, 70-72, 78-79
    In Corpus Christi, Texas, in the mid-1950s, 97-98

Tremaine, Midshipman Mark G., USN (USNA, 1945)
    As a Naval Academy midshipman in the early 1940s, 37

VA-15
    See: Attack Squadron 15 (VA-15)

VA-176
    See: Attack Squadron 176 (VA-176)

VC-33
    See: Composite Squadron 33 (VC-33)

Vietnam War
    Buildup of Navy manpower in the mid-1960s, 151-153
    Replenishment at sea in 1966-67 by the ammunition ship *Shasta* (AE-6), 161-163, 166-167

Weisner, Rear Admiral Maurice F., USN (USNA, 1941)
    Served in the Bureau of Naval Personnel in the late 1960s, 173-174

Weschler, Commander Thomas R., USN (USNA, 1939)
    In 1955 accompanied CNO designate Arleigh Burke on a trip to Hawaii, 1-8-109

Yom Kippur War
    Sixth Fleet posture during the 1973 war, 217-218

***Yorktown*, USS (CV-5)**
    Operations and crew members, 1938-40, 8-9, 14-21

Zumwalt, Admiral Elmo R., Jr., USN (USNA, 1943)
    Style as Chief of Naval Operations in the early 1970s, 209, 214

***Yorktown,* USS (CV-5)**
    Operations and crew members, 1938-40, 8-9, 14-21

Zumwalt, Admiral Elmo R., Jr., USN (USNA, 1943)
    Style as Chief of Naval Operations in the early 1970s, 209, 214